THE WORLD SERIES

The camera was present to preserve forever the conclusion to one of the most stunning defensive plays in World Series history—Bill Wambsganss's unassisted triple play for Cleveland in the top of the fifth inning of game five of the 1920 World Series. In this photo, Wambsganss has already snared Clarence Mitchell's line drive and stepped on second base (retiring Pete Kilduff, who was by then standing on third), and is about to tag a disbelieving Otto Miller for Brooklyn's third out. Umpire Hank O'Day is raising his hand to signal the completion of the historic play.

THE WORLD SERIES

An Illustrated History from 1903 to the Present

BY DONALD HONIG

CROWN PUBLISHERS, INC.
NEW YORK

Published by Crown Publishers, Inc., 225 Park Avenue South, New York, New York 10003 and represented in Canada by the Canadian MANDA Group.

CROWN is a trademark of Crown Publishers, Inc.

Manufactured in the United States of America

Library of Congress Cataloging-in-Publication Data

Honig, Donald.
  The World Series.

  Includes index.
  1. World series (Baseball)—History.   I. Title.
GV878.4.H66   1986   796.357'782   86-4495
ISBN 0-517-56182-4

10 9 8 7 6 5 4 3 2 1

First Edition

Design: Robert Aulicino

For my daughter, Catherine

By Donald Honig

NONFICTION

BASEBALL WHEN THE GRASS WAS REAL

BASEBALL BETWEEN THE LINES

THE MAN IN THE DUGOUT

THE OCTOBER HEROES

THE IMAGE OF THEIR GREATNESS (WITH LAWRENCE RITTER)

THE 100 GREATEST BASEBALL PLAYERS OF ALL TIME (WITH LAWRENCE RITTER)

THE BROOKLYN DODGERS: AN ILLUSTRATED TRIBUTE

THE NEW YORK YANKEES: AN ILLUSTRATED HISTORY

BASEBALL'S 10 GREATEST TEAMS

THE LOS ANGELES DODGERS: THE FIRST QUARTER CENTURY

THE NATIONAL LEAGUE: AN ILLUSTRATED HISTORY

THE AMERICAN LEAGUE: AN ILLUSTRATED HISTORY

THE BOSTON RED SOX: AN ILLUSTRATED TRIBUTE

BASEBALL AMERICA

THE WORLD SERIES: AN ILLUSTRATED HISTORY

THE NEW YORK METS: THE FIRST QUARTER CENTURY

FICTION

SIDEWALK CAESAR

WALK LIKE A MAN

THE AMERICANS

DIVIDE THE NIGHT

NO SONG TO SING

JUDGMENT NIGHT

THE LOVE THIEF

THE SEVERITH STYLE

ILLUSIONS

I SHOULD HAVE SOLD PETUNIAS

THE LAST GREAT SEASON

MARCHING HOME

Contents

Acknowledgments

I am deeply indebted to a number of people for their generous assistance in photo research and in gathering the photographs reproduced in this book. Special thanks are due Michael P. Aronstein, president of Card Memorabilia Associates, Ltd., for the generosity of his assistance and his cogent insights. Invaluable help was also given by the publicity staffs of many big-league ball clubs, including the following: Kip Ingle, St. Louis Cardinals; Steve Brener, Toby Zwikel, and Penn Jones, Los Angeles Dodgers; Anita Littrell, Kansas City Royals; Nancy Scully, Oakland Athletics; Julie Wagner, Baltimore Orioles.

Photo credits include:

Chicago Historical Society: pp. 10, 50, 52, 106.

UPI/Bettmann Newsphotos: pp. 37, 74, 97, 120, 125, 175, 176, 228, 231.

St. Louis Cardinals: pp. 176, 179, 184, 225, 226, 233.

Kansas City Royals: pp. 215, 233, 234.

Baltimore Orioles: p. 183.

Oakland Athletics: pp. 199, 201.

Los Angeles Dodgers: p. 222.

Nancy Hogue: pp. 210, 212, 213, 223, 227, 232.

For their good advice and wise counsel, I am indebted to these keen students of baseball history: David Markson, Lawrence Ritter, Stanley Honig, Andrew Aronstein, Allan J. Grotheer, and Douglas Mulcahy.

Introduction

Every February America's finest all-around athletes leave behind the sealed vaults of winter and head for the sunshine, to work their bodies into shape and get ready for a grueling, summer-long schedule that will determine which two of baseball's twenty-six big-league teams will qualify for the biggest sports stage of them all, the World Series. Through the fading chill of springtime and the softening days of May and June and on through the broiling proving grounds of July and August and into the crisp air of September, they play on and on, driving with skill and stamina and resolution toward the laurels of October.

It began in 1903, when the owners of the Boston Red Sox (then known as the Pilgrims) and the Pittsburgh Pirates suggested that their teams, each on the road to a pennant, meet in a postseason series of games to determine a champion for all of baseball. A world champion.

For the American League, in only its third year of operation and looked upon with disdain by the older National League, it was an opportunity to establish parity. This fact was not lost on Ban Johnson, the autocratic president of the American League. But merely getting onto the same field with the rival league was not enough. When he gave his approval to the Boston club, it was with this injunction: "You must beat them."

Boston did win that first Series, a Series that was successful both artistically and financially. The contest between the league champions had been received as a momentous occasion by press and fans alike, all of whom looked forward avidly to a meeting of the following year's pennant winners.

But there was no Series in 1904. John McGraw, manager of the pennant-winning New York Giants and a sworn enemy of Ban Johnson, refused to allow his club to meet that year's American League winners, once again the Boston club. McGraw's decision was met with a barrage of criticism from the press,

fans, and his own players (who resented losing the money that went to Series participants). The criticism was so heavy that when his Giants won again the next year, McGraw relented and brought his club into a postseason contest with the Philadelphia Athletics. From that day to this, the World Series has been an autumnal fixture on the American landscape, played without interruption, despite two World Wars and the Great Depression.

Whereas the first Series in 1903 had been a best-five-of-nine affair, from 1905 through 1918 it was a four-of-seven format. From 1919 through 1921, baseball experimented with five-of-nine, but then reverted to its more compact arrangement.

The World Series is a unique American institution, laced with classic American virtues. It is an occasion replete with opportunity; for seven games or less, all men are created equal. In World Series history the names Wambsganss, Larsen, and Amoros loom larger than those of Cobb, Hornsby, and Williams.

Nothing confers professional status more dramatically or more enduringly than World Series splendor. These rousing rites of October, carrying as they do the mystique of crowning a sovereign, have placed images upon the retina of memory of things we never saw: an easy fly ball dropping from Fred Snodgrass's glove in 1912; a bad-hop grounder vaulting over Fred Lindstrom's head in 1924; Grover Cleveland Alexander walking through the mist in 1926 to record baseball's most memorable strikeout. We can even see something that probably never happened: Babe Ruth pointing to Wrigley Field's bleachers in 1932. The jamboree culmination aura of the World Series has made them vivid and indelible.

Within these pages are the men and the moments of the World Series—nearly a century's sweep of myth and folklore in the making, often frozen by the camera in the very instant of creation. Turn the pages and see it happen.

Emotions erupt in the pressure-packed atmosphere of the World Series, when the national pastime takes center stage. Kirk Gibson exults in triumph after his eighth-inning three-run home run off of San Diego's Goose Gossage salted away the Detroit Tigers' championship in game five of the 1984 Series.

THE WORLD SERIES

I
A Brand-New American Institution
1903-1910

Fred Clarke, who managed and played the outfield for the Pirates in the 1903 and 1909 World Series.

Hugh Jennings, manager of Detroit's 1907–1909 pennant winners, but a three-time loser in World Series play.

1903

A look at the first World Series ever played reveals some insights into baseball, circa 1903. Rosters were two thirds of the size they are today, platooning was unheard of, players were heartier (allegedly), and managers were more conservative. Most clubs carried just five pitchers, and these boys, unlike their professional descendants, were not supposed to look toward the bullpen. In rugged, early-century America, a man was expected to finish what he started, and big-league pitching staffs averaged around 120 complete games. A sore arm or two, and a team was headed for the dungeon. This is exactly what happened to the Pittsburgh Pirates in that maiden World Series.

It was a 140-game schedule in 1903, and three men started 92 of those games for the Pirates—Charles (Deacon) Phillippe, Sam Leever, and Ed Doheny. By the time the Series opened, Leever had a lame arm and could pitch only sporadically, and ineffectively, and Doheny had been hospitalized because of mental problems. That left the Pirate pitching pretty much up to Phillippe, and the right-hander responded heroically, starting five of the eight games, winning three, losing two, and pitching 44 innings, a record that stands to this day.

The Boston Pilgrims had two hale and hearty right-handers, Cy Young and Bill Dinneen. Together, they started seven of eight games in the Series, Dinneen winning three and Young two.

It is probably fitting that the first pitch in World Series history was delivered by Cy Young, considered by a now vanished generation of witnesses the greatest of all pitchers. Cy was thirty-six years old at the time and a 28-game winner (as well as owner of

1

one of the game's nobler bay windows).

Baseball being an entity sometimes irreverent of its immortals, especially at World Series time, Young was combed for four runs in that very first inning, played on October 1 at Boston's Huntington Avenue Grounds. Pittsburgh went on to strafe Cy for 12 hits for a 7–3 win, with Phillippe the winning pitcher.

"Cy won't give us another game like that one again," Boston skipper and third baseman Jimmy Collins said, in a not unexpected riposte to the bumping. And he was proven right.

While Young eventually squared himself away, Pittsburgh's own icon of the diamond, Honus Wagner, went on to establish what has become a persistent October tradition; World Series time is often treacherous for the greats. Honus bumbled through the Series, making six errors, some of them costly, and batting just .222.

With Phillippe winning three of the first four games (covering six days), the Pirates seemed on their way to the title. But the Pilgrims came roaring back to take the next four in a row, Young and Dinneen getting stronger as they alternated starts, while the unfairly burdened Phillippe grew weaker.

Dinneen won the finale 3–0 in Boston, pitching a smooth four-hitter, with second baseman Hobe Ferris driving in all the runs. But the Pirates literally went down fighting. Pittsburgh's player-manager Fred Clarke did not appreciate a Dinneen pitch that came too close to his head. "So the Pittsburgh leader," went a contemporary newspaper account, "pushed a bunt down the first-base line hoping to use Big Bill's back as a rug to trample his spikes on." Boston first baseman Candy LaChance called Dinneen off the ball, scooped it up, "and fired the baseball into Clarke's back as he scooted toward first base." This provoked a brawl, and it was a half hour before the umpires could restore order.

When the game was over, the jubilant Boston fans came swarming onto the field. "They paraded their heroes behind a band while adults sang and children screamed, and the players were kept long after the final out, receiving the fans' handshakes for hours."

The Pirates, however, had a last laugh of sorts. Their owner, Barney Dreyfuss, threw his share of the receipts into the players' pot, and the Pirate players came away with $1,316 a piece to the Pilgrims' $1,182 per share.

The true significance of that first World Series was twofold: it established the American League once and for all as an equal partner with its older brother, and it captivated fans everywhere, becoming an instant institution.

1905

The achievement of Christy Mathewson in the 1905 World Series set a standard for near-flawless efficiency that has never been equaled. For young boys with strong arms and wistful dreams, this is the Series to conjure. For Mathewson, it was the most scintillating performance—the centerpiece—of a long and bejeweled career.

It was the New York Giants versus the Philadelphia Athletics—the first match-up between John McGraw and Connie Mack, who were to go on to become legends in the managerial pantheon. For the combative McGraw, it was the second of ten pennants he would win; for the "saintly" Mr. Mack, the second of nine.

McGraw's team, which he outfitted for the Series in black flannel uniforms with white trim, was led by three strong starters: Mathewson, "Iron Man" McGinnity, and Leon Ames. These three won 76 games among them, topped by Matty's 32.

Mack also had a well-armed staff: Eddie Plank, Chief Bender, Andy Coakley, and Rube Waddell. Waddell was Connie's ace, probably the fastest pitcher in baseball at the time, and a Mathewson-Waddell confrontation might well have been epic. But it was not to be. Waddell, a fun-loving free spirit, had hurt his shoulder in mid-September while playfully wrestling with a teammate. Rube's loss was a serious blow for the A's, but in the long run it probably made no difference, since not even the great Waddell could have won without runs.

Mathewson worked the opener at Philadelphia on October 9, shutting out Plank on four hits, 3–0. The next day Bender returned the favor on behalf of the A's, shutting out McGinnity and the Giants by the same score, with all three Philadelphia runs being unearned. That was it for the A's. They did not win another game in the Series, nor did they score another run.

It was Mathewson on October 12, 9–0 over Coakley; McGinnity on October 13, 1–0 over Plank; and finally Mathewson again on October 14, shutting out Bender at the Polo Grounds, 3–0.

Five games, each a shutout, with Mathewson spinning his three gems in six days. Through 27 innings, the handsome twenty-six-year-old master allowed just 14 hits and one base on balls. With the three runs surrendered by McGinnity in his game-two loss having been unearned, the Giants' pitching staff logged a 0.00 earned-run average for 45 innings of work.

If it took place today, the 1905 World Series, with its five shutouts and its team batting averages of .203 (Giants) and .161 (Athletics), would no doubt be considered dull by many fans. But seen through the more telling lens of history, that long-ago October retains an unmatched nobility of achievement. Never since has a pitcher worked more impeccably than Christy Mathewson did over those six days in October 1905.

1906

Chicago became the baseball capital of the world in 1906, when both Chicago teams, the White Sox and the Cubs, won pennants in their respective leagues and challenged each other on the shores of Lake Michigan for the world championship.

Statistically, it looked like the Cubs all the way. Frank Chance's club had set a record—as yet unsurpassed—with 116 victories and a .763 winning percentage, finishing 20 games ahead of their nearest competitor. This was the team of Tinker-to-Evers-to-Chance fame, and included third baseman Harry Steinfeldt, outfielders Frank (Wildfire) Schulte and Jimmy Sheckard, and catcher Johnny Kling. The club also boasted one of the greatest of pitching staffs in right-handers Mordecai (Three Finger) Brown, Ed Reulbach, Carl Lundgren, and Orval Overall and lefty Jack Pfiester, whose combined earned-run average was a barely visible 1.76.

The White Sox, on the other hand, were known as "the Hitless Wonders." The label was well earned, for manager Fielder Jones's team had won the pennant despite the league's lowest batting average—.230. The Sox did have four good starting pitchers, however: right-handers Frank Owen and spitballer Ed Walsh, and left-handers Nick Altrock and Doc White.

Since no one had stopped the Cubs all summer in the National League, it seemed unlikely that "the Hitless Wonders" would do it in the fall. But from out of this apparent mismatch came a startling upset and the veritable legislating of what has become baseball dogma: anything can happen in a short series.

White Sox skipper Jones was even ready to concede game one to the Cubs, holding back his best pitcher, Walsh, because Jones felt that his club could not beat Three Finger Brown. So the Sox started Altrock, and the lefty pitched a strong game and edged Brown 2–1. With the Series alternating between the Cubs' West Side Park and the White Sox' South Side Park, the Cubs took the second game at South Side behind Reulbach, 7–1. Ed pitched a one-hitter, holding the Sox hitless until the seventh inning, when Jiggs Donahue singled cleanly to center.

Walsh pitched a two-hit shutout in game three, beating Jack Pfiester 3–0. Jack yielded just four hits, but one of those was a three-run triple by third baseman George Rohe. When Brown allowed just two hits in outdueling Altrock 1–0 in game four, it looked as if "the Hitless Wonders" were determined to live up to their billing. Through the first four games they had collected just 11 hits and had an aggregate batting average of .097. Yet they had managed to hold the Cubs even through four games.

And then the White Sox began behaving in a most uncharacteristic way. In game five they suddenly erupted, unloading on Reulbach, Pfiester, and Overall for 12 hits (four of them doubles by second baseman Frank Isbell), and whipped the Cubs 8–6, despite six infield errors.

The following day "the Hitless Wonders" hurled another brick at their own image by dispatching the near unbeatable Three Finger Brown (26–6 that year) in two innings, hammering his darting curve balls for eight hits and six runs. The Sox went on to a 7–3 win behind White for the world championship.

Years later a friend was twitting a long-retired Three Finger Brown about the 1906 Series. Asked how such lollipop hitters could have roughed him up so badly, Brown responded with the standard explanation for the game's more inscrutable caprices. "That's baseball," the old man said.

1907

Frank Chance led his Cubs on another Sherman-like march through the National League in 1907, winning 107 games and finishing 17 games in front. It was basically the same team as the year before, rounded off by that awesome pitching staff, which had again posted a collective earned-run average that almost precluded losing—1.73.

Chicago's opponents in the 1907 World Series were the Detroit Tigers, who by a mere 1½ games had taken their first American League pennant. This Tiger club, managed by Hughie Jennings, was not particularly strong except on the mound, where it had three 20-game winners in Wild Bill Donovan, George Mullin, and Ed Killian, and in the outfield, where they had the powerful Sam Crawford and a twenty-year-old batting champion named Ty Cobb. Cobb was a youngster with a personality like a buzz saw, a determination to win that bordered on the psychotic, and a talent that would ultimately create parameters of achievement for all who followed him on a ball field.

The opener in Chicago ended in a 12-inning 3–3 tie, called because of darkness. The Tigers, behind Donovan, had it won until the bottom of the ninth, when, with two out, Tiger catcher Charlie Schmidt missed a third strike that allowed the tying run to score (presaging another, more celebrated, missed third strike that would occur in the ninth inning of a World Series game thirty-four years later).

That opening game was as close as the Tigers came to winning in the 1907 Series, as Frank Chance's boys labored to wipe away the stigma of losing to "the Hitless Wonders" the year before. Over the next four games Pfiester, Reulbach, Overall, and Brown allowed Cobb and the Tigers just three runs, with Brown ending it with a 2–0 shutout in Detroit, a game witnessed by just 7,370 fans. According to the newspapers, by this time Tiger fans had given up on their heroes.

The Cubs won it by playing a hustling, aggressive game typical of the dead-ball era—laying down sacrifice bunts, stealing bases (16 in the five games), and taking extra bases. It was the style of play that would find its ultimate practitioner in Cobb, but in that Series Tyrus was out-Cobbed by the Cubs. The American League's batting (.350) and base-stealing (49) champ hit just .200 and stole no bases.

1908

Frank Chance brought his Cubs to the World Series for the third straight year in 1908, but this time the Chicagoans had to fight down to the final game of the season before assuring themselves of a postseason paycheck. This was the year of the notorious "Merkle boner." With the Cubs and Giants tightly contesting for the pennant, the Giants seemed to have won a key game against their rivals on September 23 at the Polo Grounds, on an Al Bridwell single with men on first and third and two out in the bottom of the ninth. The runner on first base, however, young Fred Merkle, neglected to go all the way and touch second base (as the rules required), instead sprinting for the clubhouse in center field as the joyous crowd spilled onto the field. The Cubs' alert Johnny Evers spotted the oversight, called for the ball (it turned out to be "a" ball, since the winning hit was somewhere in the outfield), and touched second base, thus forcing Merkle and nullifying the winning run, leaving the game tied. With the crowd on the field, the umpires were unable to resume play and declared the game a tie. When the Cubs and Giants ended the regular season in a dead heat, the September 23 game was made up at the Polo Grounds on October 8. Three Finger Brown beat Christy Mathewson 4–2, and the Cubs had taken their third straight pennant.

In the American League, it was Hughie Jennings's Tigers again, by a margin as narrow as a flea's eyelash—half a game over Cleveland and 1½ games over the White Sox. The Tigers were again a solid but uninspiring team, with the exception of batting champion Cobb (.324) and Sam Crawford. The Tigers, however, again had a formidable pitching staff in Wild Bill Donovan, George Mullin, Ed Willett, and knuckle baller Ed Summers, all right-handers.

The Cubs were fielding the same unit for the third year in a row—Chance, Evers, Tinker, and Steinfeldt in the infield, Kling behind the plate, and Schulte and Sheckard in the outfield along with Solly Hofman and Jimmy Slagle. And once more the Cubs brought their magnificent pitching to bear in a short series: Three Finger Brown (29–9 that year), Ed Reulbach, Orval Overall, and Jack Pfiester.

The opening game of the 1908 Series was a replay of the 1907 opener—the Tigers blowing a ninth-inning lead to a Cub rally. With Detroit leading 6–5 in the top of the ninth, the Cubs broke out with six straight singles against Summers, scoring five times and winning the first game 10–6.

The Cubs turned to the big inning again the next day in Chicago, breaking up a scoreless duel between Donovan and Overall with six runs in the bottom of the eighth, highlighted by three stolen bases and a two-run homer by Tinker.

In game three, the big inning belonged to Detroit. The Tigers came up with a five-run fifth to more than wipe out a 3–1 Chicago lead, enabling George Mullin to coast to an 8–3 win. It was in this game that Ty Cobb enjoyed the finest World Series outing he ever had. The twenty-one-year-old Georgian rapped three singles and a double in five at bats and stole two bases. In the ninth inning he singled and promptly stole second and third, but then the hyped-up boy wonder pressed his luck and was out trying to steal home.

After the Tiger victory in game three, the Series returned to Detroit and the Cubs' pitching returned to form. Brown shut out the Tigers in game four on four hits, 3–0, and Overall closed it out the next day with a three-hit, 2–0 shutout, giving the Cubs their second straight championship. This finale of the 1908 Series was notable for two reasons: at one hour and twenty-five minutes, it was the quickest World Series game ever played, and it drew the smallest crowd ever to witness a Series game—6,210.

Frank Chance was not only an effective manager—they called him "the Peerless Leader"—but in the 1908 World Series he led by example, leading all players with eight hits, a .421 batting average, and five stolen bases. This is managing with flair.

1909

Ask yourself if this is possible: a team wins the pennant, largely on the strength of three fine pitchers whose win totals are 25, 22, and 19. The team goes into the World Series and none of its big three pitches effectively; none, in fact, wins a game. Can this team possibly win the World Series? The answer is yes, for this is just what happened in 1909.

The Pittsburgh Pirates finally broke the Cubs' grip on first place, though it took 110 victories to do it, as Frank Chance's boys went down fighting, winning 104 games. The three Pirate pitchers who had done so well throughout the season were Howie Camnitz (25–6), Vic Willis (22–11), and Lefty Leifield (19–8). Camnitz started game two, Leifield game four, and Willis game six, all of which Pittsburgh lost. The Pirates won the odd-numbered games, three of which were started, completed, and won by a rookie 12-game winner named Charles (Babe) Adams, while the other game was won by Nick Maddox, a 13-game winner during the season.

The victims of Adams's fine pitching were the Detroit Tigers, back for the third straight year as pennant winners, and for the third straight year turned away in frustration, although this time they fought it down to the seventh game, the first time a World Series had gone the limit.

The Tigers again rolled out Ty Cobb (a Triple Crown winner that year), Sam Crawford, and another strong pitching staff, topped by 29-game winner George Mullin, 22-game winner Ed Willett, and 19-game winner Ed Summers.

The 1909 Series was flavored by the confrontation of the game's two greatest players, Cobb and Pittsburgh's Honus Wagner, "the antelope and the buffalo," as one writer has described them, each a batting champion that year.

According to one story that floated out of that Series, Pirate manager Fred Clarke's ace, Camnitz, had a weakness for bottled spirits, and when Howie showed up for the opener in Pittsburgh looking a bit unsteady, Clarke decided to start Adams, a twenty-seven-year-old rookie. Babe curve-balled his way through the Tiger lineup and beat Mullin, 4–1.

Thereafter, it was my-turn-your-turn as the two teams alternated wins and losses. Adams and Mullin each won twice for their teams, while veteran Wild Bill Donovan and Nick Maddox each won a game.

So the Series came down to a seventh game for the first time. Hughie Jennings started Donovan, while Clarke brought Adams back for the third time, on two days' rest. It was a cold, damp day in Detroit, cold enough for the umpires to don overcoats. But Adams remained hot, pitching a smooth six-hitter as his mates pecked away at Tiger pitching for an 8–0 victory and Pittsburgh's first world championship.

For the Tigers and their fans it was a particularly galling defeat, their third in a row. The team, which had stolen 280 bases during the season, swiped just 6 in the Series, as opposed to the Pirates' 18, a record for a seven-game Series. Six of these thefts were by Wagner, who outplayed Cobb throughout, batting .333 to Ty's .231. For Wagner it was a triumphant farewell to Series competition; the old warhorse would never play in another. Nor would Ty Cobb ever again serve in postseason competition, despite a career that still had nineteen years to run.

1910

The Chicago Cubs were back in the World Series in 1910, winning their fourth pennant in five years and playing a club that was just launching a four-out-of-five reign of their own—Connie Mack's Philadelphia Athletics.

The teams that Mack fielded from 1910 through 1914 are among the greatest in baseball history. The 1910 edition featured the king of second basemen, Eddie Collins, and third baseman Frank Baker, who had not yet picked up his famous nickname, "Home Run." The A's also had Jack Barry at shortstop and a couple of first-rate outfielders in Rube Oldring and Danny Murphy. On the mound Connie had a prodigious winner in right-hander Jack Coombs (31–9), along with another righty who almost never lost, Chief Bender, 23–5 that year. So efficient were these two that when Connie lost his number three starter, Eddie Plank, to a sore arm just before the Series, he never worried.

It was a rousing last hurrah for Frank Chance, Joe Tinker, Johnny Evers, Harry Steinfeldt, Jimmy Sheckard, Johnny Kling, and the rest of Chicago's turn-of-the-century dynasty. Winning 104 games, they had taken an easy pennant. Injuries had slowed down some of the pitchers, but Three Finger Brown was still going strong, winning 25, while rookie Leonard (King) Cole had broken in with a 20–4 record.

Despite the loss of Evers, who suffered a broken leg late in the season, the Cubs were favored to win the Series. But it was a classic situation, one ripe for an upset—an older, fading team versus a younger, brightening one just beginning its rush to glory.

The Series opened in Philadelphia, and Connie's boys applied two rude shocks to the Cubs. In game one, Chief Bender allowed the Cubs just three hits and one unearned run in a 4–1 victory. The next day Coombs, pitching an erratic game in which he allowed eight hits and walked nine, beat the Cubs 9–3. The Cubs left 14 men on base, a Series record that has since been tied twice. The A's combed Brown for 13 hits, including four doubles in a six-run eighth that put the game away.

After a day out for travel, Mack surprised everyone by coming back with Coombs. Pitching with one day's rest, Jack coasted to a 12–5 win behind a 15-hit attack. It was now three games to none, Athletics.

The Cubs kept their heads above water in game four, but just barely. Trailing 3–2 in the bottom of the ninth, they tied it on a triple by Chance, then won it in the tenth on a base hit by Sheckard.

Chicago's fine comeback merely delayed the inevitable. In the fifth and final game, it was Coombs again, on two days' rest. Jack dueled Brown until the top of the eighth, when the Athletics ripped Three Finger for five runs and a 7–2 win, ending the Series.

Though his wins were not as immaculate, Jack Coombs had matched Mathewson's iron-armed feat of three wins in six days. The A's helped him with some lusty hitting, batting .316 as a team, a figure that stood as a World Series record until 1960. Eddie Collins led all batters with nine hits and a .429 average, while Frank Baker, also with nine hits, batted .409. Murphy drove in nine runs for the A's—still the record for a five-game Series—three of them coming on the Series' only home run, in game three.

For Frank Chance and his Cubs, it was the end of the supremacy that had brought them four pennants in five years, won with virtually the same team each time.

Boston's Huntington Avenue Grounds before the start of one of the games in the 1903 World Series. Note the band of spectators in the outfield. They were allowed to stand there during the game.

A view of Boston's somewhat ramshackle dugout during the 1903 Series. Cy Young is at the far left, while first baseman Candy LaChance is the man on the near right.

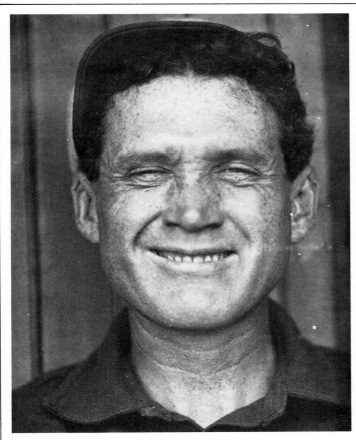

Boston's Patsy Dougherty, who hit two of the three home runs hit in the 1903 Series, both in game two.

Cy Young.

Pittsburgh's Deacon Phillippe, who started and completed five games in the 1903 World Series.

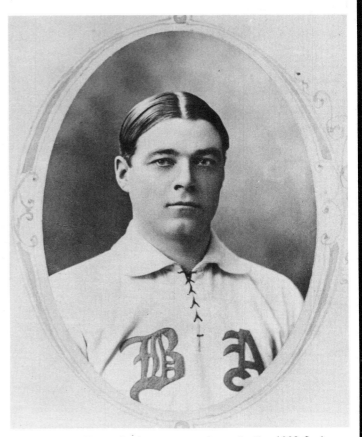

Bill Dinneen, Boston's three-game winner in the 1903 Series.

Christy Mathewson.

Dan McGann, McGraw's first baseman in the 1905 World Series. Dan's four RBIs topped all hitters in this light-hitting Series.

Ed Reulbach, who one-hit the White Sox in the second game of the 1906 World Series.

Ed Walsh.

Outfielder Topsy Hartsel, whose .294 batting average was the most respectable mark posted by an A's hitter in the 1905 Series.

The Giants' Roger Bresnahan, the man who caught all those New York shutouts against the Athletics.

Chicago White Sox southpaw Nick Altrock.

A rare action photo from the 1906 Series. It is the top of the sixth inning, the White Sox have the bases loaded, and Jack Pfiester is on the mound for the Cubs, pitching to Frank Isbell. Pfiester struck him out, but the next batter, George Rohe, tripled to left field, clearing the bases and giving the White Sox a 3–0 win.

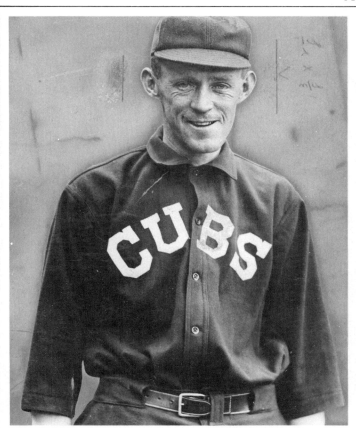

Johnny Evers, Chicago's sparkplug second baseman.

Chicago Cubs third baseman Harry Steinfeldt, who with his .471 batting average led all hitters in the 1907 World Series.

First baseman Claude Rossman, Detroit's top hitter in the 1907 Series, with eight hits and a .400 batting average.

Ed Killian, Detroit's 25-game-winning left-hander.

Wild Bill Donovan, another 25-game winner for Detroit.

Chicago Cubs shortstop Joe Tinker, who hit the only home run struck in the 1908 World Series.

Cubs manager and first baseman Frank Chance, shown here relaxing on the farm after his club's victory in the 1908 Series.

Detroit's Ed Summers, a 24-game winner who lost twice to the Cubs in the 1908 Series.

Three Finger Brown.

Frank (Wildfire) Shulte, a .389 batter for the Cubs in the 1908 Series.

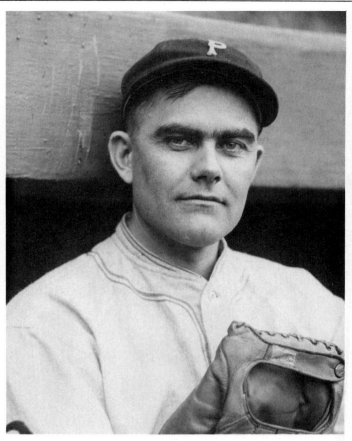

Babe Adams, Pittsburgh's three-game winner in their victory over Detroit in the 1909 World Series.

Chicago right-hander Orval Overall. He and Brown each beat the Tigers twice in the 1908 Series.

Detroit second baseman Jim Delahanty, whose nine hits were tops in the 1909 Series.

Ty Cobb.

Honus Wagner.

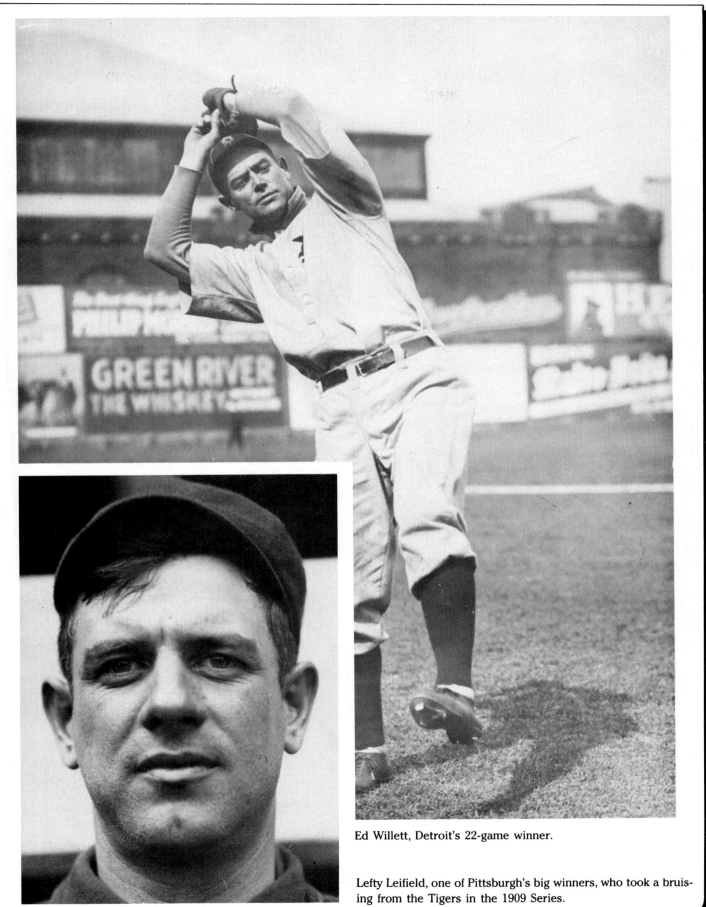

Ed Willett, Detroit's 22-game winner.

Lefty Leifield, one of Pittsburgh's big winners, who took a bruising from the Tigers in the 1909 Series.

George Mullin, Detroit's ace right-hander. The 29-game winner beat the Pirates twice.

Babe Adams.

Leonard (King) Cole, Chicago's 20-game-winning rookie in 1910.

The Athletics' Frank Baker: nine hits and a .409 batting average against the Cubs in the 1910 World Series.

Eddie Collins, top gun in the 1910 Series with nine hits and a .429 batting average.

Jack Coombs: three starts, three wins.

Danny Murphy, Athletics outfielder, who set a record for a five-game Series in 1910 with nine runs batted in.

Catcher Jimmy Archer (left) and second baseman Heinie Zimmerman of the 1910 Cubs.

II

Heading Toward Scandal
1911-1920

Connie Mack.

John McGraw.

1911

In order to be deemed great, Connie Mack contended, a team had to repeat. And repeat the Philadelphia Athletics did, taking a second straight pennant and world championship in 1911.

With the addition of Stuffy McInnis to the infield at first base, Mack now had in place his famous "$100,000 infield": McInnis, Eddie Collins, Jack Barry, and Frank Baker. (That dollar amount referred to what people believed the quartet would have been worth had Connie put them up for sale in those preinflation days of the far-reaching dollar.) In addition to a strong outfield of Danny Murphy, Rube Oldring, and Bris Lord, Mack had his three talented pitchers: Jack Coombs, following his 31-game season with a 29–12 record; Chief Bender; and the ageless Eddie Plank.

Opposing this great Athletics team was John McGraw's New York Giants, back in the Series for the first time since 1905. McGraw had .300 hitters in second baseman Larry Doyle, shortstop Art Fletcher, and catcher Chief Meyers, and a jackrabbit club that stole 347 bases during the season, still the big-league record. And John J. still had the prince of pitchers, Christy Mathewson, a 26-game winner in 1911, backed up by hard-throwing left-hander Rube Marquard (24–7).

Mathewson outpitched Bender in the opener in New York, 2–1. With the teams riding the train back and forth between New York and Philadelphia to alternate home fields, Plank edged Marquard the next day, 3–1. The winning runs came in the bottom of the sixth, when Baker shot a two-run homer over the right-field wall. This put him on the brink of gaining the most illustrious nickname in baseball.

21

Mathewson was back for game three, matched with Coombs, and quite a match it turned out to be. Matty had it 1–0 going into the top of the ninth. A look at Mathewson's World Series record up to this point might be in order. In the 1905 Series he had posted a clean slate—27 scoreless innings. In the 1911 opener he had allowed just one run, and here he had worked another eight innings of shutout ball, meaning that McGraw's incomparable ace had pitched 44 innings of World Series–pressure baseball and allowed just one run. But with one out in the top of the ninth, Frank Baker drove one into the right-field stands, tying the game. It was, up to that time, the most dramatic home run in World Series play. The A's went on to win it in the eleventh.

After that, the skies opened. Six days of rain intervened between games three and four, so that when the Series resumed the A's were facing a well-rested Mathewson. Christy's October magic, however, was not as potent as before. Behind Bender's steady pitching, the A's won, 4–2, with Baker weighing in with a pair of key doubles.

On the point of elimination now, the Giants fought it off with a gutsy ten-inning win the next day, 4–3, tying it with two in the last of the ninth and winning it with a run in the tenth when Larry Doyle scored on a sacrifice fly. Plate umpire Bill Klem later said that Doyle had missed home plate when he came sliding in; none of the Athletics noticed the omission, however, and, this being an appeal play, Klem was compelled to let the run stand.

After five tightly played games, the Athletics tore it apart behind Bender in game six, winning 13–2, flattening McGraw's boys with a seven-run seventh. Mack's team had fulfilled their skipper's definition of greatness: they had repeated.

Baker, known forever after as "Home Run," after his two key clouts, had another fine Series, leading all hitters with a .375 average. The unsung heroes for the Athletics, however, were catchers Ira Thomas and Jack Lapp. After having run wild through the National League with 347 stolen bases, the Giants were successful in just 4 of 12 steal attempts against Mack's strong-armed catchers. Overall, McGraw's club played a ragged Series, committing 16 errors and having various runners picked off, doubled up, and caught stretching, while batting just .175 against Bender, Coombs, and Plank.

1912

In 1912 the Boston Red Sox began a run that would bring them four pennants in seven years. In fact, between 1910 and 1916 the Red Sox and Athletics traded first place back and forth, the A's taking four of the pennants, the Red Sox three.

Spearheading Boston's drive to the pennant was a one-of-a-kind speedballing right-hander named Smoky Joe Wood. This twenty-two-year-old put together what is perhaps the greatest single season ever for a pitcher: a 34–5 won–lost record, a 1.91 earned-run average, 10 shutouts, and 258 strikeouts. Backing up Wood were right-handers Hugh Bedient, Buck O'Brien, and Charley Hall and lefty Ray Collins. The Red Sox also had one of the great defensive outfields in Tris Speaker, Harry Hooper, and Duffy Lewis. Player-manager Jake Stahl was a .300 hitter at first base, as was third baseman Larry Gardner.

Lining up against this Red Sox outfit were McGraw's Giants, winners of their second pennant in a row. It was one of John J.'s better clubs, with Fred Merkle at first, Larry Doyle at second, Art Fletcher at short, and Buck Herzog at third. Red Murray and Fred Snodgrass were outfield regulars, while Chief Meyers did the bulk of the catching. Christy Mathewson, Rube Marquard, and rookie Jeff Tesreau were McGraw's front three starters.

McGraw decided to start the rookie Tesreau in the opener at the Polo Grounds, but the gamble did not pay off, as Joe Wood popped his buzz ball for a 4–3 win, fanning 11, the last two of them with the tying and winning runs on second and third in the bottom of the ninth.

Alternating playing sites game by game, the two teams entrained for Boston. With Mathewson squaring off against Collins at Boston's brand-new Fenway Park, the teams played to a 6–6 eleven-inning tie, the game being called because of darkness. The Giants should have won it in ten after taking a 6–5 lead, but the Sox tied it on a Speaker triple and a dropped throw at home plate. All in all, Matty was undone by his infield, which made five errors that allowed four unearned runs.

Marquard evened the Series the next day, beating O'Brien 2–1. But then Wood beat Tesreau 3–1 and Bedient nipped Mathewson 2–1, giving Boston a commanding three-games-to-one lead.

With the waters rising around them, McGraw's club fought back. They scored five runs in the first inning for Marquard, and Rube held on for a 5–2 win. The next day they raked Wood for six in the first and coasted behind Tesreau to an 11–4 win. The stage was set for the finale in Fenway Park, with the Giants having the momentum.

McGraw started the great Mathewson, while Stahl went with Bedient. The Giants scored in the top of the third, and Mathewson nursed the run along to the bottom of the seventh. Then, with two out and men on first and second, Olaf Henriksen pinch-hit for Bedient and doubled in the tying run.

Joe Wood took over for Boston, and the youngster dueled Mathewson into the top of the tenth, when the Giants broke the tie on a double by Murray and a single by Merkle.

The last of the tenth, with Christy Mathewson just three outs away from a world championship, is one of the most memorable—and memorably fouled up —innings in World Series annals. It began with Clyde Engle batting for Wood. Clyde lifted an easy fly ball to center. Center fielder Fred Snodgrass stood under it; the ball came down, hit his glove, and bounced to the grass. Just like that. No explanations, no excuses. "I dropped it," said Snodgrass, who had to live with the flub for the rest of his life.

With Engle on second, the next batter, Harry Hooper, ripped a line drive into left center that looked like a sure triple, but Snodgrass, in a swift reversal of form, made a brilliant catch of it. "That's the one nobody ever remembers," Snodgrass said ruefully.

Pitching carefully, Mathewson walked the next batter, Steve Yerkes. Up came Tris Speaker, next to Cobb baseball's most dangerous hitter. Joe Wood, sitting on the Red Sox bench, describes what happened:

"Speaker lifted a little pop foul between first and home. The first baseman, Merkle, had the best shot at it. But instead of calling for Merkle to take it, Mathewson came down off the mound calling for Chief Meyers, the catcher. Merkle could have caught it easily, but Mathewson kept calling for Meyers, I'll never know why. You see, Merkle was coming in on the ball and the Chief was going with it. It's a much easier play for Merkle. But there was Matty, yelling for the Chief. But Meyers never could get to it. The ball dropped. It just clunked down into the grass in foul ground and lay there. We couldn't believe it. Neither could Mathewson. You never saw a man as mad as he was when the ball hit the ground. But the way we saw it, it was his own fault. He called for the wrong man."

And the Red Sox still had the right man at home plate. Speaker hit the next pitch into right field for a single, scoring Engle and sending Yerkes to third. A moment later Larry Gardner hit a sacrifice fly to right field and the Red Sox were champions.

History has remembered Fred Snodgrass as the goat of the 1912 World Series, but according to Joe Wood and his Red Sox teammates, the moment of crucial undoing came when Christy Mathewson called for the wrong man on Speaker's pop foul.

1913

For the third time in nine years the World Series featured a match-up of the two men considered baseball's premier managers— John McGraw and Connie Mack. Each man was at the very crest of his game, with McGraw winning his third consecutive pennant, while for Connie it was his third in four years.

The Giants entered the Series handicapped by injuries to two regulars, center fielder Fred Snodgrass and first baseman Fred Merkle. Merkle hobbled through the Series, and Snodgrass hardly played at all. In addition, regular catcher Chief Meyers broke a finger during pregame warm-ups prior to the start of game two. But McGraw was able to go into the Series with his usual strong pitching staff—Christy Mathewson, Rube Marquard, and Jeff Tesreau, each a 20-plus winner that year.

Mack still had his veteran pitching stalwarts Eddie Plank and Chief Bender, along with a hard-throwing youngster named Joe Bush, called "Bullet Joe" for the velocity of his fast ball. This was another hard-hitting Athletics club, with Stuffy McInnis batting .326, Eddie Collins .345, Home Run Baker .336, and outfielder Amos Strunk .305.

In the opener in New York Bender beat Marquard 6–4, with Baker driving in three runs with three hits, including a home run. Frank apparently liked his nickname and wanted to hang on to it.

In game two Mathewson and Plank matched craft and guile, and after nine innings it was as it had been at the beginning: 0–0. In the bottom of the ninth, the Giants had put on a stirring baseball version of the "goal-line stand." With none out, the A's had Strunk on third and Jack Barry on second. The next batter, Jack Lapp, grounded to first, where Hooks Wiltse, a pitcher, was filling in. Wiltse made a good stop and threw home to nab Strunk. With Barry on third now and Lapp on first, Plank grounded to Wiltse and Hooks fired home again, getting a sliding Barry. Mathewson retired the next man, and the game went into overtime. In the top of the tenth, the Giants scored three, with Matty sprinkling a bit more stardust over his legend by singling in the winning run. The final score was 3–0.

After that it was all Philadelphia. Behind Bush, Bender, and Plank, the Athletics swept games three, four, and five, with Plank closing it out with a two-hit, 3–1 victory over Mathewson.

For the Athletics, Frank Baker turned in another fine series, getting nine hits in the five games, driving in seven runs, and batting .450. For John McGraw and his Giants, the World Series was proving to be a mixed blessing—three straight appearances, three straight losses.

1914

The world of baseball, never mundane to begin with, was treated to something extra-special in 1914: a miracle. This miracle, baseball style, was fashioned by the Boston Braves. In last place in mid-July, the Braves began rumbling, generating steam and a drive that never faltered until the season was over. Winning 34 of their last 44 games, George Stallings's club swept in by 10½ games.

The Braves' miracle was shaped primarily by two prodigious winners, right-handers Dick Rudolph (27–10) and Bill James (26–7), and a solid third starter, George (Lefty) Tyler (16–14). Otherwise, the team was notable only for Johnny Evers, the former Chicago Cubs firebrand, now playing second for the Braves, and shortstop Walter (Rabbit) Maranville, light of bat but magical of glove.

Opposed to this club of spirited miracle workers were Connie Mack's seemingly invincible Philadelphia Athletics, winners of three of the last four World Series and, by all that seemed sane and logical, sure to be winners of this one also. Connie still had his brand-name pitchers Bender and Plank, wily veterans of the October shadows, abetted by a strong young staff that included Joe Bush, Bob Shawkey, and Herb Pennock. On hand also were McInnis, Collins, Barry, Baker, and the rest of Connie's unbeatables.

"Anything can happen in a short series." Once again the homey old bromide became an October summation. Not only did something happen, it happened with stunning totality: the nondescript Braves swept the best team in baseball in four.

The Braves gave Bender a bumping in the opener in Philadelphia, winning 7–1 behind Rudolph. The next day fast baller James nipped Plank in a beauty, 1–0, the run scoring on a ninth-inning single by Les Mann.

The clubs then took the train up to Boston, where the Braves had arranged to play their home games in the Red Sox' Fenway Park rather than in their own South End Grounds. Fenway's larger seating capacity meant more money for everyone. (Avarice in baseball is definitely not a latter-day phenomenon.)

The Braves took a twelve-inning tingler in game three, 5–4, after both clubs had scored twice in the tenth. The hitting star for Boston was a most unlikely customer—catcher Hank Gowdy, a .243 lightweight for the season. In this game, Hank rapped two doubles and the only home run of the Series.

The Braves completed their miracle immaculately the next day with a 3–1 win behind Rudolph, with a single by Johnny Evers driving home the world-championship runs in the fifth inning. It was the first four-game wipeout ever in a World Series.

Evers batted .438 for the Series, but the big gunner was Gowdy at .545, including three doubles, a triple, and a home run. Rudolph, James, and Tyler, who did all of Boston's pitching, held Connie Mack's boys to a collective .172 batting average. It was a season and a Series for Boston Braves fans to savor. And they were going to have to savor it for a long time. The Braves did not win another pennant until 1948.

1915

It was Boston and Philadelphia again in the Series in 1915, but instead of the Braves and the Athletics, it was the Red Sox and the Phillies.

Leading the Phillies to the pennant was one of the greatest of all pitchers, Grover Cleveland Alexander, a 31-game winner that year, the first of three consecutive 30-game seasons for Alex. The club also featured home run champ Gavvy Cravath, the burly outfielder having hit 24 one-way shots in 1915, setting a modern major-league record. First baseman Fred Luderus batted .315, second best in the league, while at shortstop the Phillies had one of the smoothest in Dave Bancroft. Running the club was freshman manager Pat Moran.

Catcher-manager Bill Carrigan's Red Sox were particularly strong on defense, with Harry Hooper, Tris Speaker, and Duffy Lewis in the outfield, Everett Scott at shortstop, Larry Gardner at third, Jack Barry at second, and Dick Hoblitzel at first. Boston was also strong on the mound, where right-handers Rube Foster and Ernie Shore and southpaws Dutch Leonard and Babe Ruth led a fine staff. It was the twenty-year-old Ruth's first full year in the big leagues, and he dazzled one and all with an 18–8 record. "He can hit, too," manager Carrigan said. In fact, Ruth's lone appearance in the 1915 Series was as a pinch hitter in the opening game. (He grounded out.)

The Phillies, behind Alexander, won the opener, beating Shore 3–1, scoring two runs in the bottom of the eighth on two walks and two infield singles.

The Series saw a notable "first" when President Woodrow Wilson journeyed up from Washington to see the second game in Philadelphia, the first time a President had attended a World Series game. The Chief Executive saw a good one, too, as Foster nipped Erskine Mayer 2–1, with Rube himself driving in the winning run in the top of the ninth with his third hit of the game.

When the clubs moved the Series up to Boston for games three and four, they played not in Fenway Park but in newly built Braves Field, which held more people; indeed, 42,300 attended the third game, a new World Series attendance record.

The teams played a pair of tight ball games in Boston. In game three, Leonard beat Alexander 2–1 on a single by Duffy Lewis in the bottom of the ninth. The following day, Shore won over George Chalmers, 2–1—the third straight 2–1 Red Sox victory.

The teams returned to Philadelphia with the Phillies down three games to one and in sad shape, having managed just 18 hits off of Boston's good pitching. Game five was an odd one, with the Red Sox hitting three home runs to back up Foster's 5–4 Series-ending victory. What was odd about this power show was that the Sox had hit just 14 home runs all year (four of them by pitcher Ruth). Hooper hit one in the third inning to tie the score at 2–2, Lewis hit a two-run shot in the top of the eighth to tie the score at 4–4, and then in the top of the ninth Hooper hit another that proved the game winner. (Over the course of the season, Lewis and Hooper had hit just two home runs apiece.)

Lewis and Hooper did the bulk of Boston's hitting,

with averages of .444 and .350 respectively. For the Phillies, who batted a mere .182 in the Series, Fred Luderus did most of what little hitting they showed, batting .438 and driving in six of his team's ten runs.

Phillies fans didn't realize it at the time, but there was a long, arid road ahead. Their ball club was not destined to win another pennant until 1950, or another World Series game until 1980.

1916

For the third consecutive season the National League sent a brand-new team to the World Series, an event that had been dominated by Pittsburgh, New York, and Chicago from its inception through 1913. After Boston in 1914 and Philadelphia in 1915 came Brooklyn in 1916. The Dodgers, under their colorful skipper Wilbert Robinson, won their first pennant since the establishment of the two-league structure in 1901. The Dodgers had two good hitters in first baseman Jake Daubert and outfielder Zack Wheat, and a 25-game winner in right-hander Jeff Pfeffer. The rest of the staff was a mélange of retreads that Robinson manipulated skillfully all season—Rube Marquard from the Giants, Larry Cheney from the Cubs, and Connie Mack's former 30-game winner Jack Coombs.

The American League sent a familiar entry to the Series—the Boston Red Sox. With Tris Speaker having been dealt to Cleveland in a salary dispute, the Sox were without a big hitter, but they were still deep in pitching, with young Mr. Ruth (23–12), followed by Carl Mays, Dutch Leonard, Ernie Shore, and Rube Foster.

The Red Sox were top-heavy favorites to win, to such an extent that a young Dodger outfielder named Casey Stengel approached some of the Sox players before the first game and whimsically asked them what they thought the Dodgers' losing share might amount to.

There was to be no upset in this World Series. The Red Sox took the first two games in Boston (again played in Braves Field to accommodate more fans). In game two, Ruth and Brooklyn's southpaw Sherry Smith engaged in the greatest pitching duel in World Series history. The Dodgers scored in the top of the first on an inside-the-park home run by Hy Myers, and the Red Sox tied it in the bottom of the third, Ruth himself knocking in the run with a ground ball. Thereafter it was zero upon zero, for ten innings. Finally, in the bottom of the fourteenth, the Red Sox won it on a pinch single by Del Gainor. Ruth had made his first impact on World Series play, hurling thirteen consecutive scoreless innings.

In game three, in Brooklyn's Ebbets Field, Jack Coombs ran his lifetime World Series record to 5–0, beating Mays 4–3 on Ivy Olson's two-run triple in the fifth inning. And that was it for the Dodgers. Leonard

and Shore held the Brooks to eight hits over the last two games, and the Red Sox had taken their fourth world championship in four tries.

Duffy Lewis and Harry Hooper again led Boston's attack, with averages of .353 and .333 respectively. The leading hitter of the Series, however, was Brooklyn's chatty Mr. Stengel, who batted .364. It was Stengel's first World Series. He would be back twelve more times—two of them as a player, ten as a manager.

1917

After several years of rebuilding, during which his club dropped to last place (in 1915), John McGraw was back on top. His squad of new faces included three winning left-handers—Ferdie Schupp, Slim Sallee, and Rube Benton. He also had a couple of solid right-handers in Pol Perritt and the veteran Jeff Tesreau. Other new faces were third baseman Heinie Zimmerman and .300-hitting outfielders George Burns and Benny Kauff.

Opposing McGraw was a ball club heading for greatness and infamy—the Chicago White Sox. Unlike the last White Sox club to play in the fall—"the Hitless Wonders" of 1906—this outfit had its share of smoking bats, among them outfielders Shoeless Joe Jackson and Happy Felsch and second baseman Eddie Collins, whom the Sox had acquired from Connie Mack. The Chicago ace was right-hander Eddie Cicotte, a 28-game winner. Behind Eddie were two more good pitchers, righty Red Faber and lefty Claude Williams.

McGraw's World Series luck remained solidly bad. He lost the opener in Chicago 2–1 to Cicotte, the winning run being a home run by Felsch in the bottom of the fourth. The loser was Sallee, despite a good effort. The next day Faber whipped Schupp, 7–2.

Home cooking seemed to revive the Giants when they returned to New York, Benton and then Schupp hurling shutouts at the Polo Grounds, pulling the Giants even at two games apiece.

Back in Chicago for game five, however, the White Sox erased a 5–2 Giant lead with three in the seventh and three more in the eighth, battering Sallee while a mesmerized McGraw watched. Winning in relief for the White Sox was Faber, his second victory of the Series. Red came back two days later at the Polo Grounds and chalked up his third win and a world championship for the White Sox, 4–2.

This final game, which handed John McGraw his fourth World Series loss in seven years, featured a memorable footrace down the third-base line. In the top of the fourth, with no score, the White Sox brought in three runs, aided and abetted by the Giants. Collins led off and reached second on Zimmerman's throwing error. The next batter, Joe Jackson, lifted an easy fly ball, which right fielder Dave Robertson dropped, Collins moving to third. Happy Felsch then grounded to the pitcher, Rube Benton. With Collins breaking down the line, Benton threw to Zimmerman, the third baseman. Catcher Bill Rariden came up to help get Collins in a rundown. But Rariden got too close to Collins, and Eddie whirled and sprinted past him before Zimmerman could throw. With neither first baseman Walter Holke nor Benton backing up, Collins raced across the unguarded home plate with a frustrated Zimmerman, ball in hand, chasing him all the way. When Zim was later derided for his footrace, he responded with a deathless line: "Who the hell was I going to throw it to? Klem?" (Bill Klem was the plate umpire.)

Chick Gandil followed these high jinks with a two-run single, and the White Sox were on their way to a 4–2 win and the title.

In the 1912 Series McGraw had seen Snodgrass drop a fly ball and then Speaker's pop foul fall untouched, costing him a Series. Now it was a pair of errors and Heinie Zimmerman's comic pursuit of Collins costing him another crack at a title. John J. might have been wondering whether October was worth all the trouble.

1918

A World Series played in early September? Yes. It happened in 1918. With the war raging on the Western Front in France, the provost marshal issued a "work or fight" order, forcing qualified draft-age men into either war-related work or military service. Baseball was declared a nonessential industry, and the major leagues were ordered to terminate their seasons on Labor Day. A two-week grace period was granted to allow that national institution, the World Series, to be played.

So it began on September 5, in Chicago, Fred Mitchell's Cubs versus Ed Barrow's Red Sox. The Cubs boasted what was probably the best pitching staff in baseball in left-handers Jim (Hippo) Vaughan (22–10) and Lefty Tyler (19–8) and right-hander Claude Hendrix (20–7). Outside of their pitching and ex-Giant Fred Merkle at first base and a scintillating shortstop named Charlie Hollacher, however, the Cubs were a run-of-the-mill club.

With several of their regulars (most prominently Jack Barry and Duffy Lewis) lost to military service, the Red Sox fielded a team just good enough to win, with pitching again their strong suit, their top hitter being pitcher–first baseman–outfielder Babe Ruth. In 95 games that year the twenty-three-year-old boomer batted .300 and slammed 11 home runs, the latter figure good enough to tie for the league lead. Being phased into the starting lineup more and more now, the young lefty posted a 13–7 record. (Though he was still pitcher enough to open the World

Series.) The staff was topped that year by 21-game winner Carl Mays, Sam Jones, and Joe Bush, all right-handers.

So the World Series opened with the American League's home run champ on the mound. Ruth pitched brilliantly, and so did Hippo Vaughan. But Babe was just a little better, winning 1–0. This effort extended Ruth's World Series scoreless-inning string to 22⅓.

Tyler beat Bush 3–1 the next day to even it out, with Lefty himself knocking in the second and third runs with a single in the bottom of the second. The next day, Mays edged the Cubs 2–1, beating Vaughan, who had come back on one day's rest and pitched well again, but just not well enough.

Because of wartime travel restrictions, the first three games had been scheduled for Chicago, the remainder in Boston. When the clubs reconvened in Boston, it was Ruth against Tyler. (In a move designed to keep Ruth out of the starting lineup, Cubs manager Mitchell had decided to throw only left-handers against the Red Sox.) Ruth pitched seven more scoreless innings, the Cubs finally breaking the spell with two in the top of the seventh, ending Ruth's scoreless-inning streak at 29⅔, a World Series mark destined to stand for 43 years. Nevertheless, the Red Sox won it 3–2, with Ruth himself knocking in the first two with a fourth-inning triple. (Boston's starting pitcher was batting sixth in the lineup.) In the top of the ninth inning, when the Cubs threatened, Joe Bush came in to put out the fire, and starting pitcher Ruth went not to the dugout but out to left field.

The Red Sox were now up three games to one and poised to clinch it when a quaint occurrence took place before game five. This was the first year that the other first-division teams were being cut in on the Series money; consequently, the shares for the players participating in the Series would be smaller. (Considerably smaller: the winners received $1,103 apiece, the losers just $671.) So the players threatened to strike unless their shares were increased. When it was pointed out to them by American League president Ban Johnson that with American boys dying in the trenches in France at that moment, their demands would look selfish, petty, and down-right unpatriotic, the players relented and the Series went on.

Vaughan, pitching for the third time in six days, hurled another strong game, and this time it was he who received the handshakes, shutting out the Red Sox 3–0.

The next day Carl Mays put the baseball season to sleep—it was September 11—by nipping Tyler and the Cubs 2–1. Both Boston runs were unearned, scoring in the third inning when Cubs right fielder Max Flack dropped a line drive with runners on second and third and two out.

It was a pitchers' Series, the winning Red Sox batting .186, the losing Cubs .210. Particularly brilliant were Boston's Ruth and Mays, each winning two games; while particularly frustrated was Chicago's Vaughan, who pitched 27 innings, allowed just three runs, and won only one of three decisions. For Boston it was now five world championships in five tries.

For those who cared to take notice of such things, the National League had followed a peculiar pattern through the 1917 and 1918 World Series. In 1917 McGraw had started left-handers six times in six games—Schupp, Sallee, and Benton. In 1918 Chicago skipper Mitchell had done the same—Vaughan three times, Tyler three times. Twelve consecutive National League World Series games started by southpaws. It was enough to make right-handers think about organizing.

1919

The 1919 pennant-winning Chicago White Sox were considered an awesome ballplaying machine, the team that had everything. Pitching: Eddie Cicotte (29–7), Claude (Lefty) Williams (23–11), plus Dickie Kerr and Red Faber. Hitting: Shoeless Joe Jackson, Eddie Collins, Happy Felsch, Chick Gandil, Buck Weaver. Sparkling defense: particularly from shortstop Swede Risberg, third baseman Weaver, center fielder Felsch, catcher Ray Schalk, and second baseman Collins.

They were heavy favorites to win the World Series from the first-time pennant-winning Cincinnati Reds. But suddenly, on the eve of the Series, the odds made a hairpin turn and switched from 3–1 White Sox to 8–5 Reds. Rumors began flying in gusts. As the "smart" money kept pouring in on the Reds, the word was out: certain White Sox players had been "reached" by New York gamblers. Seven players, to be exact: pitchers Cicotte and Williams, first baseman Gandil, shortstop Risberg, outfielders Jackson and Felsch, and utility man Fred McMullin. An eighth, Weaver, knew about the fix but said nothing. (Buck's code of silence, which he no doubt thought was honorable, cost him his career when a few years later he was barred from organized baseball along with his seven tarnished teammates.)

Cincinnati had a good if unexceptional ball club, its most notable members being center fielder Edd Roush, first baseman Jake Daubert, and third baseman Heinie Groh. The Reds' pitching was strong and deep, with southpaws Slim Sallee and Dutch Ruether and right-handers Ray Fisher, Hod Eller, Jimmy Ring, and Dolf Luque, Cuba's first truly generous gift to major-league ball.

The swindlers had been promised $100,000 (most of which they never collected). Supposedly the signal that all was set would come on the first pitch of the Series, when Cicotte would plunk Cincinnati leadoff man Morrie Rath. The first pitch indeed went into Morrie's ribs, and the charade was on.

Cicotte dumped the opener and Williams the second game. Williams, noted as a control pitcher, walked six men in game two, four of them scoring, which was enough. White Sox southpaw Dickie Kerr became one of baseball's folk heroes when he struggled to victories in games three and six despite his less-than-enthusiastic supporting cast.

With baseball experimenting with a best-of-nine Series again, the 1919 fiasco labored on through eight games. Cincinnati got strong shutout efforts from Ring and Eller, but nobody will ever know how hard Joe Jackson and his confederates were trying. In fact, the whole thing began to bear out some gritty wisdom: if you weren't confused, you didn't understand it. With the White Sox facing extinction, down four games to two, Cicotte inexplicably kept his club alive with a strong effort.

The next day, however, Lefty Williams made sure. With rumors abounding that Cincinnati was going to be handed a torrential first inning, the curve-balling Williams, ignoring Schalk's signals, lobbed batting-practice fast balls across the plate for the Cincy hitters to tee off on. Before White Sox skipper Kid Gleason could get the blatant Williams out of there, three runs had scored and another was about to. Having been given this helping hand, the Reds went on to a 10–5 win and a dubious world championship.

"They played like horseshit," observed tough old Jimmy Ring years later, and then added a true athlete's comment: "but we would have beaten them anyway."

Maybe. According to some stories, the White Sox won their three games because they were trying to induce the gamblers to come across with tardy payments. In other words, when they were trying, the Sox were able to win.

The "Black Sox scandal," as it has become known, led to the installation of Judge Kenesaw Mountain Landis as baseball's all-powerful commissioner. The severe, unforgiving judge booted the unholy seven plus Weaver out of baseball forever and imposed upon the game an image of virtue and purity. A note for those concerned about such things: in the first two games Cincinnati started left-handers Sallee and Ruether, running to fourteen the string of National League World Series games started by southpaws. The string was broken when righty Ray Fisher started game three for the Reds.

1920

One play in game five made the 1920 World Series one of the most memorable of all October pageants. Cleveland second baseman Bill Wambsganss was the man who made the famous play, leaping high for a line drive, coming down with the ball, and thus beginning an unassisted triple play that enshrined him forever in the Valhalla of Unique Baseball Moments.

Despite the fact that the Black Sox scandal had broken just two weeks before the start of the 1920 Series, the best-of-nine affair between the Indians and the Brooklyn Dodgers was a well-attended, avidly followed contest.

The Cleveland staff boasted a 31-game winner in right-hander Jim Bagby, but the real ace of the staff was considered to be right-handed spitballer Stanley Coveleski (24–12). Cleveland had another 20-game winner in righty Ray Caldwell, while late-season acquisition Walter (Duster) Mails, a lefty, had gone 7–0. Player-manager Tris Speaker, batting .388 that season, led a club that included .300 hitters Larry Gardner, Charley Jamieson, Elmer Smith, and Steve O'Neill. It was a good, solid team, one that had had to recover from the mid-August loss of its fine shortstop Ray Chapman, who died after a beaning by the Yankees' Carl Mays. Joe Sewell, who was brought in to replace Chapman, also batted over .300 in his few weeks' work.

Brooklyn skipper Wilbert Robinson had his own 20-game-winning right-handed spitballer, Burleigh Grimes, backed by a rather deep staff that included right-handers Jeff Pfeffer, Al Mamaux, and Leon Cadore and lefties Rube Marquard, Sherry Smith, and Clarence Mitchell. While the Dodgers could not match Cleveland's hitting, they did have a trio of .300 stickers in first baseman Ed Konetchy and outfielders Zack Wheat and Hy Myers.

Up until game five, it was a quiet Series, with Coveleski (twice), Grimes, and Smith pitching strong, low-score wins for their teams. Game five, however, played in Cleveland on October 10, went rushing into the history books like a tidal wave.

In the first inning, Cleveland put the first three men on base against Grimes. Cleanup man Elmer Smith then sent one of Burleigh's fast balls over the right-field fence for the first grand-slam home run ever in a World Series. In the bottom of the fourth, Jim Bagby became the first pitcher ever to homer in a World Series when he deposited a Grimes delivery among the customers in the center-field seats. Grimes left, replaced by left-hander Clarence Mitchell.

Trailing 7–0 in the top of the fifth, Brooklyn got their first two batters, Pete Kilduff and Otto Miller, aboard with singles. The batter was Mitchell. Clarence was a good-hitting pitcher, and Robinson let him hit for himself, a decision for which baseball buffs have been forever grateful.

Mitchell ripped one of Bagby's pitches for what looked like a sure single to right. Kilduff and Miller certainly thought it was on its way, for they began charging along the base lines. Bill Wambsganss, however, ran to his right, leaped high, and speared the ball. His momentum having brought him close to second, Bill stepped on the bag, then whirled to see

where Otto Miller was. Otto was conveniently close, stopped dead in his tracks, still unable to believe what was happening. Wambsganss took a step or two and put the ball on him, completing the unassisted triple play. It took the stunned crowd a few moments to realize what had happened, and then they threw their hats onto the field in tribute.

Three innings later Mitchell again came to the plate, this time with a man on first and none out. Clarence rolled into a double play, giving him the distinction of making five outs in two at bats, an all-time record for offensive futility.

Possibly they were disheartened after making so much negative history, but over the next two games the Dodgers managed only eight hits and no runs against Walter Mails and Coveleski, who wrapped it up for Cleveland in game seven to give the Indians the title.

Stanley Coveleski's pitching in 1920 stands among the finest in World Series annals. He allowed just 2 runs, 2 walks, and 15 hits in 27 innings, for an 0.67 earned-run average. Overall, the Indian staff logged an 0.88 earned-run average for 61 innings of work.

Coveleski was the eighth man to win three games in a single Series. It would be 26 years before it happened again.

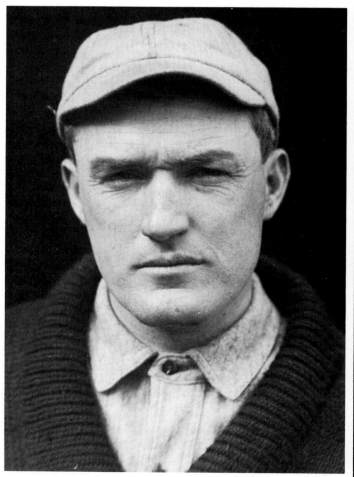

Bill Carrigan.

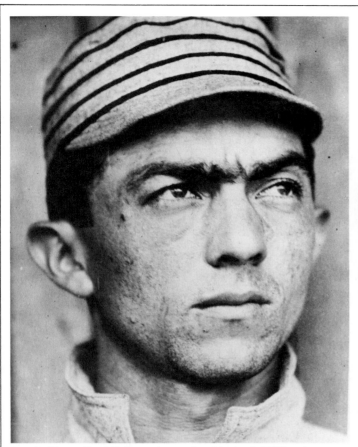

Frank (Home Run) Baker, whose nine hits and .375 batting average topped all hitters in the 1911 World Series.

The Athletics' Rube Oldring, who belted a three-run homer against the Giants in game five of the 1911 Series.

Connie Mack's shortstop Jack Barry, who slammed four doubles and batted .368 in the 1911 Series.

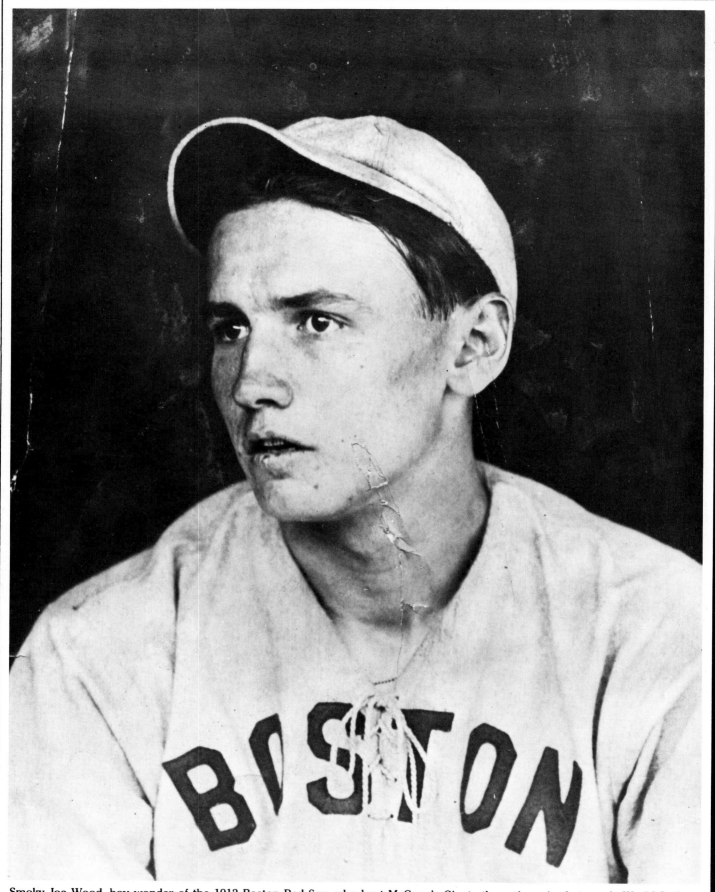

Smoky Joe Wood, boy wonder of the 1912 Boston Red Sox, who beat McGraw's Giants three times in that year's World Series.

New York Giants second baseman Larry Doyle, a .304 batter in the 1911 Series.

Christy Mathewson.

Rube Marquard, who beat the Red Sox twice in the 1912 Series.

Giants third baseman Buck Herzog, who with 12 hits and a .400 batting average led all hitters in the 1912 Series.

Tris Speaker.

Giants center fielder Fred Snodgrass, the man who made one of the most memorable errors in World Series history.

Frank Baker had another fine Series in 1913, leading everyone with nine hits, seven runs batted in, and a .450 average.

John McGraw (left) and Eddie Collins getting the 1913 World Series started with the traditional handshake. It was a good Series for Eddie, who batted .421.

Giants outfielder Tillie Shafer sliding safely into third in the seventh inning of game one of the 1913 Series, after a base hit by **Larry Doyle**. Frank Baker is a bit late with the tag, while pitcher Chief Bender is hustling over to back up.

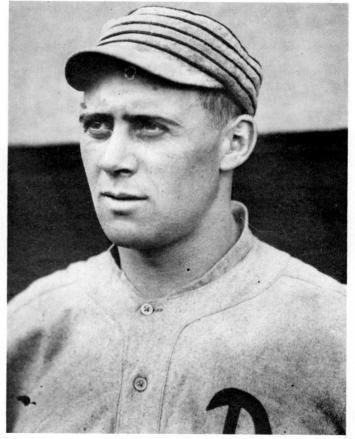

Left-hander Eddie Plank, one of Connie Mack's perennial aces.

Athletics catcher Wally Schang, a .357 hitter in the 1913 Series.

Braves catcher Hank Gowdy, hitting star of the 1914 Series.

Chief Bender, who beat the Giants twice in the 1913 Series.

The Giants' Fred Snodgrass getting back to first base after a pickoff attempt by A's catcher Jack Lapp to Stuffy McInnis. The action occurred in the third inning of game two.

A dramatic moment in the bottom of the ninth inning of game two of the 1913 Series. With the score 0–0, the Athletics' Jack Barry has just been tagged out in a rundown between home and third. Christy Mathewson is standing over Barry, catcher Larry McLean is at the left, and first baseman Hooks Wiltse, who made the play home, is in the background. The umpire is Tommy Connolly.

Boston Braves manager George Stallings sitting in the dugout at Shibe Park, Philadelphia, before the start of game two of the 1914 World Series against the A's. With him are his two ace right-handers, Bill James (left) and Dick Rudolph.

It's the second inning of the 1914 Series opener and the Athletics' Amos Strunk is out at home. Hank Gowdy is the catcher, while the umpire is ex–Red Sox pitcher Bill Dinneen.

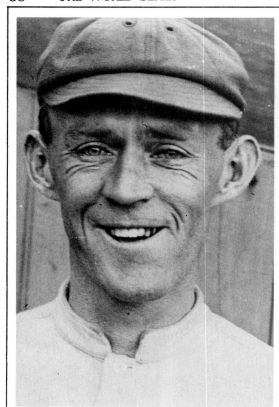

The Braves' Johnny Evers. Johnny tattooed Athletics pitching for a .438 batting average in the 1914 Series.

Boston Red Sox outfielder Duffy Lewis, top hitter of the 1915 World Series.

The third member of the 1914 Boston Braves Big Three pitching staff, George (Lefty) Tyler.

Grover Cleveland Alexander.

Boston's Tris Speaker being tagged out at second on an attempted steal by the Phillies' Bert Niehoff. The action occurred in the first inning of the second game of the 1915 Series.

Philadelphia's George Chalmers, loser of a 2–1 heartbreaker to Ernie Shore in game four of the 1915 Series.

Phillies first baseman Fred Luderus, who batted .438 in the 1915 Series. He was the only Philadelphia hitter to have any success against the strong Red Sox pitching.

Boston's Rube Foster, two-time conqueror of the Phillies in the 1915 World Series.

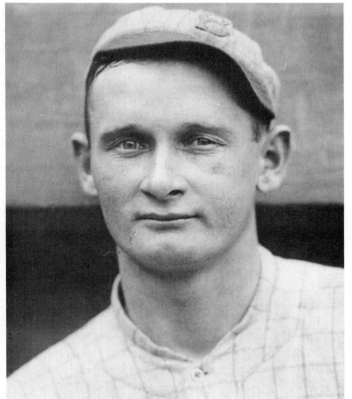

Brooklyn's Sherrod Smith, who lost the fourteen-inning duel to Babe Ruth.

Babe Ruth, one of the Red Sox' pitching heroes in their 1916 World Series victory over the Brooklyn Dodgers.

The Philadelphia Phillies' pennant-winning outfield. From left to right, Gavvy Cravath, Dode Paskert, Possum Whitted.

Boston's Tilly Walker sliding into third with a triple he hit in the first inning of the 1916 Series opener.

Brooklyn's Ivy Olson sliding into third in a cloud of dust after having been sacrificed over by Otto Miller in the fourth inning of game three. Larry Gardner is the third baseman.

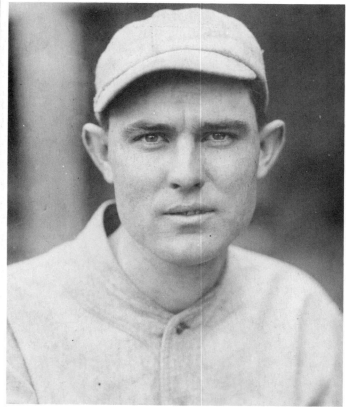

Red Sox right-hander Ernie Shore, who beat the Dodgers twice in the 1916 Series.

Red Sox southpaw Hubert (Dutch) Leonard.

The outfield of the 1916 pennant-winning Brooklyn Dodgers. Left to right, Casey Stengel, Jimmy Johnston, Hy Myers, Zack Wheat.

Boston's Larry Gardner sliding in safely after his three-run inside-the-park home run in the second inning of game four of the 1916 Series.

Red Sox manager and catcher Bill Carrigan at bat during the 1916 World Series. The Dodger catcher is Chief Meyers. Bill's choke-up grip was not uncommon in the dead-ball era.

Giants outfielder Dave Robertson. Dave had a great Series in 1917, leading everyone with 11 hits and a .500 batting average, but his costly error in game six wiped it all away.

Four members of the Chicago White Sox pennant-winning outfield in 1917. Left to right, Nemo Leibold, Happy Felsch, Shano Collins, and Shoeless Joe Jackson.

The Chicago White Sox and the New York Giants at the Polo Grounds in the 1917 World Series.

The White Sox' Red Faber, who beat the Giants three times in the 1917 World Series.

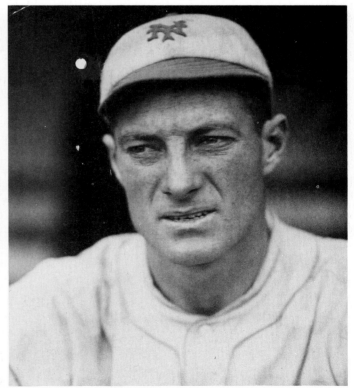

New York third baseman Heinie Zimmerman, the man who chased Eddie Collins across home plate in game six of the 1917 Series.

Action during the second inning of the third game of the 1917 Series. Chicago's Buck Weaver is sliding into second base. Buck looks out, but a moment after this photo was snapped New York's Art Fletcher dropped the ball and umpire Silk O'Loughlin called Weaver safe. The interested spectator is second baseman Buck Herzog.

Chicago's Eddie Collins, who batted .409 against the Giants in the 1917 World Series.

Babe Ruth, winner of two games over the Chicago Cubs in the 1918 World Series.

Chicago Cubs left-hander Jim (Hippo) Vaughan, who pitched brilliantly for the Cubs in the 1918 Series, but in a losing cause.

Chicago Cubs second baseman Charlie Pick, who with seven hits and a .389 batting average led all hitters in the light-hitting 1918 Series.

Red Sox right-hander Carl Mays. He matched teammate Ruth in the 1918 Series by also beating the Cubs twice.

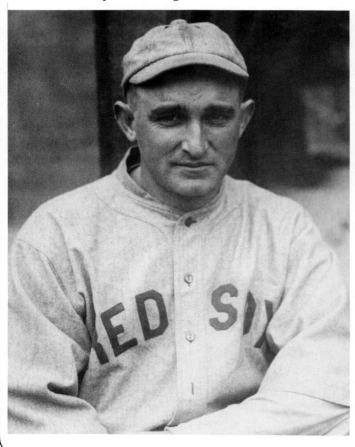

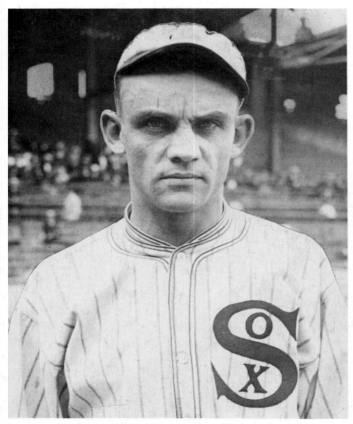

Chick Gandil, alleged by some to have been the ringleader of the 1919 cabal on the Chicago White Sox.

Eddie Cicotte, ace of the White Sox pitching staff.

Chick Gandil out stealing in the second inning of the first game of the 1919 World Series. Making the play is Cincinnati second baseman Morrie Rath.

Buck Weaver.

Claude (Lefty) Williams. He was a dubious success in the 1919 World Series swindle, losing three games.

Cincinnati's Greasy Neale out on an attempted steal in game two of the 1919 Series. Swede Risberg is making the putout. Watching from the mound is Lefty Williams.

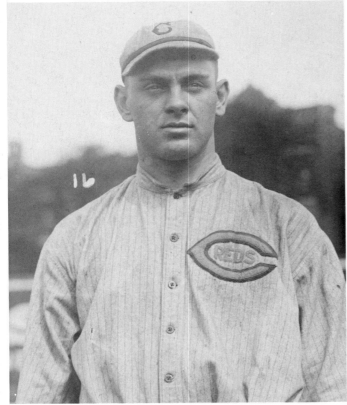

Cincinnati right-hander Hod Eller, who twice defeated the White Sox in the 1919 Series.

Brooklyn's great outfielder Zack Wheat. His nine hits against Cleveland were tops in the 1920 World Series.

Jim Bagby, 31-game winner for the pennant-winning 1920 Cleveland Indians.

Cincinnati fast-baller Jimmy Ring, who shut out the White Sox in the fourth game of the 1919 World Series.

Stanley Coveleski, Cleveland's three-game winner in the 1920 Series.

Cleveland's Elmer Smith, the man who launched the first grand-slam home run in World Series history against the Dodgers in 1920.

Brooklyn's Tommy Griffith is out at home, tagged by catcher Steve O'Neil. The action took place in the bottom of the third inning of game two of the 1920 Series.

It's the second inning of game two of the 1920 Series at Ebbets Field in Brooklyn. Cleveland's Larry Gardner, who had doubled, is being tagged out by shortstop Ivy Olson after breaking from the bag on a ground ball to pitcher Burleigh Grimes, who is running at the edge of the grass. Gardner is trying to get back to the base, but umpire Hank O'Day is about to call him out.

Bill Wambsganss is just completing his stunning unassisted triple play against the Dodgers in the top of the fifth inning of game five of the 1920 World Series. Bill has caught Clarence Mitchell's line drive and stepped on second (base runner Pete Kilduff is all the way to third base), and is about to tag a disbelieving Otto Miller. Umpire Hank O'Day is beginning to raise his hand to call the historic third out.

III
Enter Mr. Ruth and Company
1921~1930

Miller Huggins.

John McGraw.

1921

In 1921 New York City was treated to the first of the many "Subway Series" that were to entertain the city over the next 35 years. John McGraw and his Giants were back in the World Series, and facing them were their Polo Grounds tenants, the New York Yankees, winners of their first American League pennant.

The era of the lively ball had begun, the era of the Yankees, the era of Babe Ruth. In a few years the league's finest left-handed pitcher, with the Red Sox, had become an outfielder with the Yankees and baseball's greatest slugger. Ruth had put together a colossal year in 1921—59 home runs, 171 runs batted in, .378 batting average. The other large-sized socker on this first Yankee pennant winner was outfielder Bob Meusel, with 24 home runs and 135 runs

batted in. Also on the club were first baseman Wally Pipp, second baseman Aaron Ward, shortstop Roger Peckinpaugh, catcher Wally Schang, and third baseman Home Run Baker, playing out the string in New York. Manager Miller Huggins had three strong right-handed starters in Carl Mays, Waite Hoyt, and Bob Shawkey.

McGraw, taking the first of an unprecedented four straight pennants, had a heavy-hitting club that included first baseman George Kelly, shortstop Dave Bancroft, third baseman Frank Frisch, catcher Frank Snyder, and outfielders Irish Meusel (brother of the Yankees' Bob), Ross Youngs, and George Burns. Lefty Art Nehf was John J.'s ace that year, with a 20–12 record, followed by Fred Toney, Jesse Barnes, and Shufflin' Phil Douglas.

The Yankees got off to a two-game lead by identical 3–0 scores, the shutouts being pitched by Mays and Hoyt. When the Yankees jumped to a 4–0 lead in the top of game three, McGraw must have begun wondering what a man had to do to win in October. But his club roared back with four of their own in the bottom of the third, and then ripped the game apart with an eight-run seventh inning. When it was done, the Giants had a 20-hit, 13–5 win, with Burns and Snyder getting 4 hits apiece.

The Giants evened the Series in game four with a 4–2 win, a game marked by Ruth's first World Series home run. The next day, Ruth began the winning rally in a 3–1 Yankee win by leading off an inning with a bunt single. It was the last game Babe started in that Series, injuries forcing him to the sidelines.

Down three games to two in what was to be the last of the best-of-nine World Series, the Giants pounced on the Ruth-less Yankees and took games six, seven, and eight to give McGraw the championship that had eluded him in four tries since 1905. In game six, the Giants outpunched the Yanks 8–5; in game seven, Douglas outdueled Mays, 2–1; while game eight featured a classic hookup between Nehf and Hoyt.

The Giants scored in the top of the first on an error by Peckinpaugh at short, and Nehf grimly protected that run for the rest of the game. In the bottom of the ninth, Aaron Ward walked with one out. Baker rapped what seemed a sure hit on the ground to right field, but Giants second baseman Johnny Rawlings made a spectacular stop and threw Baker out at first. With Ward trying for third on the play, first baseman George Kelly made what has been called one of the great pegs in World Series history, firing across the infield to nail Ward at third.

It was a sweet victory for McGraw, particularly coming over what he considered an upstart Yankee team that was beginning to edge his Giants for primacy in New York. McGraw's pitchers, led by Nehf, Douglas, and Barnes, held the Yankees, a .300-hitting club over the season, to a .207 mark. For the Giants, Frisch, Rawlings, Meusel, Burns, and Snyder all hit well.

The best pitching in the Series was done in a losing cause. Yankee Waite Hoyt pitched three complete games, winning two and losing one, and giving up just two unearned runs, thus equaling Mathewson's 1905 performance by going twenty-seven innings and showing an earned-run average of 0.00.

1922

It was the same cast a year later—McGraw and the Giants versus Ruth and the Yankees. (One thing was different—the Series had been cut back to a best-of-seven format.) McGraw's club pounded National League pitching for a .304 batting average that summer, helping Art Nehf, Rosy Ryan, and Jesse Barnes to winning seasons. The Giants had eight .300 hitters

in the lineup, including a couple of platooning outfielders—Bill Cunningham and Casey Stengel, the latter batting .368.

Miller Huggins's club, which had won the pennant by a single game over the St. Louis Browns, had added pitchers Bullet Joe Bush (26–7) and Sam Jones, shortstop Everett Scott, and third baseman Joe Dugan, courtesy of the Red Sox. Bush and Jones supplemented the already strong starting corps of Hoyt, Mays, and Shawkey.

The Yankees may have had the edge in pitching going into the Series, but it was the Giants' pitchers who once again dominated, holding Babe Ruth and his mates to a mere .203 composite average. The Yankees, in fact, did not win a game.

After taking the opener with a three-run eighth-inning rally against Bush, McGraw saw his club play to a 3–3 tie the next day, the game called because of darkness. The umpires' decision to call the game was highly controversial; according to most estimates, there was at least 45 minutes of daylight still remaining. Feeling cheated, the fans bombarded the field with missiles. Rather than have anyone think that the called game had been a ploy to milk an extra day's receipts from the Series, Judge Landis announced that all monies taken in for the game—over $100,000—would be donated to military hospitals for disabled veterans.

With everyone placated, the Series resumed. Jack Scott, a sore-armed right-hander McGraw had picked up from Cincinnati in mid-season, shut out the Yankees 3–0 in game three. In games four and five it was Hugh McQuillen, another mid-season acquisition, and Art Nehf stopping the Yankees, 4–3 and 5–3. John McGraw and his Giants remained on top of both New York City and the world of baseball, which at that time seemed one and the same. Leading the way for the champions were Frankie Frisch with another good Series, batting .471, and third baseman Heinie Groh, who did even better at .474.

Thanks to some strategy and psychology by McGraw, Ruth suffered through his only homerless Series as a Yankee, and his worst—batting just .118. Sensing that the big guy was overeager to do well, McGraw ordered his pitchers to throw everything to Ruth low and out of the strike zone. The overanxious Babe went for the bait, popping up, grounding out, and striking out.

1923

Fed up with Babe Ruth and the Yankees and all the success and adulation they were piling up, McGraw saw to it that the upstarts were booted out of the Polo Grounds and told to build a stadium of their own. And so Yankee owner Jacob Ruppert did just that. Not only did he build Yankee Stadium, the world's most sumptuous ball park, he did it right across the Harlem River, in full view of the Polo Grounds.

Miller Huggins's crew showed that it didn't make any difference where they played—they rushed through the league to their third straight pennant, led by the cannonading of Mr. Ruth and by one of the finest pitching staffs ever assembled: Waite Hoyt, Joe Bush, Bob Shawkey, Sam Jones, and newcomer Herb Pennock.

Keeping pace with the Yankees were McGraw's Giants, winning *their* third pennant in a row. McGraw's nucleus was pretty much unchanged: Kelly, Frisch, Bancroft, and Groh in the infield, Youngs, Stengel, Cunningham, and Meusel in the outfield, and Snyder behind the plate. The pitching was so-so, with Rosy Ryan and Jack Scott the big winners with only 16 apiece, followed by McQuillen, Bentley, and Nehf.

The Giants began in fine style at Yankee Stadium, winning a memorable 5–4 game. It was a 4–4 tie going into the top of the ninth. With two out and the bases empty, Casey Stengel belted one into deep left-center and began a famous gallop around the bases, sliding into home plate ahead of the relay for an inside-the-park, game-winning home run.

The Yankees evened it in game two, 4–2, with Ruth hitting a pair of solo shots to give Herb Pennock his first World Series victory. With the clubs alternating home fields, they were back at Yankee Stadium for game three, where Art Nehf squeaked out a 1–0 win over Jones. The lone run? It was a seventh-inning home run into the right-field bleachers by Stengel. Trotting slowly around the bases this time, savoring every moment of it, Stengel thumbed his nose at the Yankee bench and made, one observer noted, "other objectionable gestures."

With a third straight World Series loss to their neighbors now looming large, the Yankee bats suddenly came alive. A six-run second inning tore open game four, and the Yanks coasted to an 8–4 win, knotting the Series. The next day Huggins's men scored seven runs in the first two innings and sailed in 8–1 behind Bush. Trailing 4–1 in the top of the eighth the next day at the Polo Grounds, they parlayed three singles and three walks into a five-run inning that carried them to a 6–4 win and the first-ever New York Yankees world championship.

For Babe Ruth the Series was a triumph and a personal satisfaction. More disciplined at the plate this time, the great man belted three home runs and batted .368. Aaron Ward led the Yankees with ten hits and a .417 average, while for the Giants Frisch had a third straight fine Series with ten hits and a .400 average.

1924

After 18 years of uncomplaining devotion and incomparable performance, a legend was finally out of the shadows of the second division and for the first time was heading for the national spotlight. Walter Johnson, ace pitcher of the consistently inept Washington Senators, had finally, at the age of thirty-six, made it to a World Series, and when he did, this gentle, humble, modest fast baller had the good wishes of sentimental fans everywhere.

It was Washington's first pennant. Driven by their boy wonder, twenty-seven-year-old second baseman and manager Bucky Harris, and armed with the good bats of first baseman Joe Judge and outfielders Sam Rice and Goose Goslin, plus solid performers like shortstop Roger Peckinpaugh, third baseman Ossie Bluege, and catcher Muddy Ruel, the Senators finally made it, edging Ruth and the Yankees by two games.

Facing Walter and the Senators were John McGraw and his New York Giants. For McGraw it was an unprecedented fourth consecutive pennant, his tenth overall, and his last. John J. did it primarily with hitting, none of his pitchers winning more than 16, but his club batting an even .300 for the season. With none of his regulars batting under .280, it was a potent lineup McGraw sent against Walter Johnson when the Series opened in Washington. That lineup, in fact, was crowded with seven future Hall of Famers: Freddy Lindstrom, Frank Frisch, Ross Youngs, George Kelly, Bill Terry, Hack Wilson, and Travis Jackson.

The 1924 Series has been called one of the greatest ever played. The opener went twelve innings and saw the Giants edge the Senators 4–3, with Johnson and Nehf going all the way. The Senators had tied it with a run in the bottom of the ninth; then the Giants scored two in the top of the twelfth, but Washington fought back for a run in the bottom of the inning and left the tying run on third.

Game two was another thriller. Trailing 3–1 in the top of the ninth, the Giants scored twice to tie, only to see the Senators win it in the bottom of the ninth on a two-bagger by Peckinpaugh.

Playing in New York now, the Giants took game three, 6–4. Washington evened the Series the next day, 7–4, thanks to a big game by Goslin. Goose collected three singles and a home run in four at bats and drove in four runs. Johnson started game five, still looking for his first World Series victory. The unsentimental Giants, however, whacked the great pitcher for 13 hits and pinned a second defeat on him, 6–2.

Back in Washington, the Senators fought to stave off elimination. Curve baller Tom Zachary outpitched Nehf for a 2–1 victory that deadlocked the Series. Both Washington runs scored on a clutch two-run single in the fifth by manager Harris.

So the stage was set for a seventh game, one that turned out to be one of the most famous of all World Series games. It began with a burst of strategy. Harris started right-hander Curly Ogden, not one of his front-line pitchers. This proved to be a ploy to get McGraw to insert left-handed-hitting Terry into the lineup. After Ogden pitched to two batters, in came lefty George Mogridge, a move designed to force Terry out of the game. (Terry, who had been eating Washington pitching alive in the Series, was then a rookie who played only against right-handed pitching.)

Despite all the maneuvering, the Giants carried a 3–1 lead into the bottom of the eighth. It was at this point that destiny made its first intervention. With the bases loaded and two out, Harris hit a sharp grounder that bounced high over third baseman Lindstrom's head, scoring the tying runs.

Walking out to pitch in the ninth for Washington was the people's choice himself, Walter Johnson, being given one last chance to win a World Series game, and with it a world championship.

Working on just one day's rest, the old fast baller whipped through four innings of shutout ball as the autumn shadows grew longer. And then, in the bottom of the twelfth, John McGraw's World Series luck turned sour again. With one out, Muddy Ruel lifted an easy pop foul behind home plate. As he went for the ball, however, Giants catcher Hank Gowdy—World Series hero for the 1914 Miracle Braves—stepped on his discarded mask and was unable to make the play. With new life breathed into his time at bat, Ruel doubled down the third-base line.

Johnson came to bat and was safe on an infield error, Ruel holding second. At this point, destiny took another, final hand. Earl McNeely grounded toward Lindstrom at third. As Freddy poised to take the ball, it struck a pebble and took a kangaroo leap over his head into left field, allowing Ruel to come around with the winning run. For baseball fans everywhere, the feeling was a mellow one: Walter Johnson—and, only incidentally, the Washington Senators—had won.

Along with Walter, the Senators had heroes in Goose Goslin, who slammed three home runs among 11 hits; skipper Harris, who collected 11 hits and hit two home runs (he had hit only one all year); and Tom Zachary, who won two games.

But it was Walter's Series, then and forever. It was all summed up by Giants pitcher Jack Bentley, known as something of a clubhouse philosopher. "Walter Johnson," said Jack, "is such a lovable character that the good Lord didn't want to see him get beat again."

Amen.

1925

Walter drew an encore in 1925, the Senators winning again for Bucky Harris. A 20-game winner for the twelfth and last time, Johnson was joined on the Washington staff by the former Cleveland ace Stanley Coveleski, 20–5 that year.

Walter and his mates were up against Bill Mc-Kechnie's Pittsburgh Pirates, in the Series for the first time since 1909, and featuring a ferocious hitting attack. This man-eating lineup, which batted .307, had George Grantham (.326) at first, Eddie Moore (.298) at second, Glenn Wright (.308) at short, Pie Traynor (.320) at third, Earl Smith (.313) catching, and Max Carey (.343), Kiki Cuyler (.357), and Clyde Barnhart (.325) in the outfield. This starting lineup had a .324 composite batting average. Pittsburgh had good though not spectacular pitching in right-handers Lee Meadows, Ray Kremer, Vic Aldridge, and Johnny Morrison and southpaw Emil Yde.

Johnson was superb in the opener in Pittsburgh, stopping the heavy-hitting Pirates on just five hits and fanning ten, winning 2–1. Pittsburgh evened it up the next day behind Aldridge, beating Coveleski 3–2 on a two-run homer by Cuyler in the bottom of the eighth.

Game three, in Washington, featured one of the most controversial plays in Series history. With two out and nobody on in the top of the eighth and Washington leading 4–3, Pittsburgh's Earl Smith drove one out toward the right-center-field bleachers. It looked like a game-tying home run, but right fielder Sam Rice, on the run, leaped up, and his momentum carried him over the fence into the bleachers at the same time that the ball struck his glove. A few moments later Rice reappeared, clutching the ball in his glove. Umpire Cy Rigler, who had to be guessing, ruled it a catch and called Smith out. The Pirates argued loudly. Since Rice had been out of view when he caught—or did not catch—the ball, no one was ever sure quite what happened when he went tumbling into the bleachers. Did he have, and maintain, possession or not? The play was a crucial one, since Washington held on to its 4–3 lead, giving them a 2–1 advantage in games.

(A half century later, there was a melodramatic coda to the story. Sam Rice lived to be an old man. Not long before his death in 1974 he let it be known that a sealed envelope containing a letter would be found among his effects, to be opened upon his death. The letter would state the truth of what happened when he dove over the bleacher wall on October 10, 1925. When Rice died, the letter, amounting now to a deathbed statement, was opened and read. In it Sam stated that he had indeed made a fair catch of Earl Smith's long drive many years before.)

Walter Johnson gave Washington a three-games-to-one bulge by shutting out the Pirates in game four, 4–0, thanks largely to a three-run homer by Goose Goslin, one of three Goose hit in the Series, for the second year in a row. The other run also came in on a home run, this one by outfielder Joe Harris, who shared Series slugging honors with Goslin by hitting three home runs.

The Pirates then dug in, and for the first time in a

seven-game Series, a team down three games to one came back and won it. Aldridge won game five, 6–3, and Kremer evened it with a 3–2 win in game six.

Johnson started against Aldridge in game seven, but Vic was quickly gone as Washington piled up an early lead. Kremer came on in relief and held the Senators while his teammates began slugging away at Johnson. Walter was belted for 15 hits, 9 of them for extra bases. Bucky Harris, displaying blind, and probably foolish, faith in his great pitcher, let Walter go all the way, down to a 9–7 defeat. The telling hit was a two-run, tie-breaking double by Cuyler in the bottom of the eighth.

Undoing Washington throughout the Series was some uncharacteristic loose play by their usually sure-handed shortstop Roger Peckinpaugh, who made eight errors, some of them costly. The eight muffs broke the record of six set by Honus Wagner in 1903. "I tell people that I once broke one of Honus Wagner's records," the whimsical Peckinpaugh said years later. "But I don't tell them what it was."

1926

When the St. Louis Cardinals, under player-manager Rogers Hornsby, won the pennant in 1926, it meant that every National League club had made it to the World Series.

The '26 Cardinals were a young, spirited team, with Hornsby at second base, Jim Bottomley at first, Les Bell at third, Tommy Thevenow at short, Bob O'Farrell catching, and Chick Hafey, Billy Southworth, and Taylor Douthit in the outfield. On the mound the Cards had 20-game winner Flint Rhem, lefty Bill Sherdel, and veteran right-handers Jesse Haines and Grover Cleveland Alexander.

Alexander, now thirty-nine years old, was a mid-season pickup from the Cubs, which had cast the once-great, now alcoholic, epileptic pitcher adrift. Alex had pitched creditably for the Cardinals (9–7) and was going to do even better in the Series, a World Series he was destined to make uniquely his own.

Miller Huggins had brought his powerful Yankee team back to the top. In addition to Ruth and Bob Meusel, the Yankees now had Earle Combs in the outfield, young Lou Gehrig at first, rookie Tony Lazzeri at second, Mark Koenig at short, and Joe Dugan at third. Heading Huggins's pitching staff were Waite Hoyt, Herb Pennock, and Urban Shocker.

It was a Series of outstanding personal performances. For the Cardinals, Bottomley, Thevenow, and Southworth each collected ten hits, as did Combs for the Yanks. Ruth, who hit four home runs, put on a show in St. Louis in game four with three, one more titanic than the other. Pennock won two tightly pitched games. But the great moment of the Series, perhaps the most storied in Series history, belonged to Alexander, in game seven.

After Hoyt had edged Sherdel 2–1 in the New York opener, Alex took game two, 6–2, on a masterful four-hitter. Haines shut the Yankees out in game three in St. Louis, 4–0, adding a dollop of whipped cream to his day with a two-run homer. It was the Babe in game four, his three long blasts leading Hoyt and the Yankees to a 10–5 win. The Yanks broke hearts in St. Louis with a 3–2, ten-inning win in game five after tying it in the top of the ninth.

Coming back to New York with a 3–2 lead in games, the Yankees ran into Alexander and a hard-hitting attack, the Cards setting up a seventh game with a 10–2 win.

Alex was in the bullpen the next day, ready to go "a few batters" if called upon. The call came in the bottom of the seventh inning. The Cardinal starter, Haines, had been pitching well, but the knuckle baller had raised a blister on his hand and could go no further. Hornsby called for Alexander, and the lean old Nebraskan walked into this situation: bases loaded, two out, Tony Lazzeri at bat, the Cardinals winning 3–2.

It was a classic confrontation: the canny, world-weary veteran versus the tough young slugger. The thirty-nine-year-old Alex pitched with all the craft and guile of a long career. He worked a fast ball too far inside, forcing Lazzeri to pull it long but foul. (Some historians have claimed it was foul by inches. But Les Bell, playing third for the Cardinals, said it was foul all the way, by 20 feet.) Alex then struck Lazzeri out on a couple of backbreaking curve balls, sealing the most famous strikeout in baseball history.

Alexander retired the Yankees in order in the eighth, then put away the first two batters in the bottom of the ninth. With two out, nobody on, and a one-run lead, the old wizard faced Ruth, who had already homered four times in the Series. Refusing to let Babe tie him, Alex pitched him carefully and walked him on a 3–2 pitch (it was Ruth's eleventh base on balls of the Series, still a record). With Bob Meusel at the plate, Ruth, unaccountably, tried to steal second. O'Farrell fired the ball to Hornsby covering, who slapped it on the sliding Ruth, and the Series was over.

1927

Legend has it that when the Pittsburgh Pirates saw the New York Yankees muscling the ball out of Forbes Field in batting practice prior to the opening of the 1927 World Series, the Pirate players were so demoralized that they lost their confidence and consequently were wiped out in four straight. The only part of this tale that is true is that they lost four straight, but it wasn't because of lack of confidence but simply that they were up against the greatest team of all time: the 1927 New York Yankees.

With Ruth peaking at 60 home runs, young Gehrig suddenly erupting with 47, with Combs, Lazzeri, and Meusel all having blazing years at the plate, and with pitchers like Hoyt, Pennock, Shocker, George Pipgras, Wilcy Moore, and Dutch Ruether, the Yankees were close to unbeatable, winning 110 games that year.

Donie Bush's Pirates, however, were no patsies, coming into the Series with a .305 team average. They now had the Waner brothers in the outfield, Paul batting .380 and his younger brother Lloyd .355 (and between them 460 hits). In addition to the Waners, the Pirates still had Pie Traynor, Glenn Wright, George Grantham, and other sure-swinging stickers. Four solid right-handers made up their starting staff: Carmen Hill, Ray Kremer, Lee Meadows, and Vic Aldridge.

The great disparity between the two teams lay in power—the Yankees had hit 158 home runs to the Pirates' 54.

The Pirates struggled gamely. They lost the opener 5–4, and were in game two until the Yankees broke it open with three in the eighth for a 6–2 win. Game three was tight until a six-run Yankee seventh inning put it away for an 8–1 win, Ruth icing it with a three-run one-way ticket into the right-field bleachers. Herb Pennock was masterly in this game, retiring the first 22 batters to face him; Pie Traynor broke up the perfect game with a clean single. Pennock finished up with a three-hitter.

Game four was another tightly contested affair, going into the bottom of the ninth tied at 3–3. Combs led off with a walk from Pittsburgh relief pitcher Johnny Miljus. Mark Koenig then outlegged a bunt. Both runners moved up on a wild pitch. Ruth was given an intentional walk, filling the bases. Miljus then pitched heroically, striking out Gehrig and Meusel. Throwing with everything he had, Johnny whipped a strike across to Lazzeri, but his next pitch went wild and Combs hustled down the line and crossed the plate, giving the Yankees a 4–3 win and the first four-game sweep since 1914.

The hitting stars for the Yankees were shortstop Mark Koenig, with 9 for 18 and a .500 batting average, and Mr. Ruth, who hit the only two home runs of the Series and drove in seven runs in the four games.

1928

For the second time in three years the St. Louis Cardinals showed up for a World Series against the New York Yankees. And show up was about all they did. The Yankees, not quite as ferocious as they were the year before (their win total had dropped from 110 to 101 as they fought off a tenacious challenge from Connie Mack's resurgent Athletics), were still the

Yankees, and this now meant Ruth and Gehrig. What these two did to the Cardinals in the 1928 Series bordered on assault and battery.

The Cardinals presented a revamped cast. Hornsby was gone, traded to the Giants for Frank Frisch. (Rogers had been unable to get along with his employer, Sam Breaden, while Frisch and McGraw had come to nurture mutual hatred.) The Cards still had Taylor Douthit and Chick Hafey in the outfield, but now veteran Rabbit Maranville was at short, Andy High at third, and Jimmie Wilson behind the plate. The pitching was still pretty much in the hands of Jess Haines, Bill Sherdel, and Grover Cleveland Alexander. Managing the Cardinals was Bill McKechnie, who had taken the Pirates to the Series in 1925 and then been canned after a third-place finish.

Miller Huggins, winning his sixth pennant in eight years, went into the Series with one of his aces, Herb Pennock, out with a bad arm and center fielder Earle Combs held to one pinch-hit appearance by a broken finger. Hug went with three pitchers—Waite Hoyt, George Pipgras, and Tom Zachary—and got four complete-game wins from them, two from Hoyt.

But it was all Ruth and Gehrig in this Series. In game one Ruth had two doubles and a single, Gehrig a single and a double. (Yankees, 4–1.) In game two, in which the Yankees wiped out Grover Cleveland Alexander, Ruth had a single and a double, Gehrig a tremendous three-run homer. (Yankees, 9–3.) In game three Ruth had two singles, Gehrig two home runs. (Yankees, 7–3.) In game four Ruth erupted with three home runs and Gehrig one. (Yankees, 7–3.)

Overall, Ruth batted .625 with ten hits, including three home runs; Gehrig batted .545 with four home runs and nine runs batted in.

For the Yankees, it was their second four-game sweep in a row, and they did it without Pennock and Combs. To make the debacle complete, an exasperated Sam Breadon demoted his manager, Bill McKechnie, to Rochester. For Deacon Bill, it seemed there was nothing in glory but grief.

1929

"Connie sure taught me a lesson that time." The speaker was Joe McCarthy, a career minor-leaguer who had finally made it to the majors in 1926 as manager of the Chicago Cubs and to the World Series in 1929.

The teacher of the lesson was Connie Mack, out of the Series for fifteen years but back in 1929 with a club to rival the '27 Yankees for firepower. Connie had Jimmie Foxx at first base, Jimmy Dykes at third, Mickey Cochrane catching, Al Simmons, Bing Miller, and Mule Haas in the outfield—all .300 hitters—and Max Bishop at second and Joe Boley at short. For pitching he had Robert Moses (Lefty) Grove, the premier fast baller of the age; George Earnshaw, a speedballing righty; and southpaw Rube Walberg.

Opposing the Philadelphia bullyboys, who had rampaged to a pennant by 18 games over the second-place Yankees, were McCarthy's Cubs, packing plenty of thunder themselves. Joe had an outfield that outhit Connie's—Riggs Stephenson (.362), Kiki Cuyler (.360), and Hack Wilson (.345). McCarthy also had a .380 hitter at second base named Rogers Hornsby. Rogers was now playing with his fourth team in four years, his grainy disposition dissolving welcome mats under his very shoes. The Cubs also had fancy-Dan glove man Charlie Grimm at first base, whose .298 average was barely noticeable on this club. On the mound McCarthy had good, tough pitchers in right-handers Charlie Root, Pat Malone, and Guy Bush.

The lesson that Connie taught Joe? It came in the opening game in Chicago. Connie had taken note of the right-handed power in Joe's lineup—all of the Cub stickers except Grimm were righties. So instead of starting one of his Big Three, Connie slipped in Howard Ehmke, a little-used veteran. It was Connie's belief that the sidearming Ehmke's combination of curves and off-speed deliveries would provide a distraction for the right-handed Cub sluggers. To everyone's amazement—except Connie's—that was exactly what happened. Ehmke not only stopped the Cubs 3–1, he established a World Series game strikeout record with 13 whiffs.

The next day the Cubs had to contend with blazers fired by Earnshaw and Grove, who relieved big George in the fifth. Together they fanned another 13 Cubs as Connie's boys ran off with a 9–3 win, Simmons and Foxx knocking in seven of the nine.

Connie came back with Earnshaw on one day's rest in Philadelphia in game three. George hurled well, fanning ten, but Guy Bush won for the Cubs, 3–1.

Game four provided the most stunning rally in World Series history, a rally that has forever epitomized the greatness of the 1929–1931 Philadelphia Athletics. Going into the bottom of the seventh the Cubs were leading 8–0, seemingly on their way to deadlocking the Series. With Charlie Root working on a three-hit shutout, this is what happened: Al Simmons hit a home run (making the score 8–1). Jimmie Foxx singled. Bing Miller got a single when center fielder Hack Wilson lost the ball in the sun. Jimmy Dykes singled, scoring Foxx (8–2). Joe Boley singled, scoring Miller (8–3). Pinch hitter George Burns popped out. Max Bishop singled, scoring Dykes (8–4). Art Nehf was now pitching for the Cubs. Mule Haas hit a drive that Wilson again lost in the sun, Haas coming all the way around for an inside-the-park home run (8–7). Mickey Cochrane walked. Sheriff Blake was now pitching for the Cubs. Simmons singled. Foxx singled, scoring Cochrane (8–8). Pat Malone was now pitching for the Cubs. Miller was

hit by a pitch. Dykes doubled, scoring Simmons and Foxx (10–8). The agony ended as Boley and Burns struck out. The most ferocious inning in World Series history was over.

To ensure their lead, the A's brought none other than Lefty Grove in from the bullpen. Lefty came out firing, fanning four of the six men he faced, and put it away.

Up now three games to one, the A's administered another embittering defeat in the next game. Losing to Pat Malone 2–0 in the bottom of the ninth with one out, this is what happened: Bishop singled. Haas hit one over the right-field wall for a game-tying homer. Cochrane grounded out. Simmons doubled. Foxx was intentionally walked. Miller then doubled, scoring Simmons with the championship run.

It had been a long dry spell, but Connie Mack was back on top of the heap again.

1930

Connie's Athletics were as torrid in 1930 as they had been in '29, taking their second straight pennant, with Lefty Grove rising to the heights of a 28–5 won-lost record.

Taking their third pennant in five years (each under a different manager), the Cardinals brought an all-.300-hitting lineup into the Series. The National League had gone completely haywire all season, ending with a .303 batting average, with the Cardinals checking in at .314. Chief among manager Gabby Street's punishers were Frankie Frisch, Jim Bottomley, Chick Hafey, and George Watkins. Street, however, lacked the front-line starters to match Grove and Earnshaw, his best being Bill Hallahan and veterans Burleigh Grimes and Jesse Haines.

But the Cardinal pitchers did surprisingly well against the hard-hitting Athletics, holding them to a .197 batting average, while Grove and Earnshaw, doing most of the pitching for Connie Mack, held the .314-hitting Cardinals to a .200 batting mark. The A's, however, hit with uncommon emphasis, 18 of their 35 hits going for extra bases, with Al Simmons and Jimmie Foxx doing the bulk of the slugging.

The Athletics took the first two games in Philadelphia behind Grove and Earnshaw, 5–2 and 6–1. With the Series moving on to St. Louis, Hallahan got the Cards back into things with a 5–0 shutout, and the following day Haines evened it up by four-hitting the A's, 4–1.

The key game in the 1930 Series was the fifth, played in St. Louis. Earnshaw dueled Grimes 0–0 through seven innings, with Grove taking over for Earnshaw in the eighth. In the top of the ninth Grimes walked Cochrane and then coughed up a home run ball to Foxx. It must have been a patented Jimmie Foxx blast, for Grimes said later, "He hit it so hard I couldn't feel sorry for myself." The A's won it 2–0.

With a day off for travel, the Series resumed in Philadelphia. Mack surprised everyone by coming right back with Earnshaw on just one day's rest. George, an ox of a man, showed no fatigue as he pitched another strong game, stopping the Cardinals 7–1, giving Connie Mack his fifth world championship, the most for a manager up to that time.

Bill McKechnie.

Outfielder George Burns, who got 11 hits for the Giants in the 1921 World Series against the Yankees, leading all hitters.

Giants pitcher Phil Douglas striking out Babe Ruth in the eighth inning of the first game of the 1921 Series at the Polo Grounds. Notice how far over third baseman Frank Frisch is playing the pull-hitting Ruth.

Yankee Mike McNally is safe at home in the top of the third inning of game five of the 1921 Series. The catcher is Earl Smith, the umpire Cy Rigler. Mike scored on a sacrifice fly.

Giants right-hander Jesse Barnes, who beat the Yankees twice in the 1921 Series.

The Giants' Frank Snyder has just smashed a home run in the second inning of game six of the 1921 Series.

Waite Hoyt, who pitched brilliantly for the Yankees against the Giants in the 1921 Series.

The Giants' Frank Frisch, a .471 hitter against the Yankees in the 1922 World Series.

The Yankees' Bob Meusel put his club temporarily ahead with this run in the top of the seventh inning of game five of the 1922 Series. Both Meusel and Giants catcher Frank Snyder are awaiting umpire Bill Klem's call.

An inning later, in the bottom of the eighth, Bob's brother Irish comes sliding across with the run that put the Giants back in the lead. Frank Frisch, who scored a moment earlier, is watching the play, as is third base coach Hugh Jennings, who has run up for a better look. The Yankee catcher is Wally Schang, and the umpire is Bill Klem.

The Giants' Heinie Groh, whose .474 batting average was the highest in the 1922 Series.

John McGraw's outfield in the 1922 World Series. Left to right, Casey Stengel, Bill Cunningham, Ross Youngs, Irish Meusel.

The Yankees' great left-hander Herb Pennock, who beat the Giants twice in the 1923 World Series.

Brothers and rivals: the Giants' Irish Meusel (left) and the Yankees' Bob Meusel. They competed against each other in the World Series in 1921, 1922, and 1923.

It seems to take five Giants to run down Babe Ruth in this action, which occurred in the seventh inning of the second game of the 1923 Series. Ruth, who had walked, was picked off first by Giants catcher Frank Snyder. Babe headed for second but was caught in a rundown between shortstop Dave Bancroft and first baseman George Kelly, who is about to put the tag on the great man. Catcher Snyder is in the foreground, while Frankie Frisch is bringing up the rear, and pitcher Jack Bentley is hustling over to back up Kelly.

Casey Stengel.

Yankees second baseman Aaron Ward, the leading hitter in the 1923 Series, with a .417 batting average.

Babe Ruth.

Goose Goslin: 11 hits, including three home runs, in the 1924 Series.

Bucky Harris, manager and second baseman of the 1924 and 1925 pennant-winning Washington Senators.

Washington's Goose Goslin has just been thrown out at first in the opening game of the 1924 World Series. Making the putout is Giants first baseman Bill Terry.

Fred Lindstrom, the Giants' eighteen-year-old third baseman who collected 10 hits in the 1924 Series.

The top of the ninth inning of game two of the 1924 Series. The Giants' George Kelly has just scored the tying run on a base hit by Hack Wilson. The upended catcher is Muddy Ruel.

Walter Johnson.

Pittsburgh's Max Carey: 11 hits and a .458 batting average in the 1925 World Series.

Washington shortstop Roger Peckinpaugh, one of the best, who in the 1925 Series proved it can happen to the best: eight errors.

Washington's Sam Rice: 12 hits and a controversial catch.

Goose Goslin slamming one of his three home runs against the Pirates in the 1925 Series, repeating his feat of the year before. The black armband on Goose's left sleeve was in honor of Christy Mathewson, who died just as the Series was starting.

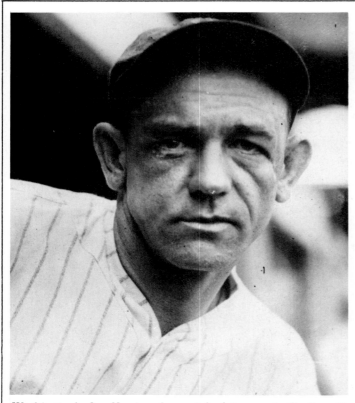

Washington's Joe Harris, who matched teammate Goslin with three homers in the 1925 Series. Joe also had eight other hits and a .440 batting average.

Pittsburgh's Ray Kremer, who beat the Senators twice in the 1925 Series.

Six Cardinals line up for the photographer prior to the opening of the 1926 World Series. Left to right: Taylor Douthit, Billy Southworth, Les Bell, Jim Bottomley, Chick Hafey, Bob O'Farrell.

Twenty-three-year-old Lou Gehrig of the Yankees, a .348 hitter in the 1926 Series.

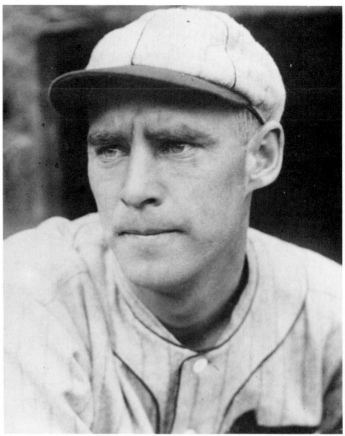

Cardinals southpaw Bill Sherdel, who lost two well-pitched games to the Yankees in the 1926 Series.

The Cardinals' Billy Southworth crossing home plate after his three-run homer in the top of the seventh inning of game two of the 1926 Series at Yankee Stadium. That's skipper Rogers Hornsby giving him a pat on the shoulder.

Herb Pennock, the man who twice outpitched Sherdel.

The Cardinals' Flint Rhem warming up for game four of the 1926 Series.

The Babe homered three times in the fourth game of the 1926 Series. This is number one, in the first inning.

Cardinals shortstop Tommy Thevenow, a light hitter who got hot in October 1926, outhitting Ruth, Gehrig, and Hornsby with a .417 batting average.

Tony Lazzeri.

Yankees shortstop Mark Koenig, who topped everybody with nine hits and a .500 batting average versus the Pirates in the 1927 World Series.

Jesse Haines, whose blistered finger forced him from the seventh game of the 1926 Series, setting the stage for Alexander.

Grover Cleveland Alexander.

New York's Bob Meusel scoring on a wild pitch by Pittsburgh's Vic Aldridge in the eighth inning of game two of the 1927 Series. Falling out of the way is batter Joe Dugan, as Aldridge runs up too late to cover the plate. Pirate catcher Johnny Gooch is returning with the ball.

Lloyd (left) and Paul Waner, the hitting marvels of the 1927 Pittsburgh Pirates.

Babe Ruth, who also made his presence felt in the 1928 Series: three home runs, three doubles, nine runs scored, ten hits, a .625 batting average.

Just two home runs were hit in the 1927 World Series. Guess who hit them?

Lou Gehrig, a one-man wrecking crew against the Cardinals in the four-game 1928 World Series. Lou hit four homers, drove in nine runs, and batted .545.

Starting pitchers for the second game of the 1928 Series at Yankee Stadium, Grover Cleveland Alexander (left) for the Cardinals and George Pipgras for the Yankees. The Yankees drove Alex from the mound in the third inning. Pipgras later said that he believed that Alex, a notorious imbiber, was either drunk or hung over before the game.

Howard Ehmke, Connie Mack's surprise starter in game one of the 1929 Series.

Yankee Waite Hoyt, who beat the Cardinals twice in the 1928 Series.

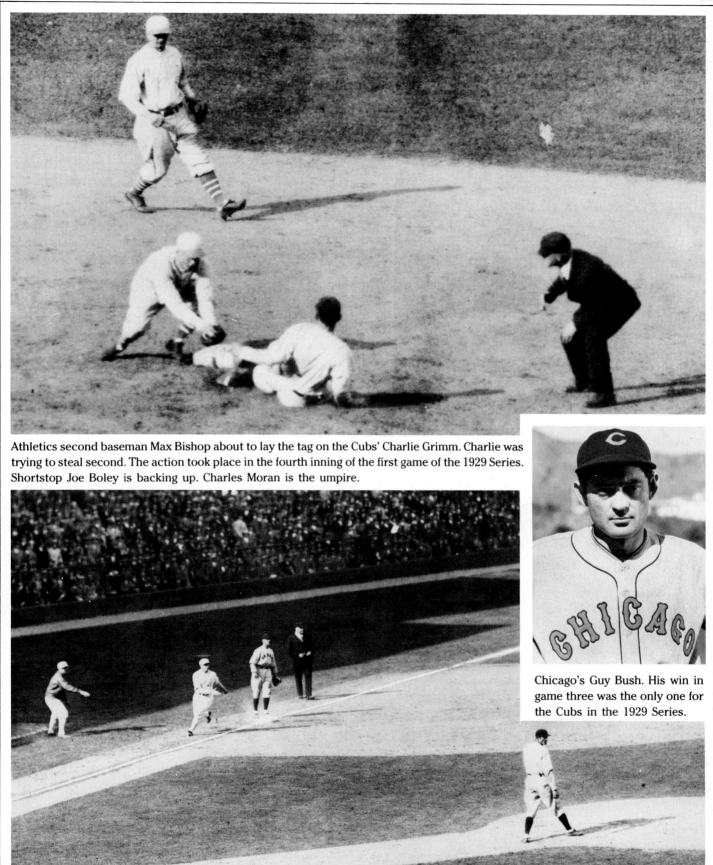

Athletics second baseman Max Bishop about to lay the tag on the Cubs' Charlie Grimm. Charlie was trying to steal second. The action took place in the fourth inning of the first game of the 1929 Series. Shortstop Joe Boley is backing up. Charles Moran is the umpire.

Chicago's Guy Bush. His win in game three was the only one for the Cubs in the 1929 Series.

It's the third inning of game three of the 1929 Series. Philadelphia's Mule Haas has just moved to third base on an error by Cubs shortstop Woody English that filled the bases. Cubs pitcher Guy Bush, on the mound, pitched out of it.

Three distinguished spectators at the 1929 World Series. Left to right, George Sisler, Babe Ruth, and the just-retired Ty Cobb.

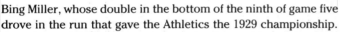

Bing Miller, whose double in the bottom of the ninth of game five drove in the run that gave the Athletics the 1929 championship.

The Athletics erupting from their dugout a few moments after Bing Miller's hit ended the 1929 World Series.

Chicago's powerful Hack Wilson, who hit well in the 1929 Series (.471), but lost those fly balls in the sun in Philadelphia's ten-run seventh inning in game four.

Hack Wilson taking an earth-shaking swing—and missing—in the 1929 Series. The catcher is Mickey Cochrane.

Al Simmons, the Athletics' big bonker, who led all hitters in the 1930 Series with a .364 batting average.

George Earnshaw, who pitched the Athletics to two victories over the Cardinals in the 1930 Series.

That's Cardinals second baseman Frank Frisch slapping the tag on the Athletics' Mickey Cochrane, who was trying to steal second base in the bottom of the first inning of the opener of the 1930 Series. Bearing witness is shortstop Charlie Gelbert, while umpire Harry Geisel is giving Mickey the bad news.

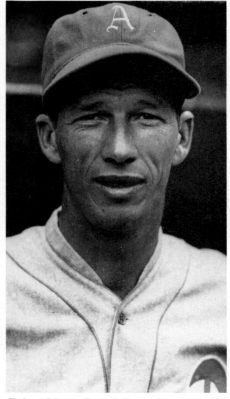

Robert Moses (Lefty) Grove, in person. He won the two games that Earnshaw didn't.

Joe McCarthy, whose Yankees won five pennants in the 1930s.

1931

The 1931 Series was a repeat performance of the previous year—the Athletics versus the Cardinals—and it was so thoroughly and engagingly dominated by a little-known Cardinal rookie that it remains one of the few October events to have a player's name billed over it: the Pepper Martin Series.

John Leonard (Pepper) Martin was a likable, unassuming, hard-playing twenty-seven-year-old outfielder. The fleet-footed Oklahoman batted an even .300 during the season, but in the Series, particularly through the first five games, he was Ty Cobb and Babe Ruth personified. "Our secret weapon," a chuckling Bill Hallahan called him years later.

For a week in October, the zealously hustling Pepper raised the spirits of a Depression-ridden country with his sharp hitting and his headfirst dives for stolen bases, driving the lordly Athletics to distraction. "What is he hitting?" the scholarly Mr. Mack asked George Earnshaw during the Series, thinking to perhaps change the pattern on Martin. "Everything we throw," Earnshaw answered ruefully.

In the opener Pepper treated the great Grove, 31–4 that year, like a batting-practice pitcher, rapping two singles and a double. The A's, however, defeated rookie starter Paul Derringer and the Cardinals 6–2, Simmons driving in three of the runs. Game two was all Pepper. With one out in the second, he stretched what should have been a single into a double, stole third, then scored on a sacrifice fly. In the bottom of the seventh he singled, stole second, advanced to third on a ground out, and scored on a squeeze play. Final score: Cards 2, A's 0, Hallahan shutting out Earnshaw.

In game three in Philadelphia, Pepper again

85

bruised the great Grove, rapping a single and a double and scoring twice in a 5–2 Cardinal win. It was a two-hitter for Burleigh Grimes.

In game four Earnshaw returned the favor, firing a two-hitter against the Cardinals, with Pepper getting both hits, a single and a double. It was a 3–0 Athletics victory. In the bottom of the sixth, Jimmie Foxx hit a home run so far over the left-field pavilion that it led one of the Cardinal relief pitchers to say later, "We were watching that ball for two innings."

With the Series deadlocked at two games apiece, Pepper personally tore apart the crucial fifth game. He hit two singles and a home run and drove in four runs in a 5–1 Cardinal victory. The winning pitcher was Hallahan, the losing pitcher old Yankee hero Waite Hoyt, now working for Connie Mack.

After five games, Martin's rampage stood at 12 for 18. But then Pepper suddenly turned mortal again, going hitless in the last two contests. The A's tied the Series in game six, 8–1, Grove once again beating Derringer, sending the Series into a seventh game.

With Pepper at rest, the Cardinals won it all in game seven, 4–2, behind a gritty performance by Burleigh Grimes, with last-out help from Hallahan.

Through a week in October, Pepper Martin had become a national hero, carving a special niche for himself in baseball lore. Overall, he batted .500 for the Series, collecting 12 hits and stealing five bases.

The 1931 World Series was the eighth and last for Connie Mack. Falling attendance and a worsening economy would force the old man to sell off his stars over the next few years, and though he would spend another 19 years managing his beloved Athletics, never again would Connie Mack be anything more than a spectator at a World Series.

1932

The 1932 World Series would have been eminently forgettable—the Yankees clobbered the Cubs in four—except for one unforgettable moment in game three, perhaps baseball's *most* unforgettable. Inevitably, it seemed, it involved Babe Ruth, now thirty-seven years old and playing in his last World Series.

Managing the Yankees was ex–Cub skipper Joe McCarthy, at the beginning of a reign that would bring him eight pennants and seven world championships in twelve years. The '32 Yankees still had some of the '27 bruisers—Ruth, Gehrig, Lazzeri, Combs—who were abetted now by catcher Bill Dickey, outfielder Ben Chapman, shortstop Frank Crosetti, and third baseman Joe Sewell. Pitching, McCarthy had Lefty Gomez and right-handers Red Ruffing, George Pipgras, and Johnny Allen.

Opposing these steamrollers was a Chicago Cubs team that included such solid men as manager–first baseman Charlie Grimm, second baseman Billy Herman, shortstop Billy Jurges, outfielders Kiki Cuyler and Riggs Stephenson, and catcher Gabby Hartnett. A stalwart quartet of right-handers did most of the Cubs' pitching: Lon Warneke, Charlie Root, Guy Bush, and Pat Malone.

What brought on the high drama of game three was a feud that had erupted between the two teams. When Jurges was put out of action with a late-season injury, the Cubs brought up from the minors ex-Yankee shortstop Mark Koenig to fill in. Koenig played exceedingly well and helped the club to the pennant. When it came to slicing up their World Series melon, however, the Cubs voted Koenig just a half share. Though it was clearly none of their business, the Yankees were rankled by what they considered the parsimonious treatment of a popular former teammate. And so began a hurling back and forth of insults, with the volume rising and the invective turning more and more sulfurous. At the center of it, as he was always at the center of everything, was Ruth.

The Cubs' collective disposition was not sweetened by a 12–6 shellacking they took in game one at Yankee Stadium. Game two also went to the Yankees, 5–2.

Chicago's Wrigley Field was the setting for game three. With nearly 50,000 Cub fans howling at the Yankees—primarily at Ruth—and the dugouts firing insults back and forth, the Yankees began a barrage early in the game that featured a three-run homer by Ruth and a solo shot by Gehrig. In the top of the fifth inning Ruth came to bat. Charlie Root, who had started and was still on the mound, whipped across two strikes. Ruth raised his arm and made a gesture. There is a welter of differing interpretations concerning this gesture: he was pointing at Root, at the Cub dugout, at the outfield wall, or he was pointing at nothing, just letting the Cubs know he still had one strike left. Whatever mysteries remain about the gesture, what happened next was colossally vivid: Ruth drove the next pitch on a mighty journey out of the ball park.

In later years Ruth would variously say either that he did call his home run that day or that he did not. In all likelihood he did not. A pitcher of Root's simmering temperament would have responded to such blatant showboating with a beanball. But it no longer matters what Ruth did or did not do; baseball legend has come to insist that he called his shot.

The Yankees ended it the next day with a 19-hit, 13–6 rollover.

Overshadowed by baseball's greatest showman in this four-game sweep of the Cubs (the Yankees' third straight sweep, following their cleaver jobs on the Pirates in 1927 and the Cardinals in 1928) were Lou Gehrig's three home runs and .529 batting average. Also buried in all the noise was Joe McCarthy's sweet revenge upon the team that had fired him at the end of the 1930 season.

1933

In 1933 the New York Giants won their first pennant since 1924, and for the first time in their history they were led into a World Series by a manager other than John McGraw. McGraw had retired the year before; he was succeeded by first baseman Bill Terry. Unlike the Giant teams of the early 1920s, the '33 club was stronger on the mound than at the plate. Only Terry, third baseman Johnny Vergez, and outfielders Mel Ott and Jo-Jo Moore delivered consistently at the plate. In screwballing left-hander Carl Hubbell and right-handers Hal Schumacher, Roy Parmalee, and knuckle baller Fred Fitzsimmons, however, Terry had what was probably the league's best pitching staff.

The Giants' rather modest hitting made the Washington Senators the Series favorites. Once more managed to success by a youthful infielder—this time it was twenty-six-year-old shortstop Joe Cronin—the Senators had a strong lineup that included outfielders Goose Goslin, Heinie Manush, and Fred Schulte, first baseman Joe Kuhel, second baseman Buddy Myer, and Cronin, one of the great hitting shortstops of all time. With Ossie Bluege at third and Luke Sewell catching, this was an exceptionally well-balanced team. Twenty-game winners Alvin Crowder and southpaw Earl Whitehill led Cronin's pitching staff.

The Series opened at the Polo Grounds, and Hubbell and Schumacher stopped the highly touted Washington hitters cold, limiting them to just five hits per game en route to 4–2 and 6–1 victories. The Senators held a 1–0 lead into the bottom of the sixth of the latter game, when the Giants broke out with six runs.

The Senators got untracked in game three, Whitehill shutting the Giants out 4–0.

The teams then played a couple of extra-inning thrillers. The Giants took a 2–1 eleven-inning nail-biter behind Hubbell. After scoring the tie breaker in the top of the eleventh on a single by shortstop Blondie Ryan, Hubbell had to face a bases-loaded, one-out situation in the bottom of the inning. With pinch hitter Cliff Bolton at bat, the unflappable Hubbell got him to ground into a game-ending double play.

The following day the Giants iced the championship on a tenth-inning home run by Ott, 4–3. The New Yorkers won it behind 4⅓ innings of airtight relief pitching by forty-two-year-old Dolf Luque, relieving Schumacher in the sixth after a game-tying three-run homer by Schulte.

New York pitching, with Hubbell and Schumacher doing the bulk of the work, had effectively stymied the Washington hitters, holding them to a composite .217 batting average. Mel Ott, with two home runs and a .389 batting average, was the Series' top hitter.

1934

In the spring of 1934 Dizzy Dean said that he and his brother Paul would win 50 games for the Cardinals. They won 49—Dizzy 30 and Paul 19. When it came to the World Series that year, the Cardinals versus the Detroit Tigers, Dizzy said that he and Paul would win two apiece. This time he hit it right on the nose.

Dizzy was the star pitcher and star personality on a raucous, hustling, hard-nosed club soon to win renown as the Gashouse Gang. Along with the Deans were player-manager Frank Frisch at second base, first baseman Rip Collins, shortstop Leo Durocher, Pepper Martin (now playing third base), outfielders Joe Medwick, Ernie Orsatti, and Jack Rothrock, and catchers Bill DeLancey and Spud Davis. Behind the Deans on the mound were right-hander Tex Carleton and southpaws Bill Hallahan and Bill Walker.

Detroit had its first pennant winner in 25 years. Bolstered by the acquisition of catcher Mickey Cochrane (who was installed as manager) from the Athletics and Goose Goslin from the Senators to go along with first baseman Hank Greenberg, second baseman Charlie Gehringer, and outfielders Jo-Jo White, Pete Fox, and Gee Walker, the Tigers presented a lineup that batted .300. They also had a strong pitching staff with 20-game winners Tommy Bridges and Schoolboy Rowe, plus Eldon Auker and Firpo Marberry, all right-handers.

Dizzy won the opener in Detroit 8–3 as a skittish Tiger infield committed five errors in the first three innings. The Tigers evened it up the next day, taking a twelve-inning pulsator, 3–2, on Goslin's single.

The Series then moved to St. Louis, where Paul Dean won game three, 4–1, but Detroit leveled it again in game four with a heavy-hitting attack, winning 10–4. In the fourth inning of this game Dizzy was inserted as a pinch runner at first base. When the next batter hit a ground ball to Gehringer, Dizzy went rushing into second to break up the double play. A good idea, except that he forgot to slide. Shortstop Billy Rogell's peg to first hit Dizzy in the head. The 30-game winner was carried off the field and taken to the hospital. "They X-rayed my head," Dean reported later, "and didn't find anything."

The Series then tipped back and forth, Bridges beating Dizzy 3–1 in game five, but Paul resetting the balance in game six, edging Rowe 4–3. The stage was set for one of the most tumultuous World Series games ever played.

The 11–0 final score tells only part of the story. The Cardinals scored seven runs in the third inning, and with Dizzy pitching at the top of his form (on one day's rest), the issue had been settled early. In the top of the sixth, Joe Medwick, running out a triple to right-center, slid hard into Tiger third baseman Marv

Owen, inciting Owen into a brief altercation. Also incited were the frustrated Tiger fans. When Medwick took his position in left field in the bottom of the inning he became the target for a barrage of bottles, fruit, vegetables, and just about anything else that could be airborne.

The only way to placate the Tiger fans, it seemed, was to remove Joe from the game, which Judge Landis did. With the score standing at 9–0 at the time, the Cardinals survived the loss of their best hitter. Dizzy completed an 11–0 blanking behind a 17-hit assault upon six Detroit pitchers.

Four hitters shared top Series honors with 11 hits apiece—Detroit's Gehringer and St. Louis's Collins, Medwick, and Martin. Pepper, playing his second and last World Series, found the October festivities pure batting practice, collecting 23 hits and batting .418 through 14 games.

But the biggest noise to come from the 1934 World Series came from Dizzy Dean. "I told you me 'n' Paul'd win four games," Diz yelled, and yelled, and yelled.

1935

Mickey Cochrane brought his club back to the Series the next year, the Tigers still looking for their first world championship. Facing them were Charlie Grimm's Chicago Cubs, who had ridden a 21-game September winning streak that carried them past the Giants and Cardinals, who had spent the summer fighting for the pennant.

The Cubs had a solid team: Phil Cavaretta, Billy Herman, Billy Jurges, and Stan Hack in the infield, Gabby Hartnett catching, and an outfield of Frank Demaree, Augie Galan, and Chuck Klein. Along with this .288-hitting lineup went a deep and talented pitching staff: right-handers Lon Warneke, Bill Lee, Charlie Root, Tex Carleton and southpaws Larry French and Roy Henshaw.

When Lon Warneke shut out the Tigers and Schoolboy Rowe 3–0 in the opener in Detroit, the Cubs seemed to be on their way. But the Tigers came back the next day and won 8–3 behind Bridges. It was a costly victory, however, as Detroit's big hitter, Hank Greenberg, broke his wrist and was lost for the rest of the Series. Moving to first base for Detroit was third baseman Marv Owen; replacing Owen at third was light-hitting Flea Clifton. Clifton went 0 for 16 in the Series, accentuating Greenberg's loss all the more.

The Tigers took game three in Chicago, 6–5 in eleven innings. After seeing the Cubs tie the game with two in the bottom of the ninth, Detroit won it in the top of the eleventh on a single by outfielder Jo-Jo White.

The Tigers came within one game of their long-sought championship the next day, when Alvin Crow-

der edged the Cubs 2–1. Detroit's winning run scored in the top of the sixth when Galan dropped Clifton's fly ball for a two-base error and Jurges made a wild throw on Crowder's grounder.

The Cubs stayed alive by winning game five, 3–1, on the combined efforts of Warneke and Lee, with a two-run homer by Klein the big blow.

Game six was played in Detroit, and Tiger fans were poised to celebrate. With Larry French pitching for the Cubs and Tommy Bridges for the Tigers, the game tipped back and forth, coming into the ninth in a 3–3 tie. Stan Hack led off for the Cubs with a triple, and a pall settled over Detroit. But Bridges bore down and fanned Billy Jurges. Cubs skipper Charlie Grimm let Larry French bat for himself, but the best Larry could do was bounce to the mound. Bridges threw him out while Hack held third. When Augie Galan flied to left, the threat was over. Forty years later Cubs second baseman Billy Herman would say wistfully, "I can still see Stanley Hack standing there on third base."

With one out in the bottom of the ninth, Cochrane singled. Gehringer then rifled a smash on a line that Cavaretta knocked down at first; while Phil made the play on Gehringer, Cochrane moved to second. Goose Goslin then dropped a soft fly ball into right-center for a single, scoring Cochrane with the winning run and sending the city of Detroit off into a loud, all-night celebration of its first world championship.

1936

The Subway Series resumed in 1936, after 13 years. It was Joe McCarthy's Yankees versus Bill Terry's Giants.

The Yankees, back in the Series after four years, had dethroned the Tigers and left the American League in a shambles, winning by 19½ games (a new league record). It was the Yankees' eighth pennant, and the first one they had taken without Ruth. Miraculously, however, the team had apparently done the impossible—they had replaced Babe Ruth. The new man was named Joe DiMaggio, and he had teamed with Lou Gehrig, Tony Lazzeri, Bill Dickey, George Selkirk, and Red Rolfe to give the Yankees an awesome attack, making it a little easier for pitchers Lefty Gomez, Red Ruffing, Monte Pearson, Bump Hadley, Pat Malone, and Johnny Murphy.

The Giants were unable to match this array of talent, though they had some good ballplayers in second baseman Burgess Whitehead, shortstop Dick Bartell, catcher Gus Mancuso, and outfielders Hank Lieber, Jo-Jo Moore, and Mel Ott. The Giants did have the best pitcher in baseball in lefty Carl Hubbell (26–6 that year, winning his last 16 decisions), backed up by right-handers Hal Schumacher and Fred Fitzsimmons.

When Hubbell defeated Ruffing 6–1 in the opener at the Polo Grounds, it marked the Yankees' first World Series loss after 12 straight wins (those sweeps in 1927, 1928, and 1932). The next day, however, was pure mayhem, Yankee style. McCarthy's men tore apart five Giant pitchers, scoring seven in the third, the inning highlighted by Lazzeri's grand-slam homer (the first in Series play since Elmer Smith's in 1920), and another six in the ninth on their way to a brutalizing 18–4 win.

Order was restored the next day at Yankee Stadium, but it was still McCarthy's club, 2–1, behind Hadley, Frank Crosetti driving in the winning run with an infield single in the bottom of the eighth.

In game four the Yankees did something no one had been able to do since mid-season—pin a loss on Carl Hubbell. With Gehrig hitting a key two-run homer, the Bronx Bombers whipped Terry's ace 5–2 behind Monte Pearson.

Needing one more to cinch, the Yankees were delayed by a 5–4 ten-inning loss to Hal Schumacher. The following day the Yankees let go with another explosive performance. Leading 6–5 going into the top of the ninth, they erupted for seven runs and headed on to a 13–5 win and the championship, having mounted their second 17-hit assault of the Series.

The Yankees batted .302 as a team through the six games of the 1936 World Series, topped by outfielder Jake Powell's ten hits and .455 average, followed by Rolfe's ten hits and .400 average. McCarthy's mound star was Gomez, with two wins.

"I remember after that Series," Joe McCarthy recalled years later, "somebody came up to me and said my club was so good it didn't look like anybody was going to beat us for a long time. I'll tell you, that fellow knew what he was talking about."

1937

The same two teams met again in the 1937 World Series, the Yankees having again run through the league, taking the pennant by 13 games, the Giants slipping in by three over the Cubs.

The Yankees had Gehrig (now in the twelfth year of his consecutive-game streak) driving in 159 runs, young DiMaggio driving in 167, and Dickey 133. Compared to this, the Giants' top RBI man was Mel Ott with 95, though the Giants did get some steady hitting from Dick Bartell, catcher Harry Danning, second baseman Burgess Whitehead, and outfielders Jo-Jo Moore and Jimmy Ripple. Hubbell and Schumacher had been joined on the pitching staff by a 20-game-winning rookie southpaw named Cliff Melton.

McCarthy's pitchers, overshadowed by the thundering bats around them, were led by 20-game winners Ruffing and Gomez, followed by Hadley, Pear-

son, and relief specialist Johnny Murphy.

Game one at Yankee Stadium was a match between 20-game-winning left-handers Gomez and Hubbell. With the Giants holding a 1–0 lead and Hubbell pitching masterfully, retiring 14 in a row, the Yankees suddenly exploded as they had the previous year, scoring seven runs in the bottom of the sixth and setting the tone of the Series with an 8–1 win.

It was 8–2 the next day, the Yankees winning easily behind Ruffing, the hard-hitting Yankee right-hander knocking in three by himself. The next day, at the Polo Grounds, McCarthy's rippers threatened to make it a sweep, coasting to a 5–1 victory by Pearson, with last-out help from Murphy.

Hubbell came back in game four on two days' rest and spared his mates the embarrassment of a wipe-out, beating the Yankees 7–3 as the Giants finally came alive with six runs in the bottom of the second. In the top of the ninth, Gehrig hit his tenth and last World Series home run.

The inevitable took place the next day, when Gomez defeated Melton 4–2, giving the Yankees back-to-back world championships and five out of five since 1928.

Gomez again won two games, running his World Series history to 5–0, while Tony Lazzeri, playing his last year as a Yankee, led all hitters with a .400 batting average.

The Yankees were the souls of efficiency in this Series. In addition to their timely hitting and strong pitching, they became the first team ever to go through a World Series without committing an error. The Yankees of that era, it seemed, were just about perfect.

1938

Joe McCarthy brought his Yankees back to the Series for the third straight year in 1938, and, if anything, the club had strengthened itself. Lazzeri had been replaced at second by Joe Gordon, a flashy fielder with a home run bat, and another young power hitter named Tommy Henrich was now in the outfield. The two youngsters supplemented the nucleus of Gehrig, DiMaggio, Dickey, Rolfe, Selkirk, and Crosetti, with Gomez, Ruffing, and Pearson still carrying the burden of the pitching.

Continuing their odd pattern of winning every three years, the Cubs, winners in 1929, 1932, and 1935, were back on top in the National League, having won a very close race with Pittsburgh. With 65 home runs to the Yankees' 174, they were no match for the New Yorkers' firepower, though they did have veteran talent at every position: Rip Collins, Billy Herman, Billy Jurges, and Stan Hack in the infield; Frank Demaree, Augie Galan, Carl Reynolds, and youngster Joe Marty in the outfield; and manager Gabby Hartnett behind the plate. Right-handers Bill

Lee and Clay Bryant were Chicago's big winners, helped along by an occasional victory by sore-armed Dizzy Dean, who had been purchased from the Cardinals that spring.

It was, in fact, Dean who provided the only real drama in an otherwise lackluster Series. After the Yankees had taken the opener in Chicago behind Ruffing, 3–1 (with Dickey going 4 for 4), Dean started the second game against Gomez. With his once mighty "express" permanently derailed, Dizzy kept the Yankee long ballers off-stride with slow curves and changes of speeds for seven innings. Leading 3–2 in the top of the eighth, however, he saw Frank Crosetti pop a two-run homer into the left-field bleachers. DiMaggio added another two-run shot in the ninth, and the Yankees, behind Gomez and Murphy, won it 6–3.

The Yankees took game three in Yankee Stadium, 5–2, behind Pearson. Joe Gordon, an eighth-place hitter on this club, drove in three runs. Joe Marty, as he had done in game two for the Cubs, went 3 for 4 and drove in all of his team's runs.

The Yankees made it a sweep in game four. With Ruffing winning again, and Crosetti driving in four runs with a double and triple, the New Yorkers worked over six Chicago pitchers for an 8–3 win, and became the first team ever to take three successive world titles.

Rookie Gordon, who batted .400, and Crosetti each drove in six runs, accounting for more than half the Yankees' total of 22. Joe Marty was the Series' top hitter, going 6 for 12 for a .500 batting average and driving in five of Chicago's nine runs.

In winning his game, Gomez ran his World Series record to 6–0. Lefty wouldn't see another October decision, and his 6–0 mark remains the best in Series history for games won without a loss.

Overlooked by jubilant Yankee fans was a subpar performance by Gehrig. Lou contributed just four singles and drove in no runs. It was an omen of impending tragedy. A few weeks into the 1939 season the "Iron Man's" consecutive-game streak would end at 2,130, and two years after that he would be dead, a victim of amyotrophic lateral sclerosis, a muscle-killing illness known thereafter as "Lou Gehrig's disease."

1939

When years later someone asked Cincinnati first baseman Frank McCormick about the 1939 World Series, in which his club played the Yankees, McCormick smiled wryly and said, "What World Series?"

It was a Series that a Yankee team ran through in four games for the fifth time in their history, giving them a record of 28 wins in their last 31 Series games, dating back to 1927.

Playing without Gehrig for the first time since 1925 (Babe Dahlgren was now on first base for the Yankees), McCarthy's team still won by 17 games, some of the slack having been taken up by rookie outfielder Charlie Keller, who batted .334. Joe DiMaggio, enjoying his peak year with a .381 batting average, Joe Gordon, Bill Dickey, and George Selkirk all drove in over 100 runs. Along with staff leader Red Ruffing (21–7), McCarthy had seven pitchers winning in double figures: Atley Donald, Lefty Gomez, Bump Hadley, Monte Pearson, Steve Sundra, and Oral Hildebrand.

The Reds, with skipper Bill McKechnie winning a pennant with his third different club (1925 Pirates and 1928 Cardinals), were a team that emphasized timely hitting, good defense, and two superb pitchers in right-handers Bucky Walters (27–11) and Paul Derringer (25–7). The Reds' big gunners were first baseman McCormick, catcher Ernie Lombardi, and outfielder Ival Goodman, along with such sharp players as Lonny Frey at second, Billy Myers at short, Bill Werber at third, and Harry Craft in center.

Ruffing and Derringer opened the Series in Yankee Stadium, and the two big righties put on a fine show. It was a 1–1 ball game into the bottom of the ninth. With one out, Keller tripled. The Reds walked DiMaggio, but Dickey ended it with a single to center.

Monte Pearson two-hit the Reds in game two, 4–0, holding the Cincinnatians hitless until one out in the eighth.

Game three, in Cincinnati, was a Charlie Keller show, the Yankee rookie hitting two home runs and driving in four runs in a 7–3 New York victory. The game was, in fact, a lethal display of Yankee power economy: getting seven runs on just five hits, with four of the hits home runs—DiMaggio and Dickey joining Keller with one-way shots.

The finale, which the Yankees took in ten innings 7–4, saw the creating of the Series' lasting image: "the Lombardi snooze." The Yankees having tied the score at four-all with two in the top of the ninth, they broke it open with three in the tenth. With Keller on first and Crosetti on third with one out, DiMaggio singled to right, scoring Crosetti. When Goodman fumbled the ball in right, Keller also scored. In coming across the plate, the muscular Keller banged into Lombardi, stunning the big catcher. Seeing Lombardi momentarily dazed, DiMaggio, ever alert, also came in to score. With nothing much else to write about this Series, the writers latched on to Lombardi's "snooze" at home, which was decidedly unfair to Ernie, who had taken quite a wallop from Keller.

Yankee Charlie Keller dominated the short Series, batting .438 in the four games, with three home runs, a triple, a double, and six runs batted in. With the Yankees having now won four straight world titles, the cry "Break up the Yankees" began rumbling through baseball America. But from Cincinnati, it was more modest. "Yankees, hell," Reds fans muttered. "Just break up Keller."

1940

The Yankees missed out on a fifth straight pennant, but just barely, finishing in third place, two games behind Detroit, the Tigers edging Cleveland by one. Detroit was a hard-hitting club, with .340 hitters Hank Greenberg and Barney McCosky in the outfield, along with power hitter Rudy York at first, veteran Charlie Gehringer at second, and Pinky Higgins at third. The Tiger ace that year was the colorful, much-traveled Bobo Newsom, backed by experienced right-handers Schoolboy Rowe and Tommy Bridges.

For the second year in a row, Bill McKechnie's Reds had ridden on the strong arms of Bucky Walters and Paul Derringer and the big bats of Frank McCormick, and Ernie Lombardi, winning the pennant by 12 games. The Reds received a blow, however, when a foot injury limited Lombardi to a few pinch-hit appearances in the Series. His place was taken by the forty-year-old Jimmie Wilson. The veteran catcher, who had recently retired, was a Cincinnati coach; he caught virtually the entire Series for the Reds, hit well, and accounted for the Series' only stolen base.

Detroit hitting swept away Derringer and the Reds in the opener in Cincinnati, 7–2, Newsom winning. Walters tied it the next day, beating Rowe, 5–3.

In Detroit, the veteran curve baller Bridges put the Tigers one up with a 7–4 victory, helped by two-run homers from Higgins and York in the bottom of the seventh. But Derringer came back in game four and tied it again with a 5–2 win. When Newsom, with the help of a tremendous three-run homer by Greenberg,

shut out the Reds 8–0 in game five, it put the Tigers on the brink of their second world championship.

The Series moved back to Cincinnati, and Bucky Walters kept his club alive with a clutch 4–0 win. Bucky helped make sure by hitting a solo homer in the bottom of the eighth.

Newsom and Derringer squared off in the deciding game, Bobo working on one day's rest. If there was a sentimental favorite, it was Bobo, whose father had died a few days before.

The Tigers took a one-run lead in the top of the third, and Newsom nursed it along to the bottom of the seventh. With time running out on the Reds, Frank McCormick led off with a double. Jimmy Ripple followed with another double, but with the slow-footed McCormick running, the Tigers had a play at the plate. Tiger shortstop Dick Bartell took the outfield relay with his back to the plate and, with the hometown Cincinnati fans roaring, was unable to hear his teammates' shouts to throw home, allowing McCormick to score.

Jimmie Wilson then sacrificed Ripple to third, and after pinch hitter Ernie Lombardi was intentionally walked, Billy Myers flied to center deep enough to score Ripple.

Derringer remained watertight, pitching Cincinnati to a 2–1 victory and the club's first world championship since the tainted win in 1919.

For the Reds, the Series had followed the pattern of their season: Derringer and Walters, Walters and Derringer, the two great right-handers each winning two games.

The Cardinals' hard-throwing lefty Wild Bill Hallahan, who defeated the Athletics twice in the 1931 World Series.

Philadelphia power plant Jimmie Foxx, who batted .348 in the 1931 Series. Of Jimmie's monumental game four home run somebody in the Cardinal bullpen said, "We were watching that ball for two innings."

Five lumbermen pose together during the 1931 Series. Left to right, Jim Bottomley, Pepper Martin, and Chick Hafey of the Cardinals, Al Simmons and Mickey Cochrane of the Athletics.

Pepper Martin doing his thing in the 1931 Series. It's the bottom of the seventh inning of game two, and Pepper has just swept in from third on a squeeze bunt by Charlie Gelbert. Mickey Cochrane looks as if he's doing a war dance with plate umpire Dick Nallin.

Al Simmons had another good Series for the A's in 1931, driving in eight runs and batting .333.

Cardinals pitcher Burleigh Grimes, who won two games in the 1931 Series, including the seventh and deciding game.

Chicago shortstop Billy Jurges.

Cubs catcher Gabby Hartnett.

Chicago pitcher Charlie Root, the man who threw the famous pitch to Babe Ruth in the 1932 World Series.

Lou Gehrig, who had another sensational Series for the Yankees against the Chicago Cubs in 1932, batting .529.

Babe Ruth being congratulated by Lou Gehrig after slamming his "called shot" home run in the 1932 World Series. Catcher Hartnett looks stunned, while umpire Roy Van Graflin seems amused.

Mr. Ruth. The 1932 World Series was his tenth and last.

The Giants' great Carl Hubbell. He beat the Washington Senators twice in the 1933 World Series, pitching 20 innings and allowing no earned runs.

Giants right-hander Hal Schumacher, who played "Prince Hal" to Hubbell's "King Carl."

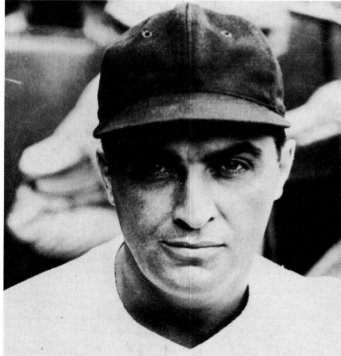

Earl Whitehill. The Washington left-hander shut out the Giants in game three of the 1933 World Series, giving the Senators their only win.

The greatest shortstop of all time showed up at the 1933 World Series, and here is Honus Wagner posing with the opposing managers, Washington's Joe Cronin (left) and New York's Bill Terry.

Joe Cronin is firing to first to complete a double play in the eighth inning of the fifth and last game of the 1933 World Series. The Giants' Kiddo Davis is the base runner, Washington second baseman Buddy Myer is watching the action, and umpire Charlie Pfirman is making the call.

The New York Giants have just won the 1933 World Series against the Washington Senators, and the winning smiles belong to New York slugger Mel Ott (left), the Series' top hitter with a .389 batting average, and first baseman–manager Bill Terry.

The veteran Dolf Luque, who pitched brilliantly in relief to win the fifth and final game of the 1933 Series for the Giants.

Detroit's Charlie Gehringer, top hitter of the 1934 World Series with a .379 batting average (tied with the Cardinals' outfielder Joe Medwick).

Detroit first baseman Hank Greenberg, leading RBI man of the 1934 Series with seven.

Gee Walker, whose pinch single in the bottom of the ninth of game two tied the score and enabled the Tigers to go on and win it in the twelfth.

Dizzy Dean (left) and his brother Paul (right) pose with Detroit's right-handed ace Schoolboy Rowe before the second game of the 1934 Series, which Rowe won in twelve innings, 3–2.

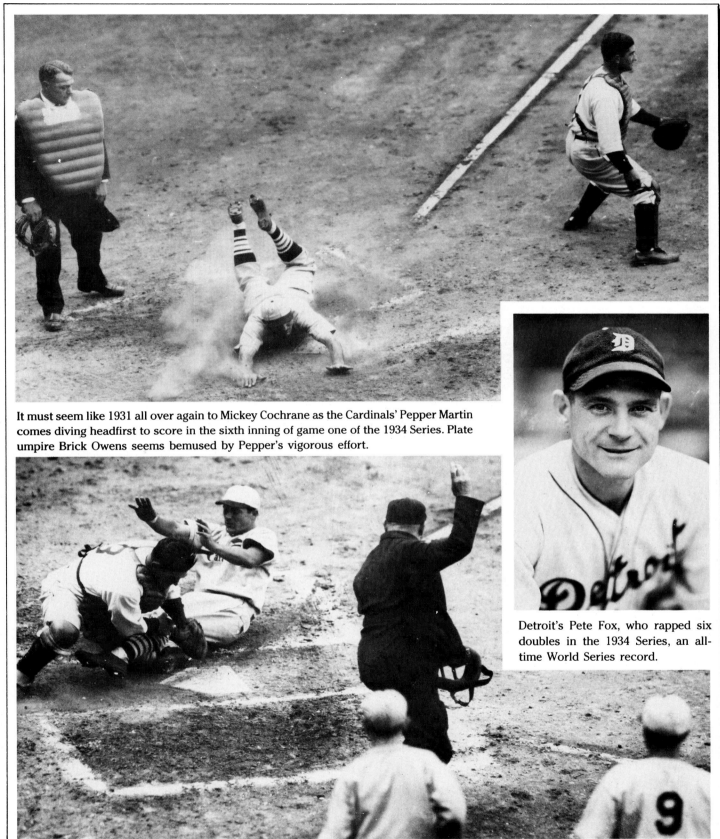

It must seem like 1931 all over again to Mickey Cochrane as the Cardinals' Pepper Martin comes diving headfirst to score in the sixth inning of game one of the 1934 Series. Plate umpire Brick Owens seems bemused by Pepper's vigorous effort.

Detroit's Pete Fox, who rapped six doubles in the 1934 Series, an all-time World Series record.

Another Cardinal heading for home, but this time Joe Medwick is not going to make it. In a rugged coming together of two rugged men, Cochrane has blocked Joe off the plate by inches and tagged him out. The action occurred in the top of the third inning of game two, 1934. Medwick was trying to score on a Rip Collins single to left, but Goose Goslin's throw was on time and on the money. Bill Klem is the umpire.

Joe Medwick.

It's game four of the 1934 Series between the Cardinals and the Tigers, bottom of the fourth inning, and pinch runner Dizzy Dean, running from first to second on a ground ball, has just been skulled by shortstop Billy Rogell's peg. Second baseman Charlie Gehringer is at the right.

Joe Medwick crashing into Detroit third baseman Marv Owen in the sixth inning of the seventh game, 1934. This is the slide that precipitated Medwick's confrontation with Owen, enraged the Tiger fans, and led to Joe's removal from the game.

Dizzy being carried off the field after being hit in the head. When a 30-game winner goes down, it's serious—attested to by the fact that at least 14 Cardinals dashed out to check on their ace.

The Cubs' sharp right-hander Lon Warneke, who beat the Tigers twice in the 1935 World Series.

Frank Demaree, who hit only two home runs all season for the Cubs, came into the 1935 Series and hit two more.

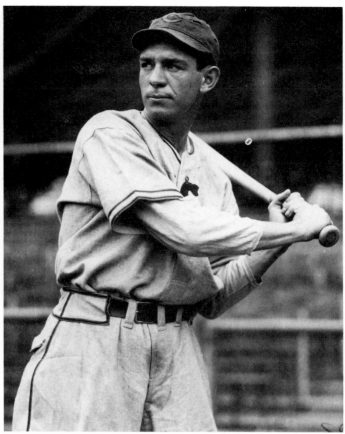

Augie Galan, a member of the Cubs' 1935 outfield.

Detroit's curve-balling right-hander Tommy Bridges, who beat the Cubs twice in two starts in the 1935 Series.

Goose Goslin, the man whose single in the bottom of the ninth inning of game six of the 1935 World Series gave the Tigers their first world championship.

Giants manager and first baseman Bill Terry reaches in vain for an errant throw from third baseman Travis Jackson as Jake Powell crosses first base. The umpire is Harry Geisel. The action occurred in the bottom of the sixth inning, game five, 1936 Series.

Shortstop Dick Bartell hit well for the Giants in the 1936 Series, with eight hits and a .381 batting average.

It's the bottom of the first inning of game six of the 1936 Series. The Giants have the bases loaded, and Mel Ott has just rifled a double down the right-field line that will score two runs. It was a good beginning, but the Yankees came back to win the game 13–5, and with it the Series.

As he had done in 1936, so did Lefty Gomez do in 1937—beat the Giants twice in the World Series.

Lou Gehrig, who enjoyed his last truly productive Series in 1937.

Lou Gehrig: another good Series in 1936, with two home runs and seven runs batted in in six games.

Giants first baseman Johnny McCarthy drew two errors on this play. First he fumbled George Selkirk's grounder, then threw wildly to pitcher Hal Schumacher, shown here trying to grab the ball with his bare hand. Selkirk ended up on second. The play occurred in the fifth inning of game three of the 1937 Series. The umpire is Bill Stewart.

Joe DiMaggio. Joe cracked his first World Series home run against the Giants in 1937.

Cliff Melton, the Giants' 20-game-winning rookie southpaw, who was roughed up by the Yankees in the 1937 Series.

Mel Ott.

Yankee ace right-hander Red Ruffing, who won two games in the Yankees' sweep of the Chicago Cubs in the 1938 World Series.

Phil Cavaretta, a .462 hitter in the 1938 Series.

Action in the first game of the 1938 Series. Chicago's Stan Hack is out at home in the third inning. He was trying to score on Billy Herman's single, but was cut down on a throw by shortstop Frank Crosetti to catcher Bill Dickey. The umpire is Charlie Moran.

Bill Dickey.

Joe Marty, the leading batter in the 1938 World Series, with a .500 batting average.

Monte Pearson, victor over the Cubs in game three of the 1938 Series.

The three top guns on Cincinnati's 1939 pennant winners. Left to right, Ernie Lombardi, Frank McCormick, Ival Goodman.

The Yankees' Joe Gordon sliding home in the bottom of the fifth inning of the 1939 Series opener in New York. Scoring all the way from first base on Babe Dahlgren's double, Gordon's run tied the game at 1–1. Catcher Ernie Lombardi is unable to get around in time. Umpire Bill McGowan and Frank Crosetti are watching the action.

Joe DiMaggio.

The Yankees' Charlie Keller, a one-man army in the 1939 World Series.

Paul Derringer, Cincinnati's hard-luck loser in game one of the 1939 World Series.

The starting pitchers for the second game of the 1939 World Series: Cincinnati's Bucky Walters and New York's Monte Pearson.

The famous Lombardi "snooze" in the tenth inning of the fourth and final game of the 1939 Series. The Reds' catcher lies dazed on the ground as DiMaggio slides across. Home plate umpire Babe Pinelli seems to be counting to ten over Ernie.

Detroit's great slugger Hank Greenberg. Big Henry had ten hits and a .357 batting average against Cincinnati in the 1940 World Series.

The Cincinnati Reds line up to oblige the photographer prior to the 1940 World Series. Left to right, Billy Werber, Mike McCormick, Ival Goodman, Frank McCormick, Jimmy Ripple, Ernie Lombardi, Lonnie Frey, Billy Myers, Eddie Joost.

Detroit outfielder Bruce Campbell, a .360 batter in the 1940 Series.

Detroit's Bobo Newsom and Cincinnati's Paul Derringer, who each made three starts in the 1940 World Series.

Walters and Billy Werber celebrating Bucky's 4–0 shutout over the Tigers in the sixth game of the 1940 Series. Werber was the Series' top hitter, with a .370 batting average.

Here's Hank Greenberg crossing the plate after hitting a three-run homer in the bottom of the third inning of game five of the 1940 Series. Hank's reception committee includes Barney McCosky (No. 21), Rudy York, and the bat boy.

V
War, Peace, and Jackie Robinson
1941-1950

It's just happened, in the top of the ninth inning of game four of the 1941 Series at Ebbets Field. Tommy Henrich has struck out, home plate umpire Larry Goetz is calling it . . . but the ball has trickled away from Mickey Owen, and the alert Henrich is on his way.

1941

The 1941 World Series remains vivid in baseball annals not because of stellar achievements but because of the simultaneous occurrence of two decidedly negative events.

The Dodgers were playing the Yankees, the first time the two intracity rivals had met in World Series play. The Yankees, with a mighty surge through the American League, highlighted by Joe DiMaggio's 56-game hitting streak, had retaken the pennant, winning by 17 games. Along with DiMaggio, Joe McCarthy had his reliable cast of regulars: Keller, Henrich, Dickey, Gordon, and Rolfe, to whom had been added rookie Phil Rizzuto at shortstop. Despite the team's 101 victories, the Yankees' top winners, Gomez and Ruffing, won just 15 apiece; but McCarthy's staff was talented and extremely deep, including Marius Rus-

so, Atley Donald, Spud Chandler, and Ernie Bonham.

In winning their first pennant in 21 years, Leo Durocher's Dodgers had edged out the Cardinals by 2½ games in a bruising, summer-long battle. The Dodgers were a team of veterans with a couple of talented youngsters mixed in. The Brooklyn infield had Dolph Camilli at first, Billy Herman at second, twenty-two-year-old Pee Wee Reese at short, and Cookie Lavagetto at third. Mickey Owen was the catcher, and veterans Joe Medwick and Dixie Walker flanked twenty-two-year-old batting champion Pete Reiser in center. Brooklyn's pitching was led by 20-game winners Whitlow Wyatt and Kirby Higbe, along with Fred Fitzsimmons, Curt Davis, and Hugh Casey.

The Series opened in Yankee Stadium, with the clubs exchanging 3–2 victories in games one and two, Ruffing winning for New York and Wyatt for Brooklyn.

111

The dark clouds began gathering for the Dodgers in game three, in Ebbets Field. With the veteran Fitzsimmons dueling young southpaw Russo, there was no score into the top of the seventh. With two out, Russo lined a drive off of Fitz's knee that broke the kneecap. The ball caromed into Reese's glove for the third out, but Fitzsimmons was through. Hugh Casey, who came out to pitch in the eighth for Brooklyn, promptly gave up four hits and two runs, and Russo hung on to win, 2–1.

If Dodger fans thought they had run into hard luck in game three with Fitzsimmons's injury, they were in for a worse jolt the next day. The Brooks were leading 4–3 with two out and nobody on in the top of the ninth. With two strikes on him, Henrich swung and missed at a wicked Hugh Casey breaking pitch (some people said it was a spitter). The ball broke so sharply that Mickey Owen could not handle it, and as it rolled away Henrich reached first. Instead of the Series being even at two games apiece, the Yankees had life.

What followed was brutal. DiMaggio singled. Keller doubled in two runs, putting the Yankees ahead 5–4. Dickey walked, and Gordon doubled in two more. Final score: Yankees 7, Dodgers 4.

"I don't think we could have beaten a girls' team the next day," Dodger Billy Herman said. The demoralized Dodgers went tamely, losing 3–1 to Ernie Bonham. The only real excitement occurred in the fifth inning, when Wyatt and DiMaggio almost came to blows on the mound as Joe was returning to the dugout after flying out. Wyatt had low-bridged DiMaggio during Joe's at bat, and as the Yankee center fielder was cutting across the infield some sharp words were exchanged. The umpires separated the men, and the game rolled forward to its—for Brooklyn—dreary conclusion.

The Yankees had won their eighth consecutive World Series, dating back to 1927. Through the eight, their won–lost record was a stunning 32–4. Once again, Joe McCarthy's boys seemed to have a stranglehold on the rest of baseball.

1942

In 1942, a young, speedy, voraciously hungry St. Louis Cardinals team under skipper Billy Southworth won 43 of its last 51 games and came from ten games behind in August to overtake the Dodgers and win a grueling pennant race. Led by Terry Moore, Enos Slaughter, rookie Stan Musial—each a greyhound in the outfield—shortstop Marty Marion, third baseman Whitey Kurowski, catcher Walker Cooper, and pitchers Mort Cooper (Walker's brother), Johnny Beazley, southpaws Ernie White, Howie Pollett, and Max Lanier, the Cardinals were a product of Branch Rickey's fertile farm system. At the age of thirty, Moore was the oldest regular.

McCarthy's Yankees were back on top for the sixth time in seven years, still spearheaded by DiMaggio, Keller, Henrich, Dickey, Gordon, and Rizzuto, with Ernie Bonham (21–5) now the ace, followed by Spud Chandler, Hank Borowy, and the thirty-eight-year-old Red Ruffing. The Yankees, basking in an aura of invincibility, were considered overwhelming favorites.

Ruffing held the Cardinals hitless in the opener in St. Louis until two out in the bottom of the eighth, when Moore singled. Meanwhile, the Yankees had pounded out a 7–0 lead, thanks in part to an uncharacteristic four errors by the Cardinals. But in the bottom of the ninth the Cardinals suddenly came to life and threw a scare into the Yankees. With a man on first and two out, they went on to score four runs and had the tying run on first base before making the third out. Many of the Cardinals later said that this outburst restored their confidence and led them to go on from there to shock the Yankees and the world of baseball by taking the next four straight.

Right-hander Johnny Beazley stopped the Yankees in game two, 4–3, Musial driving in the winning run with an eighth-inning single. With none out in the ninth inning, the Yankees had the tying run racing for third, but a great throw by Slaughter in right field nipped pinch runner Tuck Stainback and killed the rally.

With the Series shifting to New York, the Cardinals showed that they were unawed by cavernous Yankee Stadium and nearly 70,000 Yankee fans. Ernie White, pitching with a left arm so sore "you could have stuck a fork in it and I wouldn't have felt it," shut out the Yanks 2–0, with Musial in left and Slaughter in right robbing first Gordon and then Keller of home runs with spectacular catches on back-to-back plays in the bottom of the seventh.

In game four, the Cardinals stood toe-to-toe with the Yankees, finally outslugging them, 9–6. The boys from St. Louis took it all the next day behind Beazley, 4–2. It was 2–2 in the top of the ninth when Kurowski pickled one of Ruffing's pitches and sent it into the left-field stands just fair for a two-run, game-winning, Series-winning home run.

After winning eight World Series in a row, the Yankees had finally lost.

1943

It was the Cardinals and Yankees again in 1943, with both clubs having lost key players to military service. The Cardinals had seen the departure of outfielders Terry Moore and Enos Slaughter, infielder Jimmy Brown, and pitchers Johnny Beazley and Howie Pollett. Among their replacements, the Cards had infielder Lou Klein, outfielder Danny Litwhiler, and pitchers Harry Brecheen and Al Brazle.

McCarthy's Yankees had lost the services of Joe DiMaggio, Phil Rizzuto, Red Ruffing, and first baseman Buddy Hassett. The new men included first baseman Nick Etten, third baseman Billy Johnson, and outfielder Johnny Lindell.

The realigned clubs opened the Series in New York with the Cardinals slight favorites. But with the nearly unbeatable Spud Chandler (20–4 that season) on the mound, the Yankees won the opener, beating Max Lanier 4–2. The Cardinals sent out their own 20-game winning ace Mort Cooper the next day, and the big right-hander evened it out with a 4–3 win. (For Mort and his brother Walker, the game had deeper meaning, their father having died that morning.)

With wartime travel restrictions in effect, the first three games were scheduled for Yankee Stadium. Game three saw Cardinal lefty Al Brazle leading the Yankees and Borowy 2–1 going into the bottom of the eighth. Lindell led off for the Yankees with a single to center, and took second when Harry Walker fumbled the ball. Pinch hitter George Stirnweiss then dropped a bunt along the first-base line. First baseman Ray Sanders picked it up and fired it across the diamond to Kurowski at third. The ball had Lindell beat, but the big Yankee slid hard into Kurowski and jarred the ball loose. It was a key play, in the game and in the Series, for after an out and an intentional walk, Billy Johnson cleared the bases with a triple, and the Yankees went on to a 6–2 win.

When the Series resumed in St. Louis, Marius Russo silenced the Cardinal fans with a 2–1 victory over Max Lanier, with Russo himself doubling and scoring the winning run in the top of the eighth.

In game five, Mort Cooper started for the Cardinals and started brilliantly, striking out the first five Yankees he faced. Cooper continued to pitch well. However, his one lapse, in the sixth inning, cost him the game. With two out, Charlie Keller singled and Bill Dickey hit one onto the roof in right field. That was all Spud Chandler needed. The tough-minded Yankee right-hander went on to pitch a gutty ten-hit shutout, winning it 2–0. Chandler, with his two complete-game victories in which he allowed just one earned run, emerged as the Series' dominant player.

1944

The joke was that it took a World War for the St. Louis Browns to win a pennant. It happened in 1944, when the Browns, a team legendary for sustained ineptitude, took their first and only American League pennant, edging the Tigers on the last day of the season. With most of the regular major-league talent serving in the military, Luke Sewell guided his patchwork club of veterans and retreads into the only all–St. Louis World Series ever played—Billy Southworth's Cardinals having easily won their third straight pennant.

Along with shortstop Vern Stephens, first baseman George McQuinn, and outfielders Mike Kreevich and Al Zarilla, Sewell had a staff of canny right-handers in Nelson Potter, Jack Kramer, Bob Muncrief, and Denny Galehouse.

The Cardinals still had some legitimate stars on their roster in Stan Musial, Walker Cooper, Marty Marion, Whitey Kurowski, Ray Sanders, Danny Litwhiler, and Johnny Hopp, along with pitchers Mort Cooper, Max Lanier, Harry Brecheen, and rookie Ted Wilks. The Cardinals were expected to walk through the Series.

Sewell's club, however, gave a spirited account of themselves. "It was the damnedest Series," the Browns' manager said. "St. Louis fans seemed to be rooting for both teams. I've never seen games where whatever either side did got the same amount of cheering."

Galehouse defeated Cooper in the opener 2–1, on a two-run homer by McQuinn, the eventual hitting star of the Series. The Cards came back the next day to win in eleven innings, 3–2, behind four innings of brilliant shutout relief by Blix Donnelly. The Browns then took a one-game lead with a 6–2 win behind Jack Kramer, who fanned ten Cardinals.

Faced with the possibility of what would have been a most embarrassing upset, the Cardinals began clicking more efficiently. Harry Brecheen squared things at two-all with a 5–1 win in game four, helped by a single, double, and home run by Musial. In game five Mort Cooper was overpowering, striking out twelve in a 2–0 shutout, including three Brownie pinch-hitters in the bottom of the ninth. The Cardinal runs came in on homers by Ray Sanders and Danny Litwhiler.

Max Lanier and Ted Wilks teamed to win the game six clincher for the Cardinals, 3–1, two of the Cardinal runs scoring on errors. Errors, in fact, had been a problem for the Browns throughout the Series. In committing ten to the Cardinals' one, Sewell's defense had bobbled in seven unearned runs, almost half of the Cardinals' total of sixteen.

Cardinal pitching pretty much numbed the Browns' bats during the Series, holding them to a .183 average, with George McQuinn doing most of the losers' hitting, compiling a .438 batting average.

Together, the clubs struck out 92 times (the Browns 49, the Cards 43), setting a new record for a six-game Series.

1945

The Detroit Tigers got their big man back in midseason in 1945 when Hank Greenberg was discharged from the army air corps, and Big Henry belted them into a pennant with a grand-slam home run on the last day of the season.

Along with Greenberg, Steve O'Neill's Tigers had some good veteran players in first baseman Rudy

York, second baseman Eddie Mayo, and outfielders Doc Cramer and Roy Cullenbine.

In the National League, Charlie Grimm's Cubs had broken the Cardinals' three-year grip on first place, thanks to good seasons from first baseman Phil Cavaretta, second baseman Don Johnson, third baseman Stan Hack, and outfielders Bill Nicholson, Andy Pafko, and Peanuts Lowrey. A good pitching staff of Hank Wyse, Claude Passeau, Paul Derringer, and lefty Ray Prim was bolstered by the mid-season acquisition from the Yankees of Hank Borowy, who went 11–2 for the Cubs.

The curve-balling Borowy got the Cubs off to a good start with a 9–0 shutout in the opener in Detroit. In game two Detroit's hard-throwing Virgil Trucks, just a few weeks out of the navy, whipped the Cubs 4–1, thanks in large measure to a three-run homer by Greenberg. In game three the veteran Passeau put the Cubs back up by a game when he hurled a one-hit gem, shutting out the Tigers 3–0. It was the first one-hitter in Series play since Ed Reulbach's against the White Sox in 1906. Only a clean single by Rudy York in the second inning had prevented Passeau from pitching the World Series' first no-hitter.

The war was over, but some travel restrictions were still in effect; consequently, the first three games had been played in Detroit, with the remainder of the competition scheduled for Chicago.

In game four, in Chicago, Dizzy Trout evened the Series with a 4–1 victory for Detroit. The Tigers went a length ahead in game five, winning 8–4, with Greenberg slamming three doubles.

The Cubs stayed alive with an 8–7 twelve-inning win in game six. It was Stan Hack's fourth hit of the game, a bad-hop double that bounced over Greenberg's head in left field and scored pinch runner Billy Schuster from first base, that won it for the Cubs.

After a one-day rain postponement, the two teams joined for the seventh game. With their pitching staff depleted by the Tiger attack in games five and six, the Cubs were forced to start Borowy. After pitching a complete-game victory in the opener, Hank had gone five innings plus in game five, then come back the next day and pitched the last four innings of the twelve-inning win.

The toll on Borowy's arm showed immediately when the first three Tiger batters hit him for singles. The Cubs quickly brought in Derringer, but the Tiger tide had begun to roll and did not stop until five runs had scored, the last three on a crushing three-run double by catcher Paul Richards. The Tigers then coasted to an easy 9–3 win and the championship.

1946

The war was over, the stars were back, and, appropriately enough, two of the biggest made it to the 1946 World Series—Ted Williams with the Red Sox (Boston winning its first pennant since 1918) and Stan Musial with the Cardinals. For the Cardinals, it was the fourth pennant in five years, and a hard-earned one. After fighting the Brooklyn Dodgers to the first dead-heat finish in big-league history, Eddie Dyer's club took two straight in a best-of-three playoff.

Joe Cronin's Red Sox, running away with the pennant that year, had an exceptionally strong hitting attack. Led by the incomparable Williams, the Sox had second baseman Bobby Doerr, shortstop Johnny Pesky, first baseman Rudy York (recently obtained from Detroit), and outfielder Dom DiMaggio. On the mound, Boston had 20-game winners in right-handers Tex Hughson and Dave Ferriss, plus two more solid starters in Joe Dobson and southpaw Mickey Harris.

Though a bit short on power, the Cardinals had their usual verve-and-speed team, led by the .365-hitting Musial, recently converted to first base. Behind Musial were shortstop Marty Marion, second baseman Red Schoendienst, third baseman Whitey Kurowski, and outfielders Terry Moore, Harry Walker, and Enos Slaughter. The mainstays of Dyer's pitching staff were lefties Howie Pollett, Harry (The Cat) Brecheen, Al Brazle, and righties Murry Dickson and George Munger, the last recently discharged from military service.

The teams divided the first two games in St. Louis, the Red Sox taking the first 3–2 on York's tenth-inning homer, and the Cardinals resetting the balance in game two behind Brecheen's four-hitter, 3–0.

In Fenway Park for game three, Ferriss fired a six-hit, 4–0 shutout for Boston, Rudy York icing it with a three-run poke in the bottom of the first after a cautious Eddie Dyer had ordered Williams intentionally passed with a man on second and two out.

The next day the Cardinals tied a record set by the Giants in the 1921 Series by crashing out 20 hits in a 12–3 strafing of six Bosox pitchers. Slaughter, Kurowski, and catcher Joe Garagiola, batting consecutively in the lineup, each hit safely four times. In game five, however, Red Sox pitcher Joe Dobson held the Cards to just four hits in a 6–3 win. After the game the teams entrained for St. Louis, with the Red Sox needing just one win to take it all.

Screwballing Harry Brecheen won his second game of the Series, 4–1, deadlocking the clubs at three games apiece and setting up a seventh game.

Dave Ferriss started for the Sox, Murry Dickson for the Cards. The Cardinals chased Ferriss in the bottom of the fifth, and going into the top of the eighth it was 3–1 St. Louis. Boston, however, scored two to tie it up, knocking out Dickson, who was relieved by Brecheen. For the Cardinals, Slaughter opened the bottom of the eighth with a single. The next two batters went out. With Harry Walker at the plate,

Slaughter took off for second. Walker lined the pitch into left-center. Slaughter kept going at top speed, having made up his mind to go all the way. When Pesky took the relay from the outfield and turned around, he hesitated a split second—he hadn't expected Slaughter to try to score. Whether the slight hesitation enabled Enos to get in safely will never be known; but the peg was late and Slaughter slid across in a cloud of dust, completing one of the most famous circlings of the bases in World Series history.

Brecheen survived a Red Sox threat in the top of the ninth, pitching the Cardinals to a 4–3 win and the world championship. In so doing, Harry the Cat became the first three-game winner in Series competition since Stanley Coveleski in 1920.

The Series had been billed as a match-up between Williams and Musial, but neither of the stars excelled. Ted batted just .200 with five singles, swinging against an exaggerated shift put on by the Cardinals; while Stan batted .222, albeit with four doubles and a triple.

1947

Once more the World Series became a pageant for Everyman, a stage dominated by nominal spear carriers. Their names were Bevens, Lavagetto, and Gionfriddo, and they eclipsed such lights as DiMaggio, Rizzuto, Reiser, and Jackie Robinson, who that year had become big-league baseball's first black player.

The year was 1947, and the rivals were the New York Yankees under Bucky Harris and the Brooklyn Dodgers under Burt Shotton. The Yankees, in a transitional state, had veteran George McQuinn at first, George Stirnweiss at second, Johnny Lindell in the outfield, and the catching shared by Aaron Robinson and rookie Yogi Berra. These were in addition to Billy Johnson at third and brand-name performers DiMaggio, Rizzuto, and Henrich. Fast baller Allie Reynolds topped the pitching staff, followed by rookie right-hander Frank Shea, veteran Spud Chandler, and bullpen stopper Joe Page, a lefty who threw hard.

The Dodgers also had a mix of young and old. Second-year man Carl Furillo was in the outfield with Dixie Walker and Pete Reiser; rookie Robinson was playing first base that year, with Eddie Stanky, Pee Wee Reese, and Spider Jorgensen making up the rest of the infield. Bruce Edwards did the catching. Young Ralph Branca headed the staff with 21 wins, followed by Hugh Casey, Harry Taylor, and lefties Joe Hatten and Vic Lombardi.

The Yankees started with their usual postseason efficiency, taking the first two games at Yankee Stadium. Shea and Page won the opener 5–3, while Reynolds breezed through game two, 10–3.

Moving to Ebbets Field, the Dodgers took a 9–8

head-knocker. Then came game four, perhaps the most dramatic of all World Series games.

With his pitching staff having been raked over the day before, Harris started Bill Bevens, a big, erratic right-hander who had posted a mediocre 7–13 record for the season. The Dodgers gambled on sore-armed Harry Taylor, but he never got out of the first inning, loading the bases and walking in a run with nobody out. Replacing him was right-hander Hal Gregg, an unsung hero of this game. Gregg pitched out of the jam and went on to hurl four-hit ball for seven innings, yielding just one run.

Bevens, meanwhile, was pitching the strangest game in Series history. Going into the bottom of the ninth he held a 2–1 lead, the Dodger run having scored in the fifth inning on two walks, a sacrifice, and a ground out. Bevens had walked eight and allowed no hits. No pitcher had ever before taken a no-hitter into the ninth inning of a World Series game.

Bruce Edwards, the first batter, flied out. Furillo then drew Bevens's ninth base on balls. Jorgensen fouled out. Al Gionfriddo was sent in to run for Furillo, and Pete Reiser came up to hit for relief pitcher Hugh Casey. Gionfriddo then stole second. Rather than pitch to the dangerous Reiser, Harris ordered him walked; even though Pete had a broken bone in his ankle and couldn't run. "He can still swing," Harris said. Thus, a cardinal rule of baseball had been violated—the winning run had been put on. Eddie Miksis went down to first to run for Reiser.

Shotton then sent Harry (Cookie) Lavagetto up to bat for Ed Stanky. The veteran Lavagetto banged a high line drive off the right-field wall for Brooklyn's first and only hit, scoring Gionfriddo and Miksis and giving Brooklyn a stunning 3–2 win, sending Ebbets Field into paroxysms of joy.

Despite the crushing loss, the Yankees won the next day behind rookie Frank Shea, 2–1, DiMaggio's fifth-inning home run spelling the difference.

Brooklyn won a wild game six in Yankee Stadium, 8–6, to stay alive. It was in the bottom of the sixth inning of this game that Al Gionfriddo suddenly dropped upon stage center as if by parachute. With Brooklyn up 8–5 and two Yankees on base, DiMaggio launched what looked like a game-tying shot toward the left-field bleachers. Gionfriddo, however, ran far back and made a memorable one-handed grab of the ball in front of the 415-foot mark.

With the Series stretched to seven games for the third year in a row, the Yankees, behind a five-inning, one-hit relief stint by southpaw Joe Page, defeated the Dodgers 5–2. The quiet hero for the Yankees in the game was Rizzuto, with three singles that led to four runs.

For the Yankees, it was their eleventh world championship. For the Dodgers, it was now 0 for 4 in World Series play.

1948

Two veritable strangers to World Series play made it to the October pageant in 1948—the Cleveland Indians for the first time since 1920 and the Boston Braves for the first time since 1914.

The Indians, driven by the inspired play of their manager and shortstop, Lou Boudreau, had defeated the Red Sox in the American League's first pennant playoff. Swinging solid bats all year for the Indians were first baseman Eddie Robinson, ex-Yankee second baseman Joe Gordon, third baseman Ken Keltner, and outfielders Dale Mitchell and Larry Doby. Boudreau's top starters were Bob Lemon, the great veteran Bob Feller, and one-year sensation Gene Bearden, a left-handed knuckle baller with a 20–7 season he never came close to repeating.

Billy Southworth's Braves were surprise winners in the National League, beating out the more highly favored Dodgers and Cardinals, despite having only two reliable starters, Johnny Sain and Warren Spahn. Boston's offense was centered around third baseman Bob Elliott, shortstop Alvin Dark, and outfielder Tommy Holmes.

The Series' most memorable moment occurred in game one in Boston, in the bottom of the eighth inning of a scoreless duel between Feller and Sain. With Sibby Sisti on first and Phil Masi on second for the Braves with one out, the Indians pulled a pickoff play on Masi. As Boudreau ducked in behind Masi, Feller whirled and fired to second, and for a split second it looked as if Cleveland had its man. But umpire Bill Stewart, whom some people later claimed had been taken by surprise by the play and was unable to judge it clearly, called Masi safe. The Indians argued loudly and, of course, vainly. The importance of the play was made manifest a moment later when Holmes singled to left, scoring Masi with the game's only run. Feller lost a two-hitter.

Cleveland pitching remained tight, but this time in winning efforts. Lemon beat Spahn in game two, 4–1. In Cleveland for game three, Bearden continued his amazing season with a 2–0 shutout. In game four, Steve Gromek kept it going for the Indians with a 2–1 victory over Sain, Larry Doby's homer in the bottom of the third making the difference.

The Braves stayed above water by teeing off on Feller in game five for an 11–5 win, Bob Elliott hitting two home runs. But the following day the Indians, behind Lemon, with Bearden finishing it, edged the Braves 4–3. Cleveland had taken its first championship since 1920, despite a .199 team batting average for the Series.

1949

The Yankees and Dodgers met for the third time in World Series competition in 1949, both clubs having won their pennants on the last day of the season.

Burt Shotton brought in a Dodger team that was shaping up to dominate the National League for much of the next decade: Jackie Robinson, Gil Hodges, Pee Wee Reese, Roy Campanella, Carl Furillo, Billy Cox, Duke Snider, and pitchers Don Newcombe, Preacher Roe, and Carl Erskine.

The Yankees, under new manager Casey Stengel, had won in spite of a rebuilding of the team. Along with veterans Joe DiMaggio, Tommy Henrich, and Phil Rizzuto, Stengel had younger players like Yogi Berra, outfielder Hank Bauer, and infielders Bobby Brown and Jerry Coleman. It was on the mound, however, that the Yankees were strongest. They had four formidable starters in righties Allie Reynolds and Vic Raschi and lefties Eddie Lopat and Tommy Byrne, with Joe Page having another strong year operating out of the bullpen.

The Series opened in Yankee Stadium with a scorching pitching duel between Newcombe and Reynolds. With the score 0–0 in the bottom of the ninth, Henrich led off with a line-drive home run into the right-field stands, giving the Yanks a 1–0 win. The next day, Preacher Roe returned the favor, out-pitching Raschi, 1–0.

The Series moved across town to Brooklyn, where the Yankees mowed down the Brooks three straight. Game three was a 1–1 squeaker until the top of the ninth, when the Yanks scored three runs, two of them coming in on a big two-run pinch hit with the bases loaded by ex–National Leaguer Johnny Mize. Three runs were exactly what the Yankees needed, as the Dodgers scored two in the bottom of the ninth on solo homers by Campanella and Luis Olmo, but fell short, 4–3.

In game four it was the Yankees 6–4, thanks to a bases-loaded triple in the top of the fifth by Bobby Brown (the Series' top hitter, with a .500 average), the same Bobby Brown who went on to become a surgeon and later president of the American League.

Game five was all New York, the Yankees rattling base hits around Ebbets Field, enough of them to rack up a 10–6 win and another world title. The Dodgers' World Series record sank to 0–5.

1950

Fighting off challenges from the Tigers and Red Sox, Stengel's Yankees took a second straight pennant in 1950, buoyed by DiMaggio's last truly productive season and some steady hitting by first baseman Johnny Mize, second baseman Jerry Coleman, catcher Yogi Berra, and outfielders Hank Bauer and Gene Woodling, along with a superb year from MVP shortstop Phil Rizzuto. And once more the good hitting had been abetted by Stengel's deep and talented staff of starters—Raschi, Reynolds, Lopat, Byrne, and a mid-season arrival from the minor leagues, left-hander Whitey Ford, destined to become the greatest of all Yankee pitchers.

Facing this finely balanced club were Eddie Sawyer's Philadelphia Phillies, dubbed "the Whiz Kids" because of their many young players—third baseman Willie Jones, shortstop Granny Hamner, outfielders Del Ennis and Richie Ashburn, right-handed ace Robin Roberts, and left-hander Curt Simmons. Along with these younger players were catcher Andy Seminick, first baseman Eddie Waitkus, second baseman Mike Goliat, and outfielder Dick Sisler. In addition, the Phillies' pitching had been bolstered all year long by the remarkable relief work of right-hander Jim Konstanty.

In bringing Phillies fans their first pennant since 1915, Sawyer's club had had to battle into extra innings on the last day of the season, beating out the Dodgers on Sisler's three-run homer. Because of injuries and Simmons's departure for military service in September, Sawyer's pitching staff was seriously depleted, with Roberts pitching heroically down the stretch—three starts in the last five games—to put the Phillies over the top.

His starters were so exhausted by season's end that Sawyer had to open the Series by giving Konstanty his first start of the year. Big Jim pitched well but lost 1–0 to Raschi in Philadelphia, the sharp-hitting Bobby Brown scoring in the top of the fourth on a double and two fly balls.

Roberts gave the Phillies another strong effort in game two, but lost in ten innings to Reynolds, 2–1, on a home run by DiMaggio. "I'd popped him up four times in a row," Roberts said later. "I guess I got careless the fifth time. And you don't get careless with a guy like DiMaggio."

The Yankees took another close one in game three in New York. Tied 2–2 in the bottom of the ninth, the Yanks put together three two-out singles by Woodling, Rizzuto, and Coleman to win it.

Young Whitey Ford went for the sweep in game four, and with last-out help from Reynolds achieved it, 5–2. It was the most one-sided game of the tightly played Series.

"Our pitchers were worn out from the pennant race," Sawyer said, "but they held up fine. We just didn't hit. Of course, we were facing four guys named Raschi, Reynolds, Lopat, and Ford." It is doubtful whether any team, in any World Series, ever faced as potent an arsenal of arms in so short a span.

There had now been seven four-game sweeps in Series history, and six of them belonged to the Yankees, while the other had gone to the 1914 Braves.

The Yankees' Charlie Keller sliding safely into third on Bill Dickey's single in the bottom of the sixth inning of game one of the 1941 Series. The third baseman is Cookie Lavagetto, the umpire Larry Goetz.

Whitlow Wyatt, Brooklyn's ace pitcher, who hurled the Dodgers' only win in the 1941 World Series against the Yankees.

After Henrich reached first on Owen's dropped third strike, Di-Maggio singled, then Keller doubled, scoring both men. Here is Joe D. sliding in. No. 7 is Henrich. Mickey Owen is the catcher.

It's the seventh inning of game one of the 1941 Series, and the Dodgers' Pee Wee Reese has just been thrown out at third after tagging up at second and trying to advance on a pop foul down the line to third baseman Red Rolfe. Shortstop Phil Rizzuto rushed over and made the putout. Umpire Larry Goetz has just made it official.

Yankee Charlie Keller, who batted .389 in the 1941 Series.

Mickey Owen.

The Cardinals' Johnny Beazley, who beat the Yankees twice in the 1942 World Series.

Terry Moore, who scintillated in center field for the Cardinals in the 1942 Series.

Joe DiMaggio, a .333 hitter in the 1942 Series.

Stan Musial is safe at third in the midst of a six-run Cardinal rally in the top of the fourth inning of game four of the 1942 Series. The third baseman is Red Rolfe, the umpire George Barr. That baseball seems to be on the wrong side of Rolfe's glove.

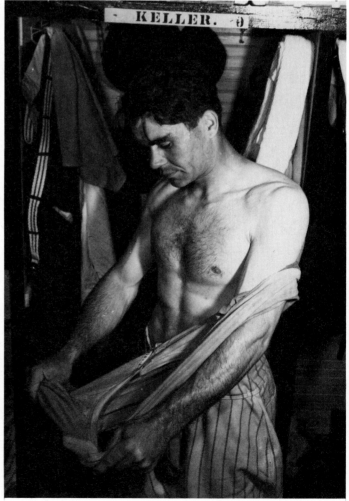

Charlie Keller, who homered twice for the Yankees in the 1942 Series.

Hank Borowy, a winner for the Yankees against the Cardinals in game three of the 1943 World Series.

George (Whitey) Kurowski. His ninth-inning home run in game five of the 1942 World Series gave the Cardinals the championship over the Yankees.

The Cardinals' great shortstop, Marty Marion. He led all hitters in the 1943 Series with a .357 batting average.

A key play in the sixth inning of the 1943 Series opener at Yankee Stadium. The Yankees' Frank Crosetti is legging out an infield single, as Cardinals first baseman Ray Sanders appears not to have possession of the ball. Umpire Beans Reardon's decision brought an argument from the Cardinals. The hit opened up a two-run inning for the Yankees, who went on to win 4–2.

The skipper and his heroes. The Yankees have just won the 1943 World Series, and Joe McCarthy (center) is rejoicing with the men who did it for him. Bill Dickey (left) hit a two-run homer, which was all right-hander Spud Chandler needed in firing a 2–0, Series-ending shutout.

The starting pitchers for the 1944 pennant-winning St. Louis Browns. Left to right, Nelson Potter, Jack Kramer, Denny Galehouse, Bob Muncrief, Sigmund Jakucki.

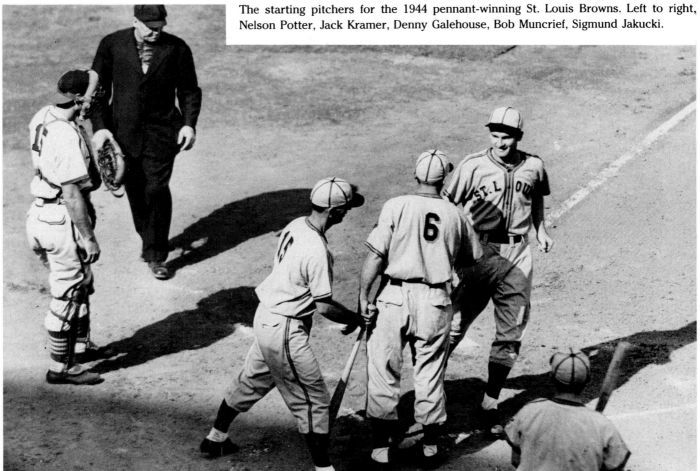

George McQuinn arriving at home plate after hitting the two-run home run that gave the Browns a 2–1 victory in the 1944 World Series opener against the Cardinals. Congratulating George are Gene Moore (No. 15), who scored ahead of him, and Mark Christman. Walker Cooper is the Cardinal catcher, Ziggy Sears the umpire. The blow came in the top of the fourth inning.

Mort Cooper, ace right-hander for the St. Louis Cardinals. He shut out the Browns in game five of the 1944 Series, fanning 12.

Sylvester (Blix) Donnelly, who pitched effectively in relief for the Cardinals in the 1944 Series.

Stan Musial. He played in four World Series with the Cardinals, with his best outing coming in 1944, when he batted .304.

Cardinals second baseman Emil Verban, who batted .412 for the Cardinals in the 1944 Series.

Hank Borowy, who appeared four times for the Cubs in the 1945 Series against Detroit, winning two and losing two.

A bit of action in the first inning of game one of the 1945 Series. The Cubs' Mickey Livingston has just been caught stealing. The Tigers' second baseman Eddie Mayo has just applied the tag. Making the emphatic call is umpire Art Passarella.

Cubs first baseman Phil Cavaretta, leading hitter in the 1945 Series with a .423 batting average. He had 11 hits, including the Cubs' only home run.

Detroit's veteran center fielder Doc Cramer, who got 11 hits and batted .379 in the 1945 Series.

Chicago's Claude Passeau, who turned in one of the finest efforts in World Series history when he one-hit the Tigers in game three in 1945.

Big Henry Greenberg played in four World Series for the Tigers and hit at least one home run in each of them. In 1945, his last Series, he hit two, plus three doubles, and drove in seven runs.

Ted Williams.

A panoramic view of the "Williams shift." The scene is Sportsman's Park in St. Louis, in the opening game of the 1946 Series. The St. Louis pitcher is making sure his fielders are in place as Williams waits at the plate. Note that center field is completely vacant.

Stan Musial.

It's game three of the 1946 Series, and Boston's Bobby Doerr has just fired to first to complete a double play on Whitey Kurowski. The man sliding is Enos Slaughter.

Harry Walker, the man whose single sent Enos on his way.

For Boston it was the arm of Dave Ferriss and the bat of Rudy York in game three of the 1946 Series. Dave (left) pitched a 4–0 shutout, while Rudy blasted a three-run homer in the bottom of the first.

Enos Slaughter completing his famous first-to-home dash in the bottom of the eighth inning of the seventh game of the 1946 Series. Roy Partee is the catcher, Al Barlick the umpire.

Enos Slaughter.

The Dodgers got out of a bases-loaded jam in the top of the first inning of game four of the 1947 Series. Here Dodgers second baseman Eddie Stanky is firing to first to double Billy Johnson after forcing Joe DiMaggio at second.

Harry Brecheen. Three victories for the Cardinals in the 1946 Series.

What is perhaps the greatest single moment in World Series history is about to happen. It is the bottom of the ninth inning of game four of the 1947 Series, at Ebbets Field in Brooklyn. Cookie Lavagetto has just swung, and on the mound Bill Bevens is watching it.

Bill Bevens. One out from glory.

Cigar in one hand and Cookie in the other, Hugh Casey, the winning pitcher in game four, congratulates Lavagetto. Overlooked was Casey's work in the 3–2 victory. Hugh came on in the top of the ninth with one out and the bases loaded and promptly fed a double-play ball to Tommy Henrich.

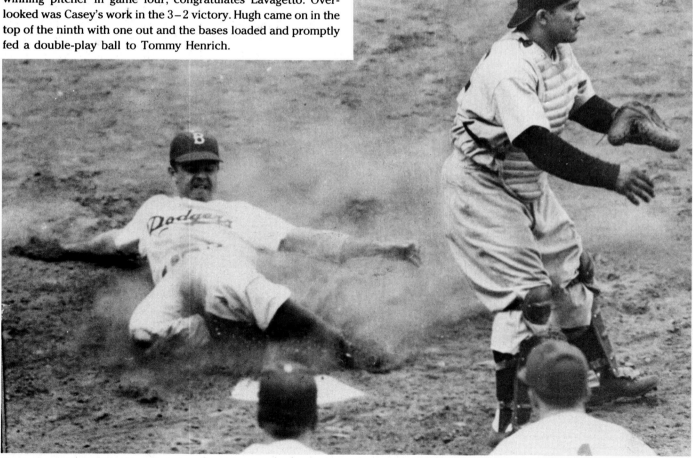

Pinch runner Eddie Miksis sliding across with the winning run on Lavagetto's hit. It has been called "the most famous run in Brooklyn Dodger history." Rookie catcher Yogi Berra waits, in vain.

Johnny Lindell of the New York Yankees, the top hitter in the 1947 struggle between the Yankees and Brooklyn Dodgers. He batted .500 with nine hits and also led with seven RBIs.

Yankee relief pitcher Joe Page, a hero of the 1947 Series, meeting the press.

The Gionfriddo catch in game six of the 1947 World Series.

Jackie Robinson was the first black to do a lot of things, including play in a World Series. The year was 1947.

It was the Boston Braves versus the Cleveland Indians in the 1948 World Series, and here's a bit of action from game two, first inning. Cleveland manager and shortstop Lou Boudreau is being thrown out at first by Braves third baseman Bob Elliott. Earl Torgeson is making the stretch for the putout.

Bob Feller, who suffered a tough 1–0 loss in the opener of the 1948 Series.

Johnny Sain (left) and Warren Spahn, aces of the Braves' 1948 pennant winners.

Left-hander Gene Bearden, one of the heroes of the 1948 world-champion Cleveland Indians.

Game six of the 1948 Series. Braves second baseman Eddie Stanky is making a midair throw to first to try to double up Jim Hegan after forcing Eddie Robinson at second, but Hegan beat the throw. Umpire Bill Stewart looks as if he's making a throw of his own. The action occurred in the top of the sixth inning.

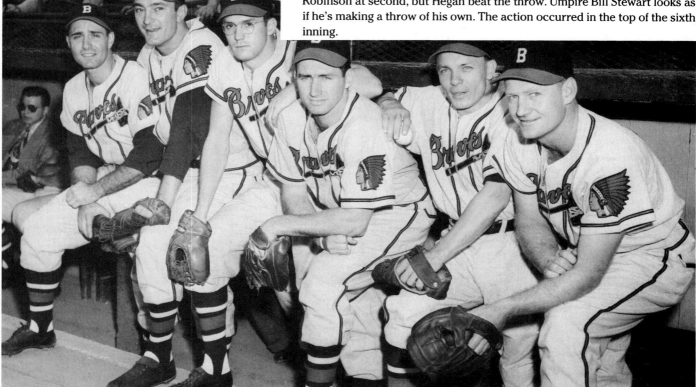

Six members of Boston's 1948 pennant winners. Left to right, Sibby Sisti, Frank McCormick, Earl Torgeson, Alvin Dark, Eddie Stanky, and Bob Elliott. Torgeson was the Series' top hitter, with a .389 batting average.

Two exuberant Dodgers working out at flag-draped Yankee Stadium before the start of the 1949 World Series. That's Roy Campanella (left) and Don Newcombe.

Allie Reynolds about to let rip in the opener of the 1949 Series against the Dodgers. The first baseman is Tommy Henrich.

Jackie Robinson getting his lead during the 1949 Series. The first baseman is Tommy Henrich.

Brooklyn's Pee Wee Reese at bat during the 1949 Series. Yogi Berra is the catcher.

The DiMaggio rip in full gear. It's the top of the ninth of game four, 1949. It looks great, but Joe struck out. The catcher is Roy Campanella, the umpire Lou Jorda.

The outfield of the 1950 pennant-winning New York Yankees. From left to right, Joe DiMaggio, Hank Bauer, Gene Woodling.

Yankees third baseman Bobby Brown, whose six hits, two triples, five runs batted in, and .500 batting average all were top numbers in the five-game 1949 World Series. Bobby later went on to become president of the American League.

The Yankees' Vic Raschi, who shut out the Phillies 1–0 in the opener of the 1950 World Series.

The great right-hander of the Philadelphia Phillies, Robin Roberts.

The Phillies' Jim Konstanty at work in game three of the 1950 Series. Joe DiMaggio is the runner at first, Eddie Waitkus the first baseman.

⌒ VI ⌒
The Yankees and the Dodgers
1951~1960

Al Lopez. If not for his Cleveland Indians in 1954 and Chicago White Sox in 1959, the Yankees would have taken every American League pennant from 1949 through 1964.

Casey Stengel (left) and Charlie Dressen.

1951

Casey Stengel's boys, in the midst of the hottest roll in baseball history now, made it three in a row in 1951. It was Joe DiMaggio's last year, but the Yankees were again on the way to replacing the irreplaceable, having brought up twenty-year-old rookie Mickey Mantle that year. Another rookie, versatile infielder Gil McDougald, also made the club that year, joining the established varsity, which still included Mize, Berra, Bauer, Woodling, Coleman, and Rizzuto. Raschi, Reynolds, and Lopat were each a year older and a year better, logging a 59–27 won–lost record among them. (Whitey Ford was in the service for two years.)

For October opponents, the Yankees drew baseball's newest "miracle" team, Leo Durocher's New York Giants. The Giants had come from 13½ games

out in mid-August to win it in a playoff with the Dodgers on Bobby Thomson's resonant last-ditch home run. Leo's miracle workers included second baseman Eddie Stanky, shortstop Alvin Dark, third baseman Henry Thompson, first baseman Whitey Lockman, catcher Wes Westrum, and outfielders Thomson, Monte Irvin, and the Giants' own twenty-year-old rookie spectacular, Willie Mays. Leo's pitching consisted mainly of a Big Three right-handed front line: Sal Maglie, Larry Jansen, and Jim Hearn, who had a composite record of 63–26.

With the Big Three exhausted by the labors of winning the playoff, the Giants opened the Series at Yankee Stadium with left-hander Dave Koslo. Shucking off the "day after" effects of their freshly minted miracle, Leo's boys got off to a 5–1 win, thanks to steady hurling by Koslo, four hits by Irvin, and a three-run homer by Dark.

Although the Yankees, behind Lopat, won game two 3–1, the win was not without its costs. Running down a fly ball hit to right-center by Mays in the fifth inning, Mantle stepped on a loose drainage cover and severely injured his knee, which drydocked him for the rest of the Series.

The Giants won game three behind Hearn, 6–2. The big play in this game came during a Giant five-run rally in the bottom of the fifth, when Stanky, apparently thrown out on a steal of second, kicked the ball out of Rizzuto's glove. A three-run home run by Lockman a few moments later sealed the issue.

After that, the Giants had no more miracles. They didn't even have a win left in them as the Yankees marched irresistibly to another world championship. Reynolds whipped them 6–2 in game four, and the next day Lopat cruised to a 13–1 laugher, which was highlighted by McDougald's grand slammer that broke open the game in the top of the third.

The wrap-up came in game six at Yankee Stadium, though in the top of the ninth the Giants showed the outlines of a miracle but were unable to fill it in. Trailing 4–1 (thanks to a three-run triple by Hank Bauer in the sixth), they scored two runs and had the tying run on second when right fielder Bauer made a sliding catch of pinch hitter Sal Yvars's line drive for the final out.

The Giants had the hitting stars of the Series—Irvin with 11 hits and a .458 batting average (plus a steal of home in game one) and Dark with 10 hits and a .417 average. But the Yankees, for the third year in a row, had everything else.

1952

Joe DiMaggio had retired, but the Yankees nevertheless won again, taking a fourth straight pennant after beating off a stubborn challenge from the pitching-strong Cleveland Indians. Along with young Mantle were those now familiar October faces belonging to Yogi Berra, Hank Bauer, Phil Rizzuto, Gil McDougald, Gene Woodling, Johnny Mize, and a spirited young second baseman named Billy Martin. Vic Raschi, Allie Reynolds, and Eddie Lopat were still winning regularly, with help this year from National League pickup Johnny Sain.

Recovering from the previous year's heartbreaking defeat, the Brooklyn Dodgers had regrouped and, under skipper Chuck Dressen, played steady, pennant-winning ball all summer. The biggest difference from 1951 was the addition to the pitching staff of a hard-throwing rookie right-hander named Joe Black. Working almost exclusively out of the bullpen, Black became the stopper the club had lacked in 1951. Dressen's cast of regulars were virtually an all-star team: Roy Campanella, Gil Hodges, Jackie Robinson, Pee Wee Reese, Billy Cox, Andy Pafko, Duke Snider, and Carl Furillo.

Dressen pulled a surprise in the opener at Ebbets Field by bypassing his regular starters Carl Erskine, Preacher Roe, and Billy Loes and going with Black. Joe came through nobly, stopping the Yanks 4–2, thanks to home runs by Reese, Robinson, and Snider. The Yankees evened it up the next day, winning behind a blistering three-hitter by Raschi, 7–1.

The Dodgers won game three in Yankee Stadium behind Roe, 5–3, the winning runs scoring on a Yogi Berra passed ball in the top of the ninth. The Yankees were right back in game four, Reynolds firing a four-hit 2–0 shutout, fanning ten.

Game five, played at Yankee Stadium, featured a memorable pitching performance by Brooklyn's Carl Erskine. Cruising along with a 4–0 lead in the bottom of the fifth, thanks in part to a two-run homer by Snider, the slender curve baller was suddenly raked for five runs, the last three on a Johnny Mize home run. Dressen, however, stayed with Erskine, and Carl rewarded his skipper's faith. The Dodgers tied the score in the top of the seventh on a Snider single and won it in the eleventh on a Snider double. In the bottom of the eleventh a leaping catch by Furillo in right robbed Mize of a game-tying home run. Erskine retired the last 19 Yankees in a row.

With their first-ever World Series title now just a game away, the Dodgers lost game six in Ebbets Field to Raschi and Reynolds, 3–2, the Brooklyn runs coming on Snider's third and fourth home runs of the Series, tying the record set by Ruth (1926) and Gehrig (1928).

Game seven came down to a single crucial play in the bottom of the seventh inning. With the help of home runs by Mantle and Woodling, the Yankees were winning 4–2. The Dodgers had the bases loaded with two out; the batter was Jackie Robinson. Jackie lifted a pop fly above the right side of the infield. It was an easy chance, but no Yankee made a move for it. With the runners churning around the bases, second baseman Billy Martin suddenly made a dash and grabbed the ball just before it hit the ground. Thereafter, lefty Bob Kuzava, in relief, held the Dodgers at bay, and the Yankees had their fourth consecutive world championship, sending the Dodgers down to an 0–6 record in World Series play.

1953

Stengel and the Yankees scaled hitherto unknown heights with a fifth straight pennant in 1953, breaking the mark of four set by McGraw's Giants in the 1920s and McCarthy's Yankees in the 1930s. Along with a highly proficient lineup headed by Mantle and Berra, the Yankees still had their veteran starters, Raschi, Reynolds, and Lopat. The ace of the staff, however, was Whitey Ford, back from two years of military service, with an 18–6 record.

Chuck Dressen's Dodgers had romped through the

National League, taking a second straight pennant with essentially the same club, the most notable addition being second baseman Jim Gilliam.

Any way you looked at it, something historic was going to happen in this World Series: the Yankees would take an incredible fifth straight, or the Dodgers would win their first.

The Yankees, hungry to make history, started the cannonading immediately, scoring four runs in the bottom of the first inning of the Yankee Stadium opener. The Yanks kayoed Dodger ace Carl Erskine and went on to a 9–5 win behind Reynolds and Sain. Stengel's troops came back the next day and won again behind Lopat, 4–2, on Mantle's two-run eighth-inning homer.

Facing a critical situation now, Dressen brought Erskine back for game three at Ebbets Field. This time the trim right-hander with the big overhand curve was superb. In defeating Raschi and the Yankees 3–2—on Roy Campanella's home run in the bottom of the eighth—Erskine broke Howard Ehmke's strikeout record by one, fanning 14 Yankees, getting Mantle four times. The following day the Dodgers drew even at two games apiece, winning 7–3 behind Loes, with Clem Labine closing it out in the ninth. Snider swung a hot bat in this game, driving in four runs with two doubles and a home run.

The Yankees won game five, 11–7, with Mantle, Martin, McDougald, and Woodling homering for the Yanks, Mantle's a booming grand slammer in the third inning.

Needing just one more win to make baseball history, the Yankees did it in dramatic style in game six at Yankee Stadium. Stengel's club was leading 3–1 in the top of the ninth when Carl Furillo slashed a clutch two-run homer down the right field line to tie the score. In the bottom of the ninth, however, with men on first and second and one out, Billy Martin rolled a single through the middle to score the winning run. For Martin, a hitting terror throughout the Series, it was his twelfth hit, setting a record for a six-game Series.

Despite being outhit by the Dodgers, .300 to .279, Stengel's club had set one of the glittering team records in all of sports history—five successive World Series championships.

1954

No doubt it seemed strange to a lot of people—a World Series without the Yankees. It wasn't that the Yankees didn't try in 1954; indeed, Stengel's club had its top winning season ever under the old man—103 victories. But this was the year that Al Lopez's Cleveland Indians set a league record with 111 wins.

The Indians had some good ballplayers in second baseman Bobby Avila, third baseman Al Rosen, first baseman Vic Wertz, catcher Jim Hegan, and outfielders Larry Doby and Al Smith. But what made Cleveland a pennant winner in 1954 was perhaps the finest pitching staff of modern times: Bob Lemon, Early Wynn, Mike Garcia, Bob Feller, Art Houtteman, the starters; Ray Narleski and Don Mossi (the only lefty in the group), the relievers.

Opposing the Indians was a snappy New York Giants team managed by Leo Durocher. While the Giants couldn't come close to matching the Indians' pitching, they did have a stronger club up and down the lineup, including a number of holdovers from the 1951 "miracle" club: Alvin Dark, Whitey Lockman, Monte Irvin, Wes Westrum, Henry Thompson, Don Mueller, and creation's greatest ballplayer, Willie Mays. On the mound, Leo had ace lefty Johnny Antonelli, Ruben Gomez, an aging Sal Maglie, and knuckle-balling relief pitcher Hoyt Wilhelm.

The 1954 World Series is remembered as the Series of both "the Catch" and Dusty Rhodes.

Rhodes was a rollicking, free-spirited, good-hit, no-field outfielder who had given Leo a .341 season as part-time outfielder and pinch hitter. In the Series he was unstoppable.

"The Catch" occurred in game one, at the Polo Grounds. It was the top of the eighth inning, the score was tied 2–2, Cleveland had men on first and second, none out, and Vic Wertz was the batter. Vic drove a tremendous drive that traveled some 460 feet out to dead center. Running endlessly, it seemed, Mays made an astonishing over-the-shoulder catch, tearing the heart out of the rally.

With the score still two-all in the bottom of the tenth, the Giants had men on first and second and one out when Durocher sent Rhodes up to bat for Irvin. Dusty popped Bob Lemon's first pitch into the air, down the right-field line, and into the lower deck some 260 feet away for a three-run homer. Wertz had hit a ball 460 feet into an historic out, Rhodes one 260 feet for a game-winning home run. So much for justice on a ball field.

In game two, Rhodes rapped a pinch single in the fifth inning that tied the score, remained in the game, and in his next at bat homered, contributing significantly to Antonelli's 3–1 win. In game three in Cleveland, Rhodes drove a two-run pinch single in the third inning, sending the Giants on to a 6–1 win.

The Giants made it a sweep with a 7–4 win in game four, despite Rhodes's sitting on the bench all the way. Durocher displayed his managerial style by relieving with his best pitcher, Antonelli, in the bottom of the eighth when the Indians threatened. Johnny fanned three of his five men and it was over.

"They say anything can happen in a short series," lamented Al Lopez. "Heck, I knew that. I just never thought it was going to be *that* short."

Outside of Rhodes, who had four hits in six times at bat, driving in seven runs, the Series' big hitter was Wertz, with eight hits and a .500 batting average.

Ironically, however, he was destined to be most re-membered as the man who hit the ball on which Mays made "the Catch."

The Giants' surprise sweep brought to an end American League domination of the World Series. The Americans had won seven straight times, and after 50 World Series held a decided 33–17 edge.

1955

"Never mind Mays's catch," Dodger fans said a year later. "What about Amoros's?"

Sandy Amoros was a little-known Cuban-born out-fielder who had batted .247 for the Dodgers in 1955. On a ball club that included Roy Campanella, Pee Wee Reese, Jackie Robinson, Carl Furillo, Gil Hodges, Duke Snider, Jim Gilliam, and 20-game winner Don Newcombe, he was little more than anonymous—until the seventh game of the 1955 World Series.

Walter Alston's great team had stormed to an easy pennant, winning by 13½ games over Milwaukee. In the American League, Stengel's Yankees were back after having missed their usual October festivity. Along with Mantle, Berra, Bauer, and McDougald, the Yankees now had Bill Skowron at first base, Elston Howard in the outfield, and Andy Carey at third. With Raschi, Reynolds, and Lopat gone, Casey's staff fea-tured Whitey Ford, fast baller Bob Turley, southpaw Tommy Byrne, and Don Larsen.

The Dodgers entered the Series with a frustrating 0–7 record in October joustings, and the way things started out, it didn't look as if much improvement was forthcoming. Helped by two home runs by Joe Collins and another by Howard, Ford won the opener in Yankee Stadium, 6–5. The next day Byrne won 4–2, knocking in the deciding runs himself with a bases-loaded single in New York's four-run bottom of the fourth.

When the Series moved to Ebbets Field, the Dod-gers began winning. Young left-hander Johnny Po-dres beat the Yankees in game three, 8–3. The Dod-gers won again the next day, 8–5, with Snider hitting a three-run homer and Hodges a two-run shot. The Brooks then went a game up with a 5–3 win, Snider hitting two more home runs, giving him four in a Series for the second time (he had hit one in the first game).

Back in Yankee Stadium, Stengel's crew held off the victory-hungry Dodgers with a 5–1 win behind Ford, all the Yankee runs coming in the first inning, the last three on an opposite field home run by the right-handed-hitting Skowron.

For game seven, Alston sent the twenty-two-year-old Podres against the veteran Byrne. The Dodgers scratched out a run in the fourth and another in the sixth, both driven in by Hodges. It was in the bottom of the sixth inning that Sandy Amoros became an all-time World Series hero.

Billy Martin opened for the Yankees with a walk, and Gil McDougald beat out a bunt. Yogi Berra, nor-mally a dead pull hitter, then lifted a long, high fly the other way—down the left-field line. Amoros, just inserted in the game after some lineup juggling by Alston in the top of the inning, made a long, long run for it and barely made the catch, the ball dropping into his straining glove near the barrier. ("He never worried a moment about crashing into it," an admir-ing Alston said later.) Amoros then relayed to a per-fectly positioned Reese, who whirled and fired to first, doubling up McDougald, who thought the ball was going to drop in. (Martin, on second, had a better angle on the play and got back to the base in time.)

Thus buoyed, Podres went on to complete a 2–0 shutout and give the Brooklyn Dodgers their first, and only, World Series triumph.

1956

For the fourth time in five years the World Series rivals were the Brooklyn Dodgers and the New York Yankees. Beginning to show some age now, Walter Alston's team had had to fight down to the last day of the season before beating out the Milwaukee Braves by one game. The Dodger lineup still presented the same core of veterans—Campanella, Hodges, Furil-lo, Snider, Robinson, Reese, Gilliam, with big Don Newcombe topping the staff with 27 wins, followed by Roger Craig, Carl Erskine, Clem Labine, and a man they had acquired in an early-season deal with Cleveland, Sal Maglie, the former Giant ace. One thing was missing for the Dodgers, however: Yankee-killer Johnny Podres was in the navy.

Securely on his winning track again, Stengel had received a mighty, Triple Crown season from Mantle, plus the usual array of base hits from Skowron, Ber-ra, Bauer, McDougald, and a newcomer at second base, Bobby Richardson. Along with Ford, Stengel's pitching included Tom Sturdivant, Bob Turley, Bob Grim, southpaw Bobby Shantz, and the erratic right-hander Don Larsen.

Maglie won the opener 6–3, thanks to a three-run homer by Hodges. Brooklyn took a wild second game in Ebbets Field, 13–8, despite a grand slammer by Berra.

Moving to Yankee Stadium for game three, Sten-gel's club won 5–3 behind Ford, thanks to a three-run homer in the bottom of the sixth by the old National Leaguer Enos Slaughter, now with the Yan-kees. Tom Sturdivant evened it out in game four, 6–2, getting home run help from Bauer and Mantle.

In game five, Stengel started Larsen, who had been kayoed in the second inning of game two. Maglie started for the Dodgers and pitched a fine five-hitter, but nobody remembers that, for this was the day that Don Larsen uncorked his perfect game. Pitching with no windup, the big right-hander saw 27 men and retired them all, throwing just 97 pitches. In the second inning Jackie Robinson lined a ball off of third baseman Andy Carey's glove, but McDougald recovered at short and threw to first just in time to nip Jackie. In the fifth inning Mantle made a fine running one-handed catch of a Gil Hodges liner. These two plays were as close as the Dodgers came to getting a base hit. And only once, to the game's second batter, Reese, did Larsen get to a three-ball count. The final batter Larsen faced was pinch hitter Dale Mitchell. Larsen fanned him on a called third strike, a pitch Mitchell claimed was "a yard outside." It was a 2–0 win, with Mantle's fourth-inning homer and a run-scoring single by Bauer in the sixth giving Larsen his margin.

The next day, Turley and Labine, normally Brooklyn's top relief pitcher, displayed more mound mastery. The Dodgers won it in the bottom of the tenth, 1–0, on a single by Robinson, with both pitchers going all the way. Turley had been especially brilliant, allowing just four hits and fanning 11.

After two games of high drama, the Yankees blew it all away in game seven at Ebbets Field. They shelled Newcombe early on a couple of Yogi Berra home runs and went on to a 9–0 win behind young right-hander Johnny Kucks, with a seventh-inning grand slammer by Skowron assuring the Yankees the championship.

The Yankees were noted for their firepower, but in the end it was their pitching that conquered the hard-hitting Dodgers. In the final three games, hurled by Larsen, Turley, and Kucks, the Dodgers were held to just seven hits and one run in twenty-seven innings.

1957

With age finally bringing to a close the Brooklyn Dodger reign in the National League, the club that had been knocking at the door the past few years at last pushed itself through and into first place. Fred Haney's Milwaukee Braves included two of modern baseball's classic stars—southpaw Warren Spahn and outfielder Henry Aaron. At thirty-six years of age, Spahn headed a strong staff that included right-handers Bob Buhl and Lew Burdette. Aaron's 44–home run bat was the centerpiece in an attack that featured third baseman Eddie Mathews, first baseman Joe Adcock, second baseman Red Schoendienst, shortstop Johnny Logan, catcher Del Crandall, and outfielders Andy Pafko and Wes Covington.

The American League had run what had now become its usual pennant race—the Yankees finishing first and the rest of the teams elsewhere. Stengel had taken eight pennants in nine years. In addition, the Yankee farm system had coughed up another gem to sparkle next to Mantle, Berra, Skowron, Howard, and the rest. The new man was twenty-year-old Tony Kubek, who delighted Stengel by playing infield and outfield with equal dexterity and batting .297.

The opening game, in New York, matched two of history's noblest left-handers, Ford and Spahn. Whitey and the Yankees came away with a 3–1 win. The following day Burdette evened things up with a 4–2 win for the Braves.

Yankee power erupted in game three in Milwaukee, the New Yorkers taking advantage of 11 walks served up by Haney's pitchers and banging away to a 12–3 win. Kubek, a Milwaukee native, belted two home runs and drove in four runs.

Game four was a spirited affair. With Spahn on the mound, the Braves took a 4–1 lead into the top of the ninth. Spahn retired the first two men, but then Berra and McDougald singled and Howard stunned the Braves with a game-tying three-run homer. The game went into the top of the tenth, and the Yankees scored a run on Bauer's triple. The Braves, however, were not finished. Pinch hitter Nippy Jones led off and was hit on the foot by a pitched ball. Plate umpire Augie Donatelli's view had been obstructed, and it wasn't until he was shown the ball, with a smudge of black polish from Jones's shoe, that he waved Nippy to first base. A sacrifice, followed by a double by Logan, tied the score. A moment later Mathews homered over the right-field fence, giving Milwaukee a 7–5 win.

Burdette gave the Braves a three-games-to-two edge by outpitching Ford 1–0 in game five. Back in New York, the Yankees tied the Series at three-all with a 3–2 win, thanks to Turley's strong pitching and home runs by Berra and Bauer.

When illness prevented Spahn from taking his turn in the seventh game, Milwaukee skipper Fred Haney brought back Burdette with two days' rest. Lew more than did the job. Armed with a four-run top of the third, he went on to pitch his second shutout of the Series, giving Milwaukee the championship with a 5–0 win.

Henry Aaron led all hitters with 11 hits, three of them home runs, seven runs batted in, and a .393 batting average. But the Series dazzler was Burdette, hurling three complete-game wins for the first time since Stanley Coveleski did it for Cleveland in 1920. Lew allowed just two runs in his 27 innings, for an 0.67 earned-run average.

1958

After winning their pennants with comparative ease, the Yankees and the Braves squared off again in the 1958 Series. In winning for the ninth time in ten years, Stengel had carved his name in the highest managerial echelons. This time Casey did it by juggling a pitching staff that was a bit thin on front-line talent. Only Turley and Ford won more than nine games. Stengel, however, had the services of an intimidating fireballing relief pitcher in Ryne Duren.

Like Stengel's, Fred Haney's club had changed little from the previous year, with Aaron and Mathews leading the hitters and Spahn and Burdette the pitchers. And for the second year in a row, the clubs played a gripping seven-game Series.

The Braves opened quickly, winning the first two games in Milwaukee, 4–3 in ten innings, behind Spahn, and then a 13–5 runaway in game two behind Burdette. The Braves iced the second one quickly with a seven-run first, topped by Burdette's three-run homer. Mantle homered twice in this game, while Bauer hit homers in both of the first two games.

Needing a win desperately now, Stengel sent Larsen to the mound in game three in New York, and the big right-hander came through, winning 4–0, with late-inning help from Duren. All four Yankee runs were driven in by Bauer with a single and his third home run in three games.

Warren Spahn was masterful in game four, stopping the Yankees on two hits, 3–0. Along the way, Spahn held Bauer hitless, ending Hank's 17-game World Series hitting streak, the longest ever in Series competition.

One defeat from elimination now, the Yankees sent Turley to the mound in game five, and the hard-throwing right-hander stopped the Braves cold, 7–0, the Yankees rushing across six runs in the bottom of the sixth. In this game the Yankees finally beat Burdette after four straight losses to him.

Back in Milwaukee for game six, the Yankees saw their ace Ford kayoed in the second inning, but tight relief work from Art Ditmar and Duren kept them in the game. At the end of nine it was tied 2–2, one of the Yankee runs coming on Bauer's record-tying fourth home run. In the top of the tenth McDougald led off with a homer, and the Yankees went on to score another run on Skowron's single. This second run proved to be the winner, as the Braves scored one and had the tying run on third when Turley came in to get the final out.

The seventh game saw Larsen start against Burdette. When Larsen looked shaky in the bottom of the third, Stengel brought Turley in for the third game in a row. Turley and Burdette dueled away at a 2–2 tie to the top of the eighth. Suddenly, with two out, the Yankees erupted. Berra doubled, Howard singled him in, Andy Carey singled, and then Bill Skowron rocked Milwaukee with a three-run homer, giving the Yankees a 6–2 lead they did not relinquish. The comeback victory gave Stengel seven world titles, tying him with Joe McCarthy.

1959

In 1957 the Dodgers and Giants deserted New York and brought big-league baseball to the West Coast. Two years later, in 1959, the Dodgers treated their new fans to a World Series, winning an unexpected pennant after a dismal seventh-place finish in 1958. In order to win it, Walter Alston's transplants had to defeat the Braves in a best-of-three playoff after finishing in a first-place tie. The Dodgers took it in two straight, thwarting Milwaukee's quest for a third successive pennant.

In their previous seven World Series appearances the Dodgers had drawn the Yankees as opponents, but in 1959 the scenario had changed. Al Lopez, whose Cleveland Indians had won the last non-Yankee pennant in 1954, had once more stopped the Stengel express, this time with a light-hitting, fast-running, good-pitching Chicago White Sox team that was nicknamed "the Go-Go Sox."

The Sox had Luis Aparicio at short, Nelson Fox at second, Sherman Lollar behind the plate, Al Smith and defensive whiz Jim Landis in the outfield, and Ted Kluszewski, a late-season acquisition from the National League, at first. Lopez's pitching was first-rate. His old Cleveland ace Early Wynn headed a staff that included lefty Billy Pierce and righties Bob Shaw, Dick Donovan, and bullpen stoppers Turk Lown and Gerry Staley.

Alston had Gil Hodges at first, Charlie Neal at second, Maury Wills at short, Jim Gilliam at third, Duke Snider, Wally Moon, and Don Demeter in the outfield, and John Roseboro behind the plate. The pitching was led by Don Drysdale, followed by Johnny Podres, Roger Craig, Sandy Koufax, and reliever Larry Sherry.

The light-hitting White Sox stunned the Dodgers in the opener in Chicago, winning 11–0 behind Wynn, with the big Kluszewski unloading two home runs. The Dodgers were trailing 2–1 in the top of the seventh in game two when they suddenly long-balled Bob Shaw. With two out and nobody on, pinch hitter Chuck Essegian tied it with a long home run. Gilliam walked, and Neal hit his second homer of the game, giving Los Angeles a 4–2 lead. Sherry came in and held the game for the Dodgers, who won it 4–3.

The Series then moved to Los Angeles, to the Dodgers' temporary home, the lopsided Los Angeles Coliseum, a stadium built for anything but baseball. Before 92,394 sun-baked fans, the Dodgers edged the Sox 3–1, Drysdale winning and Sherry again saving it, the winning runs being driven in on a two-run pitch-hit single by old Brooklyn hero Carl Furillo. The Dodgers went up three games to one the next day with a 5–4 win on Hodges's eighth-inning home run, with Sherry pitching the last two innings to pick up the win.

Playing in front of over 92,000 fans for the third game in a row, the White Sox stayed alive with a 1–0 victory, Shaw and Donovan over Koufax, Chicago's run scoring on a double play in the fourth.

The Series returned to Chicago, where the Dodgers wrapped it up easily, 9–3, tearing it open with a six-run fourth. Unnerved after hitting Landis in the head with a pitch in the bottom of the fourth, Podres was replaced by the tireless Sherry, who pitched 5⅔ innings of scoreless ball to win his second game to go along with his two saves. Almost as important to the Dodgers as Sherry's arm was that of catcher Roseboro, who stopped the Sox' running game cold, holding the go-go boys to just two stolen bases.

1960

The final statistics say the New York Yankees won the 1960 World Series against the Pittsburgh Pirates. The Yankees batted .338 over the seven games, the Pirates .256; the Yankees hit 10 home runs, the Pirates 4; the Yankees more than doubled the Pirates' output of runs, 55 to 27. Nevertheless, the telling statistic reads: Games, Pirates 4, Yankees 3.

It was Casey Stengel's tenth pennant in his twelfth, and last, year as Yankee manager. Hitting 193 home runs over the course of the season, the Yankees looked more fearsome than ever, particularly with the addition of Roger Maris in right field.

The Pirates under poker-faced Danny Murtaugh had won their first pennant since 1927. Murtaugh's club was led by right fielder Roberto Clemente and shortstop Dick Groat. Along with these two were second baseman Bill Mazeroski, third baseman Don Hoak, first basemen Dick Stuart and Rocky Nelson, catchers Smoky Burgess and Hal Smith, and outfielders Bill Virdon and Bob Skinner. Murtaugh's big winners were Vern Law and Bob Friend, backed up by relief star Elroy Face.

The Series opened in Pittsburgh, with Law and Face combining to stop the Yankees 6–4. In game two, however, Mickey Mantle and his friends devoured Pirate pitching with 19 hits (two of them homers by Mickey) and a 16–3 win. The Pirates popped 13 hits of their own, making a two-club total of 32, a record for a Series game.

The Yankees continued the bombardment in game three in New York. Bobby Richardson, who had hit only one home run all year, capped a six-run first inning with a grand slammer. Bobby later drove in two more runs with a single, giving him a Series-record six RBIs in one game. The Yankees won 10–0 behind Whitey Ford.

The Pirates came back, winning game four 3–2, again behind Law and Face, the key hit being a two-run single in the fifth by Virdon. Bill also saved the game with a remarkable leaping catch in center of Bob Cerv's drive with two men on in the seventh.

The Pirates also won game five, 5–2, Harvey Haddix winning and Face once more saving it. Pittsburgh now held a three-games-to-two advantage.

The Yankee bats cranked up again in game six in Pittsburgh, Ford coasting to a 12–0 shutout behind a 17-hit assault on six Pirate pitchers. The allegedly light-hitting Richardson slugged two triples and drove in three more runs in this game.

The seventh game of the 1960 World Series stands as one of the most exciting Series games ever played. Murtaugh started Vern Law, looking for his third win, while Stengel countered with Bob Turley. At the end of six innings the score was 5–4 New York, thanks to a three-run homer by Berra in the top of the sixth. The Yankees added two more in the top of the eighth to make it 7–4, and with lefty Bobby Shantz working on five innings of one-hit shutout ball, it looked like a Yankee wrap.

Gino Cimoli opened the bottom of the eighth for Pittsburgh with a pinch single. Then came baseball's most memorable bad bounce since the ball that vaulted over Fred Lindstrom's head in the seventh game of the 1924 Series. Bill Virdon hit what looked like a double-play ball to Kubek at short. The ball took an erratic hop and hit Tony in the throat, flooring him and putting men on first and second with none out.

Groat then singled to score Cimoli, leaving men on first and second. Shantz left, replaced by right-hander Jim Coates. A sacrifice moved both runners up. Rocky Nelson flied out, the runners holding. Clemente then beat out an infield chopper to Skowron at first base when Coates was slow in covering the bag, scoring Virdon to make it 7–6. Hal Smith, who had taken over behind the plate in the top of the inning, then lined a three-run shot over the left-field wall, making it 9–7 Pittsburgh. Right-hander Ralph Terry came in for New York and retired the side.

The Yankees, however, came right back in the top of the ninth to tie, thanks to a clutch single and some heads-up base running by Mantle. Richardson opened the inning with a single and moved to second on a single by pinch hitter Dale Long. After Maris fouled out, Mantle singled, scoring Richardson and sending Long to third, where Gil McDougald ran for him. Berra then laced a blazing grounder that Nelson speared behind first. Rocky stepped on the bag and turned to throw to second to get Mantle. But with the force removed, Mickey dove back to the bag, barely eluding Nelson's tag, and the tying run scored.

So the teams went into the bottom of the ninth tied at nine-all. The first batter was Bill Mazeroski. Terry threw a ball, and then a strike, which Mazeroski belted over the left-field wall, sending the Pirates, their fans, and the city of Pittsburgh into delirium. It was the first, and thus far only, World Series that ended with the dramatic resonance of a home run.

There were heroes galore in the 1960 Series. For the Yankees, Richardson had 11 hits and a record 12 runs batted in, Skowron 12 hits, and Mantle 10 hits, with 3 home runs and 11 runs batted in. For the Pirates, Law won two games, while Face saved three. But the 1960 World Series will always belong to the one swing of the bat of Bill Mazeroski.

Irvin has just stolen home in the top of the first inning of the 1951 Series opener between the Giants and the Yankees. Bobby Thomson, the batter, has fallen out of the way, while Yogi Berra is whirling around to get the bad news from umpire Bill Summers.

The New York Giants' Monte Irvin, the hitting star of the 1951 World Series. Monte had 11 hits and batted .458.

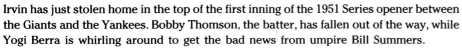

The Giants' Sal Maglie looks all alone out there in game four of the 1951 Series, but in reality Sal is surrounded by eight teammates and 49,010 paying customers.

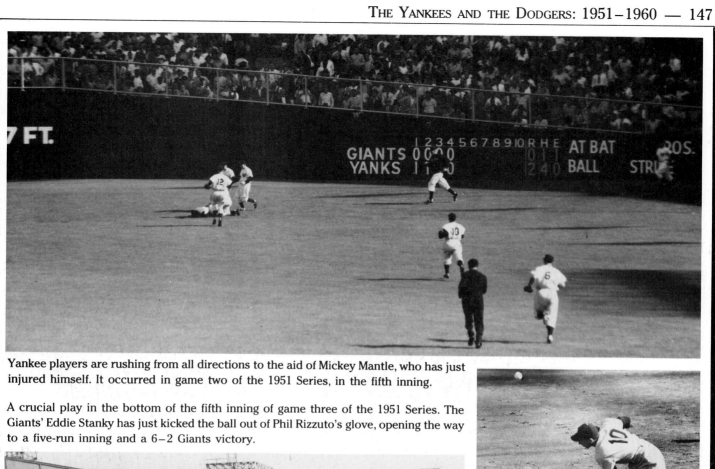

Yankee players are rushing from all directions to the aid of Mickey Mantle, who has just injured himself. It occurred in game two of the 1951 Series, in the fifth inning.

A crucial play in the bottom of the fifth inning of game three of the 1951 Series. The Giants' Eddie Stanky has just kicked the ball out of Phil Rizzuto's glove, opening the way to a five-run inning and a 6–2 Giants victory.

It's a grand-slam home run for the Yankees' Gil McDougald in the top of the third inning of game five of the 1951 Series. The blow broke a 1–1 tie and sent the Yankees on to a 13–1 win. The pitcher is Larry Jansen. The scene is the Polo Grounds.

Dodgers first baseman Gil Hodges, who had a wretched Series in 1952, going 0 for 21.

The Yankees' Vic Raschi, who beat the Dodgers twice in the 1952 Series.

Five Dodgers celebrating the team's victory over the Yankees in game one of the 1952 World Series. Front, left to right, Duke Snider, manager Charlie Dressen, Jackie Robinson. Rear, Joe Black (left) and Pee Wee Reese. Snider, Robinson, and Reese homered in the game, while Black was the winning pitcher.

Mickey Mantle had his first great Series in 1952, getting ten hits and batting .345.

Brooklyn's Carl Erskine delivering his first pitch in game five of the 1952 Series. The batter is Gil McDougald.

Yankee speedballer Allie Reynolds, who beat the Dodgers twice in the 1952 Series.

Yankees second baseman Billy Martin making his do-or-die catch of Jackie Robinson's pop fly with the bases loaded in the bottom of the seventh inning of game seven of the 1952 Series. Robinson, in the foreground, is running toward first base, while shortstop Phil Rizzuto (who autographed this picture) is in the background holding his breath.

Big John Mize of the New York Yankees: three home runs and a .400 batting average in the 1952 Series.

A bit of right-field larceny by the Dodgers' Andy Pafko in the bottom of the second inning of game five in 1952. The victim was Gene Woodling.

Billy Martin, hero of the 1953 World Series with 12 hits, eight runs batted in, a .500 batting average, and the single in the bottom of the ninth that won it all.

Yogi Berra, one of the stars for the Yankees in the 1953 Series, with a .429 batting average.

It looks as if it's going to be an awfully close play at third base in the top of the seventh inning of the opening game of the 1953 World Series, between the Yankees and Dodgers. With Dodgers on first and second and none out, Billy Cox laid down a bunt. Yankee catcher Yogi Berra scooped it up and fired to Gil Mc-Dougald at third as first baseman Joe Collins (No. 15) came running over. Umpire Bill Stewart called the Dodgers' Gil Hodges out. Dodger skipper Charlie Dressen is the third base coach.

It's the top of the fourth inning, game two of the 1953 Series. Dodger Carl Furillo has barely eluded Yogi Berra's diving tag to score on Billy Cox's double. No. 14 is Gil Hodges.

Yankee second baseman Billy Martin has forced a sliding Gil Hodges and is throwing to first to complete the double play on Carl Furillo. The umpire is Bill Grieve. The action occurred in the second inning of the third Series game in 1953.

Brooklyn's brilliant third baseman Billy Cox backhanding a scorcher off the bat of Yankee Hank Bauer in game five, 1953. The bases were loaded at the time, with two out. Looking back is base runner Phil Rizzuto.

The heroes of Brooklyn's game four victory in 1953. Left to right, relief pitcher Clem Labine, Jim Gilliam (three doubles), Duke Snider (two doubles, a homer, four RBIs), and winning pitcher Billy Loes.

Brooklyn's Carl Erskine. His 14 strikeouts in game three in 1953 set a World Series record.

Cleveland's great pitching staff in 1954. Left to right, Bob Lemon, Mike Garcia, Early Wynn, Bob Feller.

Three New York Giants outfielders showing off their World Series rings. Left to right, Willie Mays, Don Mueller, and Dusty Rhodes. Dusty came to bat six times in the 1954 Series against Cleveland, got four hits, two of them homers, and drove in seven runs.

The Mays catch in the 1954 Series.

After making his over-the-shoulder grab, Willie whirls and fires the ball back to the infield.

Vic Wertz, who batted .500 in the 1954 Series.

A bit of byplay from the 1955 World Series. The Dodgers had men on first and second when Pee Wee Reese grounded to Billy Martin; Billy fed it to Phil Rizzuto, who has come far across the bag and is now firing to first to complete the double play. Jim Gilliam, who looks as if he slid trying to upset Rizzuto, is the man on the ground. The umpire is Jim Honochick. It took place in the fourth inning of game one.

Brooklyn's Duke Snider, who hit four home runs in the World Series against the Yankees in 1955.

The Dodgers' Sandy Amoros is churning up the dust of Ebbets Field as he slides safely home, scoring on a double by Jim Gilliam. The action occurred in the third inning of game four, 1955. Yogi Berra is the catcher, Frank Dascoli the umpire.

The Amoros catch in game seven of the 1955 World Series. "He never shied away from the barrier," said Dodger skipper Walter Alston. "That was the key thing."

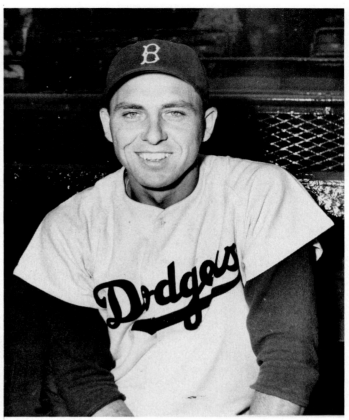

Yogi Berra, who once again put the slug on the Dodgers in the 1956 Series. Yogi batted .360 and had ten runs batted in.

Brooklyn's Gil Hodges, who drove in eight runs in the 1956 Series against the Yankees.

Mickey Mantle taking his rips against the Dodgers in the 1956 Series. Mickey hit three home runs in the seven games.

Johnny Podres, Brooklyn's pitching hero of the 1955 Series.

Don Larsen about to deliver the final pitch of his perfect game against the Dodgers in the 1956 Series. Second baseman Billy Martin is in the background. The story is vividly laid out on the scoreboard.

Don Larsen.

Brooklyn's Clem Labine, who defeated Bob Turley 1–0 in ten innings in game six of the 1956 Series.

Johnny Kucks, who pitched the shutout for the Yankees in the seventh game of the 1956 Series.

The Milwaukee Braves' Lew Burdette at work against the Yankees in the 1957 World Series. Lew was outstanding, pitching three complete-game victories, two of them shutouts.

Eddie Mathews being mobbed by his Milwaukee teammates after his tenth-inning home run broke up the fourth game of the 1957 Series and gave the Braves a 7–5 win.

Milwaukee's Bill Bruton, leading hitter of the 1958 Series with a .412 batting average.

Milwaukee's Henry Aaron, the top hitter of the 1957 Series, with three home runs, 11 hits, seven RBIs, and a .393 batting average.

The Yankees' Hank Bauer, the heavy gunner of the 1958 Series against the Braves with a record-tying four home runs. Hank had ten hits and drove in eight runs in the Yankees' comeback win.

Warren Spahn, the Milwaukee Braves' great left-hander, who beat the Yankees twice in the 1958 Series, including a two-hit shutout in game four.

The Yankees made a spirited comeback against the Braves in the 1958 Series, winning the last three games. Fireballer Bob Turley was involved in all three, winning two and saving one.

You're looking at the largest crowd ever to watch a World Series game—92,706, sitting in the sunshine and watching game five of the 1959 World Series between the Chicago White Sox and Los Angeles Dodgers, in Los Angeles.

Ted Kluszewski. The veteran National Leaguer joined the White Sox late in the 1959 season, helped them to the pennant, and had a great Series—three home runs, ten runs batted in, and a .391 batting average.

The White Sox' ebullient second baseman Nelson Fox, who batted .375 in the 1959 Series.

Action at second base in the first inning of game four of the 1959 Series. Chicago's Luis Aparicio is successfully stealing while the Dodgers' Maury Wills awaits the throw. The white blur in front of Maury's glove is the ball.

The Dodgers' bullpen dynamo of the 1959 World Series, Larry Sherry. He appeared four times, winning two and saving two.

Bill Mazeroski.

Yankee second baseman Bobby Richardson, who in the 1960 Series against the Pirates batted .367 and set an all-time record with 12 runs batted in.

Pirates reliever Roy Face on the mound at Yankee Stadium in the fourth game of the 1960 Series.

Pittsburgh's Vernon Law pitching to leadoff batter Bobby Richardson as the seventh game of the 1960 Series gets under way. The catcher is Smoky Burgess, the umpire Bill Jackowski. No. 9 is second baseman Bill Mazeroski, who would be heard from later in the game.

Vernon Law, Pittsburgh's 20-game winner, who beat the Yankees twice in the 1960 Series.

Whitey Ford, who twice shut out the Pirates in the 1960 Series.

Roger Maris (left) and Mickey Mantle, the New York power duo in the 1960 Series. Roger slammed two home runs, Mickey three. Mickey also drove in eleven runs and batted .400.

Yankees shortstop Tony Kubek has just been hit in the throat by Bill Virdon's bad-hop grounder in the bottom of the eighth inning of the seventh game of the 1960 Series. Bobby Richardson, who picked up the ball, is calling for time out.

Bill Mazeroski, about to be hemmed in on all sides by admirers after his stunning home run in the bottom of the ninth inning of game seven, the 1960 World Series.

Walter Alston.

Ralph Houk.

1961

The Yankees dismissed Casey Stengel after the 1960 Series, saying the seventy-year-old skipper was too old to manage. Replacing Stengel was Yankee coach Ralph Houk. It was in a way a thankless job, since the Yankees had the best team in baseball and were expected to repeat, with or without a manager.

And repeat they did, with the most thunderous home run barrage in baseball history. The Yankees belted a record-smashing 240 home runs in 1961. The top men were Roger Maris with a record 61, Mickey Mantle with 54, Bill Skowron with 28, Yogi Berra with 22, Elston Howard with 21, and part-time player Johnny Blanchard with 21. The club won 109 games, Whitey Ford winning 25. Behind Whitey were Ralph Terry, Bill Stafford, and left-handed reliever Luis Arroyo.

Winning in the National League for the first time in 21 years were Fred Hutchinson's Cincinnati Reds. With outfielders Frank Robinson, Vada Pinson, and Wally Post, first baseman Gordy Coleman, and third baseman Gene Freese, the Reds had some pop, but nothing to compare with the Yankees'. Cincinnati had a 20-game winner in righty Joey Jay and two talented starters in Bob Purkey and lefty Jim O'Toole.

This was a World Series that went according to form. The Yankees were supposed to dominate and they did, despite having Mantle limited to two games because of injuries.

A limited burst of power—homers by Howard and Skowron—and Ford's two-hit shutout gave the Yankees the opener in New York, 2–0. The Reds came back the next day with Jay to stop the Yanks, 6–2. That was Cincinnati's high-water mark.

The Series resumed in Cincinnati, and the Yankees

took a closely played game 3–2 on Maris's home run in the top of the ninth, after Blanchard had tied it with a pinch-hit homer in the eighth.

In game four, Ford and Jim Coates combined on a 7–0 blanking. It was in this game that Ford made World Series history by extending his string of consecutive scoreless innings to 32 before leaving the game with an ankle injury in the sixth. Ford's achievement broke Babe Ruth's long-standing record of 29⅔ goose-egg innings pitched in the 1916 and 1918 Series.

The Yankees won it all in game five, and emphatically, with five runs in the first and another five in the fourth, going on to a 13–5 pasting of eight Cincinnati pitchers. Starring was Hector Lopez with a triple, a home run, and five runs batted in.

The victory gave Ralph Houk the distinction of becoming just the third manager in history to win a world championship in his freshman season, following Bucky Harris in 1924 and Eddie Dyer in 1946.

1962

For the second time in eleven years the Giants stole a pennant from the Dodgers with a four-run ninth-inning rally in the final game of a playoff. After finishing in a first-place tie, the two transplanted West Coast teams were forced into a playoff. After dividing the first two games, the Dodgers saw a 4–2 lead melt away into a 6–4 Giants victory in the top of the ninth.

Alvin Dark's Giants had a murderous lineup, with outfielders Willie Mays, Felipe Alou, Harvey Kuenn, first baseman–outfielder Willie McCovey, first baseman Orlando Cepeda, and catcher Tom Haller. Rounding out the club were shortstop Jose Pagan, second baseman Chuck Hiller, and third baseman Jim Davenport. Juan Marichal, Jack Sanford, and southpaws Billy Pierce and Billy O'Dell were the starters.

Matched against this lumber squad were Ralph Houk's Yankees, winning their third straight pennant. They were by now a squad of familiar faces—Mantle, Maris, Skowron, Richardson, Howard, Lopez, Clete Boyer, Kubek—and newcomer Tom Tresh. Ford, Terry, and Stafford were Houk's three top starters.

With the Giants having hit 204 home runs during the season and the Yankees 199, it looked like a wide-open Series.

The second transcontinental World Series opened in San Francisco with a 6–2 Yankee win for Ford, in the course of which Whitey's scoreless streak was ended at 33⅔ innings by a Giant run in the bottom of the second.

Sanford squared it for the Giants the next day with a 2–0 shutout, helped by a tape-measure blast by McCovey far over the right-field fence.

The Series picked up in New York, with Stafford pitching the Yankees to a 3–2 win. The Giants evened it in game four with a 7–3 victory, thanks largely to a seventh-inning grand-slam home run by Chuck Hiller. The Yankees went one up again in game five, Terry beating Sanford 5–2 on a three-run bonker by Tresh in the bottom of the seventh.

The Series then moved back to San Francisco, where things were suspended by three days of rain. When the skies finally cleared, Pierce beat Ford with a three-hitter, 5–2, setting the table for a seventh game.

The finale pitted Terry against Sanford, and both men hurled brilliantly. The Yankees eked out a run in the top of the fifth on a double play, and it was that run that Terry nursed along into the bottom of the ninth.

Pinch hitter Matty Alou led off by beating out a bunt. Terry dug in and struck out Felipe Alou and Chuck Hiller. Mays then doubled to right field, and only a fine pickup and throw by Maris held Matty Alou at third. With the winning runs on second and third and the tough Willie McCovey at the plate, Terry must have had a late-afternoon nightmare about Bill Mazeroski and the 1960 Series. The nightmare became a near reality when McCovey scorched a line drive, but directly at Richardson. Bobby grabbed it, and with it another Yankee world title.

Despite all the thunder in the bats of the respective clubs, it had turned out to be a pitchers' Series, the winning Yankees batting a composite .199 to the Giants' .226.

1963

If the 1963 World Series proved anything, it was that great pitching can make for a mighty dull Series. Great pitching was what Walter Alston's Los Angeles Dodgers got from left-handers Sandy Koufax and Johnny Podres and right-hander Don Drysdale in the Series against the Yankees. With pitching of this caliber, plus an outstanding reliever in southpaw Ron Perranoski, the Dodgers needed just enough hitting, and just enough was what they got from outfielders Frank Howard, Tommy Davis, Willie Davis, first baseman Ron Fairly, third baseman Jim Gilliam, shortstop Maury Wills, and catcher John Roseboro.

Ralph Houk, making it 3 for 3 as a manager, guided his club to its fourth straight pennant. Although an injured Mickey Mantle and Roger Maris did not hit with the authority they had in the past, they were picked up by Richardson, Kubek, Howard, Tresh, and newcomer Joe Pepitone at first base (replacing Bill Skowron, now with the Dodgers). On the mound, Whitey Ford and Ralph Terry had been joined by two fast ballers, righty Jim Bouton and lefty Al Downing.

Dodger pitching set the Series pattern in the opener in Yankee Stadium, when the near-unhittable Koufax not only whipped the Yankees 5–2 but set a new Series strikeout record of 15 in so doing. Roseboro gave Koufax all he needed with a three-run homer off Ford in the second inning. The next day Podres, with ninth-inning help from Perranoski, stopped the Yankees 4–1.

Things became even quieter when the two teams journeyed to Los Angeles. In game three Drysdale pitched a masterful three-hitter—"One of the greatest pitched games I ever saw," said Walter Alston—and nipped Bouton 1–0. The Dodger run scored in the bottom of the first on a Gilliam walk, a wild pitch, and a single by Tommy Davis.

With Koufax pitching against Ford in game four, it was a match-up of premier left-handers. The Dodgers scored first in the bottom of the fifth on a monumental Frank Howard home run. The Yankees tied it on a Mantle homer in the top of the seventh. But in the bottom of the inning, Gilliam grounded to Clete Boyer at third and got all the way around to third base when Pepitone lost Boyer's peg in the white-shirted background. Gilliam scored a moment later on Willie Davis's sacrifice fly. Koufax went on to hold the Yankees for the final two innings, for a 2–1 victory and a Dodger world championship.

The powerful Dodger pitching had lived up to its reputation, limiting the Yankees to just four runs in four games and holding Houk's heavy artillery to a .171 batting average.

1964

For the second time in their pennant-studded history, the Yankees made it five straight, clinching on the next-to-last day of the season. Adding spice to this streak was the fact that it was accomplished under three different managers—Casey Stengel, Ralph Houk, and now Yogi Berra, who had assumed the job when Houk was moved up to the general manager's office.

The Yankee squad had remained fairly intact for several years, with the only significant addition in 1964 being right-handed pitcher Mel Stottlemyre to the pitching staff.

Winning a close race in the National League were the St. Louis Cardinals under Johnny Keane, the Cards finishing one game ahead of both Philadelphia and Cincinnati, who tied for second. Keane's club fielded some first-rate talent: Bill White at first, Dick Groat at short, Ken Boyer (brother of the Yankees' Clete) at third, Tim McCarver behind the plate, and Curt Flood, Mike Shannon, and the mercurial Lou Brock in the outfield. Keane's front three starters were lefties Ray Sadecki and the veteran Curt Simmons, and fast baller Bob Gibson, on the brink of superstardom now.

The Yankees not only lost the opener in St. Louis 9–5, they also lost the services of their starter and ace for the rest of the Series when Whitey Ford had to leave the game with a sore arm. The next day, young Stottlemyre drew them even with an 8–3 win over Gibson.

The teams reassembled in Yankee Stadium, where the Yanks won game three in dramatic fashion. Bouton and Simmons had dueled tenaciously for eight innings and a 1–1 tie. Simmons left in the top of the ninth for a pinch hitter. With the game still tied in the bottom of the ninth, Keane sent knuckle-balling relief pitcher Barney Schultz to the mound. Schultz, who had saved the opener for Sadecki with three good innings of relief, threw just one pitch, and Mantle ripped it into the right-field stands for a game-winning homer. Besides being a game-winner, Mickey's shot was also historic—it was his sixteenth in Series play, breaking the record he had held jointly with Babe Ruth.

The home run was the big weapon again the next day. With the Yankees leading 3–0 in the top of the sixth, Ken Boyer hit one with the bases loaded, giving St. Louis all its runs in a 4–3 win that tied the Series. The following day, the Cardinals again turned the Yankees' favorite weapon against them. After Tom Tresh had dramatically tied the game with a two-out, two-run, bottom-of-the-ninth homer off of Gibson (who fanned 13 in this game), McCarver cracked a three-run shot in the top of the tenth to give Gibson and the Cards a 5–2 win and a three-games-to-two lead.

Back in St. Louis for game six, it was home run power again. Mantle and Maris hit solo shots, but the big blast came when Pepitone belted a grand slammer in the top of the eighth to ice an 8–3 Yankee win for Bouton, pushing the Series into a seventh game.

It was Gibson against Stottlemyre in the finale, each on two days' rest. At the end of five innings Stottlemyre was gone and the Cardinals held a 6–0 lead. Mantle cut it in half with a three-run homer in the top of the sixth, but Gibson, laboring at the end, hung on for a 7–5 win, giving the Cardinals their first championship since 1946.

Along with Mantle's home runs, two other World Series records of note had been set—Bob Gibson with 31 strikeouts in 27 innings, and the Yankees' Bobby Richardson with a new mark of 13 hits.

The day after the Series, the Yankees fired manager Yogi Berra. Soon after that, in a move almost equally as stunning, they hired as manager the man who had recently defeated them—the Cardinals' Johnny Keane, who had resigned as skipper of the world champions.

1965

It had been the most remarkable run of success in sports history. Between 1921 and 1964 the New York Yankees had won 29 pennants. But now the dynasty was over. Age, injury, and a suddenly less-than-productive farm system had all conspired to bring it to an end.

Winning in the American League in 1965 were Sam Mele's Minnesota Twins, a team that included the loud bats of third baseman Harmon Killebrew, first baseman Don Mincher, catcher Earl Battey, shortstop Zoilo Versalles, and outfielders Jimmie Hall, Bob Allison, and Tony Oliva. Mele had two big winners on his staff, right-hander Jim (Mudcat) Grant and lefty Jim Kaat.

The Twins' opposition in the 1965 Series were Walter Alston's Los Angeles Dodgers. Where Mele's team muscled home their runs, Alston's ground them out with bunts, sacrifices, and steals. What little hitting the Dodgers got came from second baseman Jim Lefebvre, shortstop Maury Wills (his 94 stolen bases were the Dodgers' biggest offensive weapon), third baseman Jim Gilliam, and outfielders Ron Fairly and Lou Johnson. Once more, the Dodgers' strength lay on the mound, particularly in Sandy Koufax (26–8) and Don Drysdale (23–12), backed up by southpaw Claude Osteen and a strong bullpen.

The Series opened in Minnesota, with the Twins doing the near impossible—they beat Drysdale and Koufax back-to-back, Grant winning 8–2 and Kaat 5–1.

In Los Angeles for game three, a game the Dodgers dearly needed, Osteen notched a 4–0 shutout in what turned out to be the Series' pivotal game.

In games four and five the Twins felt the full fury of Drysdale and Koufax, Don stopping them 7–2 and striking out 11, Sandy shutting them down 7–0 and fanning 10. In the latter game, the Dodgers' Willie Davis became the first man to steal three bases in a Series game since Honus Wagner did it in 1909.

When Jim Grant beat the Dodgers for the second time in game six, 5–1, it sent the Series into seven games. Grant not only pitched a strong game, he sealed it with a three-run homer in the bottom of the sixth.

Mele started Kaat in game seven, while Alston was torn between Drysdale with three days' rest and Koufax with two. The Dodger skipper decided to go with "the greatest pitcher I ever saw." Koufax did not disappoint. With his curve ball not working to his satisfaction, the great left-hander fired mostly fast balls, and they were good enough for a three-hit, 2–0 victory with ten strikeouts. The Dodgers scored their runs in the top of the fourth on a home run by Lou Johnson, a double by Fairly, and a single by Wes Parker. It was enough to give Alston his fourth world title, more than any other National League manager.

As they had all season, the Dodger hitters drove in just enough runs to win; and as they had all season, the Dodger pitchers frustrated the opposing hitters, limiting the hard-hitting Twins to just 20 runs in the seven games and holding them to a .195 batting average.

1966

Walter Alston's Dodgers got into the Series again in 1966, but a reading of the box scores suggests that they forgot to bring their bats with them. After scoring single runs in the second and third innings of the opener in Los Angeles, they were shut out for the remaining thirty-three innings of the Series, bowing to a Baltimore sweep.

Managed by ex-Yankee Hank Bauer, the Orioles were a superb team that included outfielders Frank Robinson, Paul Blair, Curt Blefary, first baseman Boog Powell, second baseman Davey Johnson, shortstop Luis Aparicio, third baseman Brooks Robinson, and catcher Andy Etchebarren. On the mound, Bauer had lefty Dave McNally, Jim Palmer, Wally Bunker, and a deep bullpen that included right-handers Moe Drabowsky, Stu Miller, Dick Hall, Eddie Fisher, and Eddie Watt.

Alston's feather-duster lineup had Wes Parker, Maury Wills, Jim Lefebvre, Tommy Davis, Willie Davis, Ron Fairly, Lou Johnson, and Johnny Roseboro. Pitching was again the Dodgers' strength, with Koufax and Drysdale topping a staff that included Claude Osteen, rookie right-hander Don Sutton, and relief pitchers Ron Perranoski and Phil Regan.

With Koufax worn out from having pitched the pennant clincher on the last day of the season, Drysdale opened the Series for the Dodgers against McNally. Big Don got off poorly, throwing home run balls to Frank Robinson and Brooks Robinson in the top of the first inning. The three runs the Orioles scored in this inning were more than the Dodgers were to score in the entire Series. When McNally was removed after walking three Dodgers in the third, Drabowsky came in and began the goose egg roll, pitching 6⅔ innings of scoreless one-hit ball, fanning 11. The Orioles won 6–2.

In game two, Koufax was unglued by three errors in the top of the fifth by his center fielder, Willie Davis (two dropped flies and a wild throw), which sent across three unearned runs and set up a 6–0 blanking by young Jim Palmer.

In game three in Baltimore, Bunker outlasted Osteen and Regan for a 1–0 win, the run being Paul Blair's fifth-inning home run. The fourth and final game was a repeat performance—Baltimore 1–0 on a home run, this time by Frank Robinson in the bottom of the fourth. It was all Dave McNally needed as he outpitched an effective but frustrated Drysdale.

Although the Orioles were held to a .200 batting average in the Series, they looked almost thunderous compared to the anemic Dodger hitters, who set World Series records for futility with two runs, 17 hits, 23 total bases, and a microscopic .142 batting average.

1967

It was the year of Boston's "Impossible Dream," the year when the Red Sox rose from a ninth-place finish in 1966 to win the American League pennant on the last day of the season. It was the year of Carl Yastrzemski, who in 1967, his manager Dick Williams said, "was the greatest ballplayer I ever saw." The Triple Crown–winning Yastrzemski hit, ran, threw, and fielded like a man possessed, all season long. He was backed up by first baseman George Scott, shortstop Rico Petrocelli, and outfielder Reggie Smith. The ace of Williams's staff was Jim Lonborg, followed by Jose Santiago, Gary Bell, Lee Stange, and reliever John Wyatt, all right-handers.

Winners in the National League were Red Schoendienst's St. Louis Cardinals, with strong front-line pitching from Bob Gibson, Nelson Briles, Dick Hughes, and young left-hander Steve Carlton. The run producers in the St. Louis lineup were first baseman Orlando Cepeda, catcher Tim McCarver, outfielders Lou Brock, Roger Maris, and Curt Flood, and second baseman Julian Javier.

With Lonborg having had to pitch on the last day of the season, Williams had to open the Series in Boston with Santiago, with Gibson going for the Cardinals. Jose pitched well, but Gibson simply was better, nipping the Red Sox 2–1 and fanning ten, the lone Red Sox run coming on Santiago's homer. The Cardinals' winning run scored in the top of the seventh on Brock's fourth single of the game, his second stolen base, and two ground outs.

Lonborg was ready for game two at Fenway, firing a brilliant one-hit 5–0 shutout. The lone Cardinal hit came with two out in the top of the eighth when Javier doubled. The Red Sox offense was all Yastrzemski, Carl cracking two homers and a single and driving in four runs.

Nelson Briles gave the Cardinals a solid outing in game three in St. Louis, stopping the Red Sox 5–2. Gibson was back in game four, putting his club up three games to one with a 6–0 blanking. But Boston's big man, Lonborg, kept the Sox breathing with a three-hit, 3–1 win. Big Jim had allowed just four hits in his two games.

Back in Boston, Williams, faced with a thinned-out pitching staff, took a deep breath and started Gary Waslewski, a seldom-used right-hander who had won just two games all season. The gamble worked, Waslewski keeping his club in the game until the bullpen took over in the sixth inning. Helped by two Rico Petrocelli home runs and one each by Smith and Yastrzemski, the Red Sox banged out an 8–4 win, snarling the Series.

Each club rolled out their big man for game seven, Gibson for the Cardinals, Lonborg (on two days' rest) for the Red Sox. Lonborg began tiring early, and the Cardinals kept strafing him, Gibson weighing in with

a home run of his own. The crushing blow came in the top of the sixth when Javier hit a three-run homer for St. Louis. The keyed-up Gibson pitched a strong 7–2 win—his third of the Series—with a three-hitter and ten strikeouts.

The other Series standout along with Gibson was Lou Brock. The winged-footed Cardinal outfielder batted .414, led with 12 hits, and set a World Series record with seven stolen bases, which were, oddly enough, the only bases stolen by the Cardinals in the entire Series.

1968

The Cardinals coasted to a second straight pennant in 1968, and when the Detroit Tigers did the same in the American League, it set up a confrontation between the game's two dominant pitchers—St. Louis's Bob Gibson and his 22–9 record and stunning 1.12 earned-run average and Detroit's Denny McLain and his 31–6 record and 1.96 ERA.

Red Schoendienst's Cardinals fielded the same club as the previous year (the Cardinal lineups for the seventh game of the 1967 Series and the first game of the 1968 Series were identical, down to and including Gibson).

Mayo Smith's Tigers had a veteran lineup that carried some punch, particularly from catcher Bill Freehan, first baseman Norm Cash, and outfielders Willie Horton, Jim Northrup, and Al Kaline. With Kaline injured for part of the season, Smith's outfield alignment had been Horton, Northrup, and Mickey Stanley, a light-hitting but fine-fielding center fielder. But the Tiger manager wanted to get the sixteen-year veteran Kaline into the Series, so he moved Stanley to shortstop and Northrup to center and inserted Kaline in right. The gamble paid off, Stanley playing a steady shortstop and Kaline becoming one of the Series' hitting stars, with a .379 batting average.

The match-up between the scowling Gibson and the flamboyant McLain in St. Louis in game one was all Gibson, and then some. The Cardinal ace not only blanked the Tigers 4–0, but broke Sandy Koufax's one-game Series strikeout record with 17. In game two, the Tigers' second-best pitcher, the portly southpaw Mickey Lolich, put the Tigers on the boards with a strong 6–1 effort. The light-hitting Lolich stunned himself and everyone else by slamming a home run—his first ever in the big leagues—in the third inning.

When the teams moved to Detroit, the Cardinals won game three, 7–3, using three-run homers by Tim McCarver and Orlando Cepeda to do it. It was Gibson and McLain again in game four, and the Cardinals took a commanding three-games-to-one lead as the fireballing Gibson burned out the Tigers again, 10–1, fanning ten and hitting a home run of his own. Lou Brock slugged a double, triple, and home run—

getting three hits for the second game in a row—and drove in four runs.

The Cardinals started off game five as if they meant to make this a five-game Series, Cepeda hitting a three-run homer off Lolich in the top of the first, but Mickey steadied, tightened up, and held on. He blanked the Cardinals the rest of the way while his mates caught up and passed the Cardinals, 5–3. Once more Brock had three hits, but this time in a losing cause.

With McLain coming back in game six after two defeats, the Tigers settled it early and emphatically, scoring ten runs in the top of the third, four of them rolling across on Jim Northrup's grand-slam homer. McLain coasted to a 13–1 victory, tying the Series.

Game seven matched Gibson and Lolich, each seeking his third win. In winning his last two starts in the 1964 Series, all three in the 1967 Series, and his first two in this one, Gibson had now won seven straight World Series games, a new record. Today he was trying to extend that record.

Gibson and Lolich dueled grimly through six scoreless innings. Then, with two out and nobody on in the top of the seventh, Cash and Horton singled. Northrup smashed a long drive to center. Curt Flood lost the ball in the crowd background for a moment, took a few steps in, slipped, and then turned and vainly pursued what became a game-smashing triple. Freehan scored him a moment later with a double. The Tigers went on to a 4–1 win and the championship, with Lolich becoming the second pitcher in two years to hurl three complete-game World Series victories, defeating the man who had done it a year before—Bob Gibson.

For the Cardinals, both Gibson and Brock glittered in defeat. Gibson set a new Series record with 35 strikeouts, while Brock tied Bobby Richardson's mark with 13 hits, tied his own record with 7 steals, and batted a robust .464. For the Tigers, sentimental favorite Al Kaline collected 11 hits, drove in 8 runs, and batted .379. The 1968 World Series, however, will always be remembered as the Mickey Lolich Series.

1969

In 1914, the "Miracle" Braves won the pennant, coming from last place in July. In 1951, the "Miracle" Giants won the pennant, coming from 13½ games out in August. And in 1969, the "Miracle" Mets won the pennant, coming from, well, nowhere.

They were a team of youthful self-believers, managed by former Brooklyn hero Gil Hodges and galvanized by twenty-four-year-old Tom Seaver, team leader and 25-game winner. Behind Seaver were southpaw Jerry Koosman, Gary Gentry, Nolan Ryan, and relief pitchers Tug McGraw and Ron Taylor. The tight-knit Mets unit included catcher Jerry Grote, shortstop Bud Harrelson, first basemen Donn Clen-denon and Ed Kranepool, third baseman Wayne Garrett, second baseman Ken Boswell, and outfielders Tommie Agee, Cleon Jones, and Ron Swoboda.

The team had finished ninth the year before—the highest they had ever gone in their brief history, which began in 1962. Opening the 1969 season, they were 100-to-1 shots to win the pennant, and even that, Seaver said, "was being charitable."

Ironically, or maybe fittingly, this most unlikely of pennant winners met in the Series one of the most powerful clubs of modern times—Earl Weaver's 1969 Baltimore Orioles. This club had an infield of Boog Powell, Davey Johnson, Mark Belanger, and Brooks Robinson; an outfield of Frank Robinson, Paul Blair, and Don Buford; Andy Etchebarren and Elrod Hendricks behind the plate; and starting pitching to match the Mets': Jim Palmer, Dave McNally, Mike Cuellar, and Tom Phoebus, with Eddie Watt, Dick Hall, and lefty Pete Richert in the bullpen.

Top-heavy favorites to win it all, the Orioles defeated Seaver 4–1 in the opener in Baltimore, Cuellar handling the Mets easily. Koosman evened it up for the Mets the next day, pitching an almost airtight two-hit, 2–1 victory, with last-out relief from Ron Taylor. The Mets scored the winning run on a two-out single in the top of the ninth by Al Weis, a .215-hitting utility infielder.

In New York for game three, the Mets blanked the Orioles 5–0 behind the combined pitching of Gary Gentry and Nolan Ryan. Tommie Agee not only clubbed a home run for the Mets, but also made two spectacular grabs in the outfield: one on Hendricks with two men on in the top of the fourth and another on Blair with the bases loaded in the top of the seventh. The two catches rate high in anyone's treasury of World Series moments.

Game four was another match-up of Seaver and Cuellar. Seaver nursed Clendenon's second-inning solo homer into the ninth inning. Then, with one out, singles by Frank Robinson and Powell put Orioles on first and third. Brooks Robinson sent a screamer into right field. Only one man in the ball park thought it could be caught—right fielder Ron Swoboda. Swoboda made a diving, tumbling catch, holding the Orioles' rally to a single run.

In the bottom of the tenth inning, Grote doubled to lead off and Rod Gaspar ran for him. Weis was intentionally walked. J. C. Martin, hitting for Seaver, dropped a bunt, which reliever Pete Richert came in and fielded. Richert's peg struck Martin on the wrist and rolled away, allowing Gaspar to come around and score the winning run. The Orioles argued that Martin had run out of the base line and hence should have been declared out and the ball dead; news photos the next day indicated that Martin might indeed have run out of the base line. But the decision stood, and the Mets had a 2–1 win and a three-games-to-one advantage.

It seemed inevitable now. The Mets could do no wrong. Their bagful of clutch hits, breaks, great plays, and small miracles seemed inexhaustible. And it all held up for one more game. Koosman, off to a shaky start in game five when he gave up three runs in the top of the third—two of them on a Dave McNally home run—hung on and pitched steadily, waiting for his teammates to catch up. They did. Clendenon hit his third home run of the Series with a man on in the sixth to make it 3–2. In the seventh, Al Weis, with only two home runs all year, tied the game with a solo shot. Then in the bottom of the eighth, doubles by Grote and Swoboda and an infield error gave the Mets two runs. Koosman remained tough, and the Mets won it 5–3.

The Orioles had won 109 games during the regular American League season, but the Mets' pitching staff rendered them virtually harmless, holding them to a .146 team average for the Series, lowest ever for a team in a five-game Series.

For some people, 1969 is remembered for the breathtaking sight of men walking for the first time on the moon. For others, however, the most incredible event of the year took place right here on earth, in Shea Stadium, New York.

1970

Two young managers destined to become among the most dominant of their era brought their teams head-to-head in the 1970 World Series. It was Earl Weaver's Baltimore Orioles, with their second straight pennant, meeting Sparky Anderson's Cincinnati Reds.

These were exceptionally strong clubs. The Orioles were again led by Frank Robinson, Brooks Robinson, and Boog Powell, and the pitching of Palmer, Cuellar, and McNally, each a 20-game winner in 1970.

Cincinnati's strong attack was led by catcher Johnny Bench, first baseman Lee May, third baseman Tony Perez, shortstop Dave Concepcion, and outfielders Pete Rose, Bobby Tolan, and Bernie Carbo. Cincinnati's top pitchers were Gary Nolan and Don Gullett, a hard-throwing nineteen-year-old lefty who had joined the club late in the season. The Reds' 20-game-winning southpaw Jim Merritt was hampered by a sore elbow and pitched only one inning in the Series.

Determined to erase the impression left by their upset loss to the Mets the year before, the Orioles came from a 3–0 deficit to take the opener in Cincinnati, 4–3. The critical inning was the last of the sixth, the game tied at three apiece. In this inning, Brooks Robinson began a pattern of stunning defensive heroics when he robbed Lee May of a double with a darting stab of a ball that seemed headed down the left-field line. Then Carbo walked and went to third on a single by Tommy Helms. Pinch hitter Ty Cline topped a ball in front of the plate, and suddenly three men were in a pileup. Plate umpire Ken Burkhart had come out to call the ball fair; base runner Carbo plowed into him; Oriole catcher Elrod Hendricks, who fielded the ball, dove to tag Carbo. Burkhart, in no position to call the play, called Carbo out. Photos showed Hendricks tagging Carbo with his glove while holding the ball in his right hand. Burkhart's decision stood. An inning later, Brooks Robinson broke the tie with a home run, and Baltimore held on to win it.

The Reds jumped off to the lead again in game two, 4–0 after three innings. But again the Orioles came back, scoring five in the top of the fifth and going on to a 6–5 win.

Playing at home for game three, the Orioles threatened to make it a sweep with a third straight win, 9–3, the game highlighted by pitcher Dave McNally's grand-slam home run in the bottom of the sixth. In this game Brooks Robinson made three more instant-replay gems in the field and also cracked a pair of doubles. The Series was turning into a Brooks Robinson extravaganza.

The following day Brooks went 4 for 4, including a home run, but the Reds stayed alive, winning 6–5 on a three-run homer by Lee May in the top of the eighth.

Struggling desperately to stay above water, the Reds started game five with a three-run first inning against Cuellar, but that turned out to be the sum total of their scoring. The Orioles, souls of efficiency in this Series, scored two runs in each of the first three innings and pulled away to a 9–3 win and the championship.

Baltimore's .292 team batting average for the five games pointed up the weakness in Cincinnati's pitching, with Paul Blair batting .474 for the O's and Brooks Robinson .429 with two home runs, six runs batted in, and a glove that had snapped around third base like a whip all through the Series.

A bit of leather larceny by Yankee third baseman Clete Boyer, who got to his feet and threw out the Reds' Frank Robinson. The action occurred in the sixth inning of game two, 1961.

The Yankees' Bobby Richardson had another outstanding Series against the Cincinnati Reds in 1961, batting .391 and leading with nine hits.

The Yankees' Hector Lopez, who drove in seven runs against the Reds in the 1961 Series.

Cincinnati's Joey Jay on the mound at Yankee Stadium, pitching winning ball for the Reds in game two, the only game they won in the 1961 Series.

Whitey Ford, who beat the Reds twice in the 1961 Series, and along the way established a new record for consecutive scoreless innings pitched in a World Series.

A nervous moment for the Giants' Willie Mays in the second inning of the 1962 Series opener in San Francisco. Willie was taking his lead off third when Yankee pitcher Whitey Ford suddenly fired to Clete Boyer. Willie barely got back. Umpire Jim Honochick called the play. A few moments later Willie scored on Jose Pagan's two-out bunt single, snapping Ford's World Series scoreless-inning streak at 33⅔.

Unbothered by the spikes of the high-sliding Orlando Cepeda, the Yankees' Bobby Richardson fires on to first in a vain attempt to nip the Giants' Ed Bailey. The play took place in the fourth inning of game three, 1962.

Willie McCovey, whose line drive in the bottom of the ninth inning of game seven almost won the 1962 Series for the Giants.

Yankee right-hander Ralph Terry. His clutch 1–0 win in game seven in 1962 wiped away the stigma of the Mazeroski home run.

The Giants' Chuck Hiller, who blasted the Giants to a win in game four of the 1962 Series with a grand-slam home run.

Los Angeles southpaw Sandy Koufax, who defeated the Yankees twice in the 1963 World Series, including a record-shattering 15-strikeout performance in game one.

The Dodgers' Don Drysdale, who three-hit the Yankees 1–0 in game three of the 1963 Series.

The Yankees' Elston Howard, the only New Yorker to make much of a dent on Dodger pitching in the 1963 Series. He had five hits and batted .333.

The Dodgers' Tommy Davis, leading sticker of the four-game 1963 Series with six hits and a .400 batting average.

Ken Boyer of the Cardinals, whose grand-slam home run in game four of the 1964 Series gave St. Louis its 4–3 win.

Bobby Richardson. The Yankee second baseman set an all-time World Series record with 13 hits in 1964.

Bob Gibson, who won two and lost one in the 1964 Series against the Yankees, fanning 31 in 27 innings.

Bob Gibson and third baseman Ken Boyer in exuberant embrace as the Cardinals defeat the Yankees for the 1964 world championship.

Action in game seven of the 1964 World Series. Tim McCarver of the Cardinals sliding home on the front end of a double steal in the fourth inning. Mike Shannon stole second on the play. The catcher is Elston Howard.

A lineup of the Minnesota Twins' prime timbermen, winners of the 1965 American League pennant. Left to right, Rich Rollins, Harmon Killebrew, Bob Allison, Don Mincher, Jimmy Hall, Tony Oliva.

Southpaw Claude Osteen (right) won a crucial game for the Dodgers when he shut out the Twins in game three, 1965. With Osteen is his batterymate, Johnny Roseboro, who drove in two runs in the 4–0 Los Angeles win.

Los Angeles outfielder Ron Fairly, who had 11 hits and batted .379 in the 1965 Series.

Minnesota's Jim Kaat pitching to the Dodgers' Lou Johnson in game two of the 1965 World Series. The catcher is Earl Battey.

Jim (Mudcat) Grant, who started three games and won two of them for the Twins in the 1965 Series.

Lefthanders Jim Kaat (left) and Sandy Koufax, who started against each other in games two, five, and seven of the 1965 Series. Sandy won game five and the decisive game seven.

The Dodgers' Maury Wills demonstrating the agility a shortstop sometimes needs in order to ply his trade. After taking the feed from second baseman Jim Lefebvre, Wills is upended by the Orioles' Curt Blefary, but still manages to fire to first base to complete the double play. The action occurred in the second inning of the fourth and final game of the 1966 Series.

Baltimore right-hander Moe Drabowsky, who pitched 6⅔ innings of one-hit, 11-strikeout relief ball in the Orioles' opening-game victory over the Dodgers in the 1966 World Series.

Another baby Oriole, right-hander Wally Bunker. The twenty-one-year-old shut out the Dodgers in game three of the 1966 Series, 1–0.

Dodgers center fielder Willie Davis robbing Baltimore's Boog Powell of a home run with a sensational leaping catch in the fourth inning of game four, 1966, played at Baltimore.

Orioles center fielder Paul Blair depriving the Dodgers' Jim Lefebvre of what might have been a game-tying home run in the eighth inning of the fourth and final game of the 1966 Series.

The Cardinals' Lou Brock, who was dynamic in the 1967 World Series against the Red Sox, getting 12 hits, stealing seven bases, and batting .414.

After a sensational 1967 season, Carl Yastrzemski kept right on going for the Red Sox in the World Series, getting ten hits, including three home runs, and batting .400.

The Cardinals' Lou Brock about to dive in headfirst for one of the eight runs he scored in the 1967 Series. The Red Sox catcher is Elston Howard.

Boston's Jim Lonborg, who won two games in the 1967 Series—a one-hitter in game two and a three-hitter in game five—but lost the finale to Gibson. He is shown here pitching in game two. Shortstop Rico Petrocelli is in the background.

Winning pitcher Bob Gibson about to shake hands with catcher Tim McCarver after the Cardinals' victory over the Red Sox in game seven of the 1967 World Series.

Lou Brock: another great Series in 1968 against Detroit, with a .464 batting average, seven stolen bases, and a record-tying 13 hits.

Detroit's Al Kaline, who batted .379 in the 1968 Series.

St. Louis Cardinals ace Bob Gibson.

Detroit's Mickey Lolich at work in the 1968 World Series, in which he defeated the Cardinals three times.

Southpaw Mike Cuellar, who notched Baltimore's only victory in the 1969 Series with the Mets.

Jim Northrup connecting for a grand-slam homer in Detroit's mammoth ten-run third inning in game six of the 1968 Series. The pitcher is the Cardinals' Larry Jaster, the catcher Tim McCarver, the umpire Bill Haller.

The Mets have just won the 1969 World Series, and catcher Jerry Grote is embracing winning pitcher Jerry Koosman. Tom Seaver (No. 41) has run out to join in the celebration.

The Mets' great Tom Seaver pitching at Shea Stadium against the Orioles in game four of the 1969 Series.

The Swoboda catch in the top of the ninth inning of the fourth game of the 1969 Series.

The play that ended game four of the 1969 Series. It's the bottom of the tenth inning, and Orioles pitcher Pete Richert's peg is about to hit the wrist of the Mets' J. C. Martin (No. 9) and bound into right field, allowing the winning run to score.

Mets left-hander Jerry Koosman, who twice defeated the Orioles in the 1969 World Series.

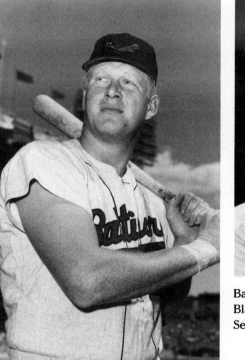

Baltimore's peerless center fielder Paul Blair, the leading hitter of the 1970 World Series with a .474 batting average.

Cincinnati's Lee May, who excelled in a losing cause in the 1970 Series, batting .389 and driving in eight runs.

John (Boog) Powell, Baltimore's power-hitting first baseman, who hit two home runs in the 1970 Series.

Brooks Robinson has just completed a routine Brooks Robinson play, robbing Cincinnati's Johnny Bench. The larceny took place in the sixth inning of game three, 1970.

Baltimore third baseman Brooks Robinson, who was nothing short of spectacular throughout the 1970 World Series against the Cincinnati Reds, both at bat and in the field. He collected nine hits and batted .429.

Sparky Anderson.

Earl Weaver.

1971

"We always knew how good he was," said one National League player, "but it took the 1971 World Series to show the rest of the country." The man he was talking about was Pittsburgh's proud, brooding, extravagantly talented right fielder, Roberto Clemente. Clemente did it all in the Pirates' pulsing seven-game victory over a seemingly invincible Baltimore team in 1971—playing a flawless right field, intimidating Oriole runners with his arm, and batting .414.

Clemente was the heart of a mayhem-laden Pirate lineup that was weighted with outfielders Willie Stargell and Al Oliver, first baseman Bob Robertson, second baseman Dave Cash, third baseman Richie Hebner, and catcher Manny Sanguillen. These bashers helped carry skipper Danny Murtaugh's staff of right-handed starters, led by Dock Ellis, Steve Blass, Bob Moose, and Nelson Briles.

In winning their third straight flag, Earl Weaver's club had built an image bordering on the awesome. The Orioles were Boog Powell, Davey Johnson, Mark Belanger, Paul Blair, Brooks Robinson, Don Buford, Frank Robinson, Merv Rettenmund; and this year the Baltimore pitching outdid even itself with four 20-game winners on the staff: Jim Palmer, Dave McNally, Mike Cuellar, and Pat Dobson.

The Orioles started out by performing like the favorites they were, McNally winning the opener in Baltimore 5–3, bolstered by a three-run homer by Rettenmund and solo shots by Frank Robinson and Buford. The Orioles looked as if they were gearing up for a runaway when they crushed the Pirates 11–3 the next day, giving Palmer an easy win.

When the Series moved to Pittsburgh, the Pirates seemed to draw new life. With Steve Blass pitching a three-hitter and Bob Robertson hitting a three-run homer, the Pirates took game three by a 5–1 score. Game four was historic—the first night game in

189

World Series history. Pat Dobson started for the Orioles and lefty Luke Walker for the Pirates. Walker was kayoed in the first inning, and Bruce Kison came on for the Pirates and pitched 6⅓ innings of one-hit ball; the Pirates won it, 4–3, with Clemente rapping three hits. The Pirates made it a sweep at home, winning game five 4–0 behind Nelson Briles's sparkling two-hitter.

Back in Baltimore, the Orioles resumed home-team dominance and tied the Series at three-all by edging the Pirates 3–2 in ten innings. The winning run in the bottom of the tenth scored on a walk to Frank Robinson, a single by Rettenmund, and a sacrifice fly by Brooks Robinson.

It was Blass and Cuellar in game seven. Clemente, who hit in all seven games, gave the Pirates a 1–0 lead with a fourth-inning home run. Pittsburgh added another in the top of the eighth; the Orioles came back with one, making it 2–1. Blass, however, surrendered nothing more, and closed the Series with a 2–1 four-hitter.

Blass, with two strong wins in which he gave up just 7 hits in eighteen innings, and Clemente, with 12 hits and a .414 batting average, ended up as the twin heroes of Pittsburgh's 1971 World Series victory.

1972

The Oakland Athletics began their remarkable domination of baseball in 1972, winning the first Athletics pennant since Connie Mack's Philadelphia edition of 1931. Dick Williams's team was top-heavy with pitching, his fine staff headed by Jim (Catfish) Hunter, John (Blue Moon) Odom, southpaws Ken Holtzman and Vida Blue, and Rollie Fingers, perhaps the greatest of all relief pitchers. With a .240 team batting average, the A's drew most of their offensive sustenance from outfielders Reggie Jackson and Joe Rudi, shortstop Bert Campaneris, first baseman Mike Epstein, and third baseman Sal Bando. With Jackson injuring himself in the championship series against Baltimore, the Athletics were forced to play the Series with their biggest cannon on the sidelines.

Representing the National League in the 1972 World Series were Sparky Anderson's Cincinnati Reds. The Reds sharply contrasted with the A's— light on pitching (Gary Nolan with 15 wins was their ace) but with hitting to spare. With Joe Morgan now at second base, the club had Tony Perez, Pete Rose, Johnny Bench, and Bobby Tolan.

The hero of the 1972 Series, however, turned out to be Oakland's second-string catcher, Gene Tenace, who during the season had hit five home runs and batted .225. He won the opener for the A's in Cincinnati single-handedly, hitting home runs his first two times up and driving in all the runs in Oakland's 3–2 win. His bat was silent the following day in Oakland's 2–1 victory, the hero being Joe Rudi with a third-

inning home run and in the bottom of the ninth a spectacular leaping backhanded catch on a drive by Denis Menkle that saved the game for Hunter.

Tight pitching continued to dominate in game three, the Reds' Jack Billingham putting his club in the win column with a 1–0 win over Odom, the Reds scoring in the top of the seventh on a single by Cesar Geronimo. The Reds were going for a Series tie in game four when a bottom-of-the-ninth Oakland rally snatched it away from them. Going into the ninth trailing 2–1 (Oakland's run coming on Tenace's third homer, in the fifth inning), the Athletics' bench came to the rescue. With one out, pinch hitter Gonzalo Marquez singled, Tenace singled, pinch hitter Don Mincher singled to tie it, and then a third pinch hitter, Angel Mangual, singled to win it.

The pattern of one-run decisions continued in game five. After trailing 3–1 to Tenace's fourth homer, a three-run shot in the bottom of the second, the Reds began pecking away, finally going ahead 5–4 in the top of the ninth on Pete Rose's single. In the bottom of the ninth the A's threatened to tie it. With men on first and third and one out, pinch runner Odom was cut down at the plate trying to score on a pop foul to Morgan behind first base.

Back in Cincinnati, the Reds evened things at three games apiece with the only runaway of the Series, an 8–1 pasting of Williams's hitherto parsimonious pitching staff.

Game seven saw Odom starting for the A's against the Reds' Billingham. By the time it was over, the A's had employed four pitchers, the Reds five. A three-base error by Tolan and Tenace's single gave the A's an unearned run in the top of the first. Cincinnati tied it in the bottom of the fifth, but the A's came back in the top of the sixth to score two—a double by the sizzling Tenace was the key blow—and went on to a 3–2 win and the championship.

The 1972 World Series was virtually a one-man show. Oakland's Gene Tenace hit four home runs, batted .348, and, most extraordinary, drove in 9 of his team's 16 runs. A quiet hero was reliever Rollie Fingers, who was called on in six of the seven games, winning one, losing one, and saving two.

1973

The Oakland Athletics took their second straight pennant in 1973, and again it was primarily on the strength of their pitching. Dick Williams had three 20-game winners in Catfish Hunter, Vida Blue, and Ken Holtzman, plus the bullpen magic of Rollie Fingers. Most of the club's offense was generated by Reggie Jackson, Gene Tenace, Sal Bando, Bert Campaneris, Joe Rudi, Billy North, and designated hitter Deron Johnson. (This was the first year the DH was used, and it was exclusive to the American League. In 1976 the DH was allowed in the World Series for the first time, to be used in alternating years.)

The vagaries of divisional play brought the New York Mets back into the World Series. After having won their division with an 82–79 record, the Mets prevailed over the Cincinnati Reds in the championship series despite the Reds' 99–63 record. The light-hitting Mets had John Milner, Felix Millan, Bud Harrelson, and Wayne Garrett in the infield, Cleon Jones and Rusty Staub in the outfield, and Jerry Grote catching. Playing his last big-league season for the Mets was the legendary but now forty-two-year-old Willie Mays, bowing out with tired legs and a .211 batting average. Yogi Berra's club had three strong starters in Tom Seaver, Jerry Koosman, and Jon Matlack, plus a solid bullpen stopper in Tug McGraw.

The Series opened in Oakland with the A's nipping Matlack 2–1, both Athletic runs scoring in the bottom of the third and being unearned because of an error by Millan at second.

Game two was a wild twelve-inning affair that the Mets won with four in the top of the twelfth, 10–7, after the A's had tied it six-all with two runs in the bottom of the ninth. The Oakland rally had a melancholy aspect to it. Pinch hitter Deron Johnson lifted a fly ball to center that Mays should have put away easily, but the veteran tripped and stumbled, letting the ball drop for a double that ignited the rally. Later, in the top of the twelfth, Willie redeemed himself with a clutch two-out single—the last hit of his major-league career—that broke the tie. After that, two errors by Oakland second baseman Mike Andrews cost three more runs. The Mets fought off an Oakland rally in the bottom of the inning to win the longest game (by time) in World Series history—four hours and thirteen minutes.

After the game, A's owner Charley Finley, in a fit of pique, removed Andrews from the team's roster, claiming Mike was injured. It was apparent to all, however—especially Andrews's incensed teammates and manager Dick Williams—that the owner was punishing Andrews for his errors. Commissioner Bowie Kuhn intervened, restoring Andrews to the roster and rebuking Finley.

The two clubs went right back into extra innings in game three in New York, with Oakland taking this one, 3–2, in eleven. The Mets evened the Series the next day, 6–1, thanks to some lusty hitting by Staub, who went 4 for 4, including a home run, and drove in five runs. The following day it was the Mets again, 2–0, on a combined shutout by Koosman and McGraw.

Trying to stave off elimination, the A's beat Seaver and the Mets 3–1 in game six in Oakland. Reggie Jackson fired the first real shots of his "Mr. October" nickname in this game, with three hits and two runs batted in.

A pair of southpaws, Matlack for the Mets and Holtzman for the A's, started game seven. In the bottom of the third the A's drove Matlack from the mound, scoring four runs on a pair of two-run homers by Campaneris and Jackson. The A's bullpen—first Fingers and then Darold Knowles, appearing for the seventh time in the Series—picked up in the sixth inning and carried the club to a 5–2 win and its second straight world title.

After the Series Oakland manager Dick Williams, fed up with Finley's interference, which had been capped off by the Andrews episode, announced his resignation.

1974

The Oakland Athletics, managed now by Alvin Dark, made it three pennants in a row in 1974. The cast remained pretty much the same, with Reggie Jackson still the principal rocket launcher and Hunter, Blue, Holtzman, and Fingers dominating the mound.

Walter Alston's Los Angeles Dodgers had undergone a complete facelift since the club had last appeared in a World Series, eight years before. The infield quartet that was going to remain intact until 1981 was now in place—Steve Garvey at first, Davey Lopes at second, Bill Russell at short, and Ron Cey at third. Alston's good-hitting outfield included Bill Buckner, Jim Wynn, and Willie Crawford, while Steve Yeager and Joe Ferguson shared the catching. While they had lost lefty Tommy John to a mid-season arm injury, the Dodgers still had ace right-handers Andy Messersmith and Don Sutton and rubber-armed righty reliever Mike Marshall, who astonished everyone with 106 appearances during the season.

The Series opened in Los Angeles, with the A's nipping the Dodgers 3–2. Dark used Holtzman, Fingers, and then Hunter to get the final out—quite an array of pitching to fire in a single game. The Dodgers won their only game of the Series in game two, 3–2 behind Sutton, with Marshall getting a save. L.A.'s winning margin was a two-run homer by Ferguson in the bottom of the sixth.

The first all-California World Series then moved up the coast to Oakland. Pinched for pitching, Alston started veteran lefty Al Downing against Dark's ace, Hunter. Downing pitched creditably, but a miscue in front of the plate by Ferguson in the bottom of the third gave the A's two unearned runs and set Oakland up for a 3–2 win. The Athletics kept rolling along methodically with a 5–2 buttering of the Dodgers in game four, thanks to a four-run sixth inning that put it away, the key blow being a two-run single by pinch hitter Jim Holt.

The Series came to a conclusion the next day with a 3–2 Oakland victory. The winning run for the A's came across in the bottom of the seventh on a tie-breaking Joe Rudi home run off of Marshall, the only run scored against Marshall, who maintained his iron-man reputation by appearing in all five games, pitching nine innings. For the A's, the ubiquitous Fingers appeared four times, winning one and saving two.

In winning, the Athletics became the only team besides the Yankees to win the World Series more than twice in succession. An interesting footnote to the 1974 Series: it was the third in a row in which no starting pitcher had worked a complete game. The age of the relief pitcher had most emphatically arrived.

1975

It has been called the greatest of modern World Series, with its sixth game considered by many the most exciting Series game ever.

The Boston Red Sox had made it to the top of the American League by defeating the Oakland A's in the championship series and thus thwarting Oakland's bid for a fourth straight world title. Manager Darrell Johnson had a potent lineup, with rookie sensation Fred Lynn, Carl Yastrzemski, Dwight Evans, Carlton Fisk, Denny Doyle, Rick Burleson, Cecil Cooper, and Bernie Carbo. (Another slugger, rookie Jim Rice, missed the Series with an injury.) And the Red Sox, for a change, had some strong pitching to go with their big bangers. The staff was topped by the colorful veteran Luis Tiant, Rick Wise, Reggie Cleveland, southpaws Bill Lee and Roger Moret, and righty relievers Jim Willoughby and Dick Drago.

Winning 108 games and the National League pennant (taking their division by 20 games) was Sparky Anderson's Cincinnati Reds — "the Big Red Machine." The club was regarded by some as perhaps the greatest in National League history. It had a lineup flooded with talent: Pete Rose, Joe Morgan, Johnny Bench, Dave Concepcion, Ken Griffey, George Foster, Tony Perez, Cesar Geronimo. On the mound Sparky had Gary Nolan, Jack Billingham, left-handers Don Gullett and Fred Norman, and a deep bullpen consisting of Pedro Borbon, Clay Carroll, Rawley Eastwick, and lefty Will McEnany.

The opener in Boston was a peculiar game. The Red Sox won it 6–0 behind Tiant, scoring all their runs in the bottom of the seventh, shattering the scoreless duel between Luis and Gullett. Going all the way, Tiant racked up the first complete game in World Series play since Steve Blass did it in the finale of the 1971 Series.

Cincinnati came back the next day, snatching a win away from Bill Lee and the Sox with two runs in the top of the ninth on clutch hits by Concepcion and Griffey for a 3–2 edging.

Game three, in Cincinnati, provided fireworks and controversy. Each club hit three home runs, the most dramatic being Dwight Evans's two-run shot in the top of the ninth that tied the score 5–5. In the bottom of the tenth, with the score still tied, one of the most hotly debated plays in Series history occurred. Geronimo led off for the Reds with a single. Ed Armbrister was sent up to hit for Eastwick. Ordered to sacrifice, he laid one down in front of the plate. Rushing out to field the ball, Fisk collided with Armbrister and then threw the ball into center field. The Red Sox argued vociferously that there had been interference, but home-plate umpire Larry Barnett disagreed. When the decibel count had been lowered, Geronimo was on third and Armbrister on second. Rose drew an intentional walk, and after an out, Morgan singled in the winning run.

Tiant drew the Sox even in game four, again going the distance, throwing 163 pitches in a gritty 5–4 win. His mates gave Luis another big inning when they scored all their runs in the top of the fifth.

The Reds went a game up by taking game five 6–2, thanks to strong pitching by Gullett and two home runs and four RBIs by Tony Perez, who had come into the game 0 for 14 in the Series.

A day of travel back to Boston and then three days of rain enabled the Red Sox to bring Tiant back against Nolan in game six. Fred Lynn sent the Sox off flying in the first inning with a three-run homer. The Reds tied it with three in the top of the fifth, then punched away for two more in the seventh and one in the eighth for a 6–3 lead. In the bottom of the eighth the Red Sox had two on and two out. Bernie Carbo was sent up to pinch-hit. The former Red sent a shock wave through New England when he blasted a Rawley Eastwick pitch into the center-field bleachers for a game-tying three-run homer. (Carbo had also pinch-hit a homer in game three.)

In the bottom of the ninth the Red Sox loaded the bases with none out, the ripest situation in baseball, yet failed to score when George Foster threw Denny Doyle out at the plate after taking Lynn's fly ball in short left. After an uneventful tenth inning, the sparks flew again in the top of the eleventh. With one out and Griffey on first, Morgan sent a high line drive screaming out to right field. What looked like a home run was hauled down in front of the bleachers with one hand by a leaping Dwight Evans, who then fired back to the infield to double up Griffey, who had gone all the way around to third.

The game moved on to the bottom of the twelfth, still tied 6–6. Fisk led off, facing right-hander Pat Darcy, Cincinnati's record-tying eighth pitcher of the game. Fisk lifted Darcy's first pitch high along the left-field line, then stood at home plate using gestures and body English to try to guide the ball fair. It was fair — just — striking high against the foul pole for the game winner. It was "the most momentous home run in Red Sox history."

Left-handers Gullett and Lee were matched in the

decisive seventh game. Boston scored three in the bottom of the third, thanks to four walks by Gullett, and the Red Sox seemed headed for their first championship since 1918. The Reds, however, scored two in the top of the sixth on Tony Perez's third homer of the Series, and then tied it with one in the seventh. The score was still tied going into the top of the ninth, with lefty Jim Burton pitching for Boston. Griffey led off with a walk. Geronimo sacrificed him to second. Pinch hitter Dan Driessen grounded out, Griffey moving to third. Pete Rose walked. Then Joe Morgan dropped a single into short center, scoring Griffey with what proved to be the deciding run. Cincinnati 4, Boston 3, in runs, and in games.

This drenching, furiously entertaining World Series left baseball America agreeing with one observer's summation: "The Reds won, but the Red Sox didn't lose."

1976

The drought ended for Yankee fans in 1976. After 12 years of deprivation, the Yankees were back on top. With their former second baseman Billy Martin managing, the team had swept through their division and then taken the championship series in five games from Kansas City on Chris Chambliss's ninth-inning home run. Along with first baseman Chambliss, the Yankees' new look included Willie Randolph at second, Graig Nettles at third, Thurman Munson catching, and Lou Piniella, Mickey Rivers, and Roy White in the outfield. The Yankees had a well-rounded pitching staff with starters Catfish Hunter, Ed Figueroa, Dock Ellis, and Doyle Alexander and relievers Sparky Lyle and Dick Tidrow.

It was a good team, but they ran smack into a great one: Sparky Anderson's Big Red Machine. What kind of apparatus was this machine? Well, in 1976 it was a meat grinder, with the same neon-light names as the year before: Rose, Bench, Morgan, Foster, Perez, Concepcion, Griffey.

In 1939 the Yankees had rolled over another Reds team in four straight. For long-remembering Cincinnati fans, revenge came 37 years later.

In game one in Cincinnati, Don Gullett and the Reds handled the Yankees with ease, winning 5–1. Game two was the only interesting affair of the Series. It was a 3–3 tie going into the bottom of the ninth. With two out and nobody on, Griffey reached second when shortstop Fred Stanley threw away his ground ball. After Morgan was intentionally passed, Perez singled to left to win it.

The Series moved to New York then, but the locale was the only thing that changed, the Reds taking game three easily, 6–2. Game four was even less of a challenge for the Reds as they swept the slate clean with a 7–2 win that brought Cincinnati its second successive title. The game was a one-man power

display by Johnny Bench. The Cincinnati catcher hit two home runs and drove in five runs. Overall, Bench's hitting dominated for the Reds. Getting two hits in each game, he batted .533 and drove in six runs. For the Yankees, the hitting of Thurman Munson was the lone bright light. The Yankee catcher batted .529 with nine hits, hitting safely in his last six times at bat, tying a Series record set by Goose Goslin in 1924. Another record was tied by Cincinnati's .313 team batting average, which equaled the four-game Series mark set by the 1932 Yankees.

The 1975–1976 Reds were the first National League team since the 1921–1922 New York Giants to win two World Series in a row.

1977

The Yankees repeated in 1977, with the help of free-agent acquisitions Don Gullett and Reggie Jackson. Adding the hard-throwing Gullett and later Mike Torrez to a staff that already included Catfish Hunter, Ed Figueroa, young southpaw Ron Guidry, and relievers Sparky Lyle and Dick Tidrow gave Billy Martin one of the strongest pitching lineups in the big leagues. The addition of Jackson made an already potent batting order even more so. Rounding out the new faces was shortstop Bucky Dent, purchased from the White Sox.

Moving aside the Big Red Machine and returning to the top were the Los Angeles Dodgers, guided by freshman skipper Tom Lasorda. Lasorda's lineup carried unprecedented dynamite—four 30-or-better home run hitters: Steve Garvey, Ron Cey, Reggie Smith, and Dusty Baker. This hitting provided support for left-handers Tommy John and Doug Rau, right-handers Don Sutton, Burt Hooton, and Rick Rhoden, and knuckle-balling righty reliever Charlie Hough.

The Series opened in New York, with the Yankees carrying off a 4–3 win in twelve innings on a double by Willie Randolph and a single by Paul Blair, who had entered the game as a defensive replacement for Jackson in right field in the ninth inning. In game two, Martin gambled on a sore-armed Catfish Hunter, but Catfish didn't have it. Smith and Cey tagged him for two-run homers early in the game, and Hooton coasted to a 6–1 win.

The Series moved to Los Angeles, and the Yankees took game three, 5–3, opening up on Tommy John for three runs in the first inning. Mike Torrez won it, despite giving up a three-run homer to Baker in the bottom of the third. The following day the Yankees again struck early, raking Doug Rau for three runs in the top of the second. Ron Guidry made them stand up, going all the way for a 4–2 win and a three-games-to-one Yankee bulge. In this game Reggie Jackson's bat began to warm up, the chesty slugger rapping a double and a home run.

The Dodgers sent the Series back to New York with a 10–4 win behind Sutton in game five, Steve Yeager's three-run homer being the big blow for L.A. Jackson again homered for the Yankees. Reggie was now primed for his prodigious one-man show in New York.

Burt Hooton started game six for the Dodgers against Torrez. The Dodgers jumped out to a 2–0 lead in the first inning on a triple by Garvey. The Yankees tied it in the bottom of the second on Chris Chambliss's two-run homer, but the Dodgers edged ahead 3–2 on Smith's solo shot in the third. The rest of the game belonged to Jackson.

In the bottom of the fourth Reggie lined Hooton's first pitch into the right-field stands for a two-run homer. In the bottom of the fifth he drove the first pitch from Elias Sosa into the seats for another two-run homer, his fourth of the Series, tying the record held jointly by Babe Ruth, Lou Gehrig, Duke Snider, Hank Bauer, and Gene Tenace. In the bottom of the eighth, with the Yankees up 7–3, Reggie picked on the first pitch thrown by Charlie Hough and sent it on a long journey into the center-field bleachers. Jackson's third home run of the game tied a Series record set by Ruth in 1926 and again in 1928, and his fifth home run of the Series established a new record for postseason slugging.

With Torrez going all the way, the Yankees won it 8–4 and regained the championship they had last won in 1962.

Jackson's record-shattering slugging overshadowed Torrez's two complete-game victories and just about everything else that occurred in the 1977 World Series. For the six games Reggie batted .450, hit his landmark five home runs, scored a record ten runs, and drove in eight. The legend of "Mr. October" had taken wing.

1978

The Yankees maintained their old habit of winning pennants in bunches with a third straight flag in 1978. In doing so, they had to overcome their own turmoil, which saw the tempestuous Billy Martin resign as manager on July 24 after disputes with Reggie Jackson and owner George Steinbrenner. Martin was replaced by the firm but placid Bob Lemon. The Yankees then had a torrid second half, winning 52 of their last 73, coming from 14 games behind in July to end in a tie at the top of the eastern division with the Red Sox. After defeating the Sox in a dramatic one-game playoff, the Yankees went on to beat Kansas City in the championship playoff for the third straight year and their thirty-second pennant.

Along with the steady hitting of Jackson, Munson, Nettles, Chambliss, Piniella, and Randolph, the Yankees received a sensational 25–3 season from Ron Guidry, 20 wins from Ed Figueroa, and overpowering

bullpen performances from free-agent signee Goose Gossage.

In the National League, Tom Lasorda, with essentially the same lineup as the year before, made it two for two, beating out the Reds with a late-season rush. The Dodgers had strengthened their pitching by bringing up right-handed fast baller Bob Welch and signing lefty reliever Terry Forster as a free agent.

The Series opened in Los Angeles, with the Dodgers applying an 11–5 shellacking to Figueroa and three other Yankee pitchers. The big man for the Dodgers was Davey Lopes, with two home runs and five runs batted in, while for the Yankees Jackson picked up where he had left off the year before with two singles and a home run.

The Dodgers made it two straight the next day with a 4–3 win that featured a tingling ninth-inning shootout between Jackson and reliever Welch. With two men on and two out and young Welch firing bullets, Jackson ran the count to 1–2, fouled off two blazers, took ball two, fouled off another, took ball three, and then, with the runners going, swung and missed for strike three, ending the gripping confrontation and the game. Overshadowed by this classic duel were the heroics of Dodger Ron Cey, who had driven in all four Dodger runs, three on a sixth-inning home run. (Jackson had driven in all three Yankee runs—two on a double and the other on a ground out.)

So the Dodgers journeyed to New York with a 2–0 lead in games. In game three Lasorda's men got plenty of runners on base, but kept making the mistake of hitting the ball to Graig Nettles. The Yankee third baseman made two spectacular stops to retire the Dodgers in the fifth and sixth innings, each time with the bases loaded. The Yankees won 5–1 behind Guidry, with Nettles having saved at least five runs with his glove work.

In game four, Reggie Jackson, who had been pivotal at home plate both hitting and striking out, now became the center of attention as a base runner. In the last of the sixth, with the Dodgers up 3–1 thanks to a Reggie Smith homer, the Yankees had Munson on second and Jackson on first and one out. Lou Piniella hit a double-play ball to shortstop Bill Russell. Russell picked it up, stepped on second, and fired on to first. The ball, however, struck Jackson on the hip and caromed into right field, allowing Munson to score. The Dodgers argued that Reggie had interfered deliberately and should have been called out, nullifying the run. The argument went up the chute like so much smoke.

The disputed run became critical when the Yankees tied the game in the bottom of the eighth and then won it in the tenth on Piniella's two-out single, evening the Series at two games apiece.

The Yankees ran away with game five, pounding out an 18-hit, 12–2 victory behind young Jim Beattie, with Thurman Munson driving in five runs.

The next day, behind Hunter and Gossage, the Yankees won their twenty-second championship, beating the Dodgers 7–2. Jackson hit a home run in the top of the seventh for New York's final two runs, a blow that gave Reggie a measure of personal satisfaction, for it came off of Bob Welch, the young fast baller who had won their *High Noon* confrontation in game two.

The Yankees as a team batted .306 in this Series, setting a new record for a six-game Series. A pleasant surprise for them had been young second baseman Brian Doyle, filling in for the injured Willie Randolph. Doyle batted .438. Also going beyond expectations was shortstop Bucky Dent, with ten hits, seven runs batted in, and a .417 batting average. And once again there was "Mr. October." Jackson rapped two homers, batted .391, and led with eight runs batted in.

1979

In a repeat match-up of the 1971 Series, the 1979 October pageant saw the Pittsburgh Pirates meet the Baltimore Orioles. The unifying slogan of Bill Virdon's Pirates was "We are family!" The paterfamilias of this tight-knit club was its thirty-nine-year-old slugging first baseman, Willie Stargell. Devoted to Willie and his inspiring leadership were some ace ballplayers like third baseman Bill Madlock, catcher Ed Ott, shortstop Tim Foli, second baseman Phil Garner, and outfielders Dave Parker, Bill Robinson, and Omar Moreno. While the Pirate pitching staff was the first ever to go into a World Series without a 15-game winner, it did have an array of hurlers with high winning percentages in left-hander John Candelaria and righties Bruce Kison, Jim Bibby, and Bert Blyleven, and two solid relief pitchers in Enrique Romo and Kent Tekulve.

Baltimore's longtime resident dugout genius Earl Weaver had a typical Baltimore club: solid hitting, good defense, and a deep pitching staff. The O's had Eddie Murray at first, Rich Dauer at second, Doug DeCinces at third, Kiko Garcia and Mark Belanger at short, Rick Dempsey catching, and Ken Singleton, Al Bumbry, and Gary Roenicke in the outfield, along with DH Lee May, who would see virtually no action in this non-DH-year Series. Starting for the Orioles were left-handers Mike Flanagan and Scott McGregor, and righties Jim Palmer, Steve Stone, and Dennis Martinez, while the bullpen had southpaw Tippy Martinez and right-handers Don Stanhouse and Sammy Stewart.

After a one-day postponement of the opener, the Orioles came out smoking, scoring five runs in the bottom of the first inning, helped by a throwing error by Garner. DeCinces capped the outburst with a two-run homer. Flanagan nursed the five runs to the end, winning 5–4. The Pirates squared it off the following

night on a ninth-inning run-producing single by pinch hitter Manny Sanguillen, which gave Virdon's men a 3–2 win.

With the Series moving to Pittsburgh, the Orioles ripped the Pirates in games three and four, each time employing the big inning to do it. In game three it was a five-run fourth, keyed by a bases-loaded triple by Garcia, who went 4 for 4. The Orioles won it 8–4 behind McGregor. In game four it was a six-run eighth that turned around a 6–3 deficit and gave the O's a 9–6 win. In that inning Weaver's pinch hitters made the skipper look like a genius: John Lowenstein and Terry Crowley each smashed two-run doubles.

Facing a desperate situation now, the Pirates fought back with a 7–1 win in game five behind the combined pitching of Jim Rooker and Blyleven, helped along by Madlock's four singles.

Back in Baltimore, Candelaria and Palmer were in a scoreless deadlock when the Pirates jolted the Orioles' great right-hander with two in the seventh and two more in the eighth for a 4–0 win, setting up a seventh game.

The game was a pulse-racer, the Pirates using four pitchers and the Orioles six, five of them in the top of the ninth. Going into that inning, the Pirates held a 2–1 edge, gained on Stargell's third home run of the Series, a two-run belt in the sixth that erased the lead Rich Dauer had given Baltimore with a third-inning homer. The Pirates began pecking away in the top of the ninth, and Weaver, in an attempt to stem the tide, began running pitchers in and out: Tim Stoddard, Mike Flanagan, Don Stanhouse, Tippy Martinez, Dennis Martinez. But this assembly line could not prevent the Pirates from scoring two more runs. Tekulve retired the Orioles in the bottom of the ninth, and the Pirates had a 4–1 victory and a comeback World Series championship.

With a .323 team batting average, the Pirates had a fistful of heroes. With 12 hits and a .500 batting average, Garner tied Pepper Martin (1931) and Johnny Lindell (1947) for the highest average for a seven-game Series. Pittsburgh's year-long hero, Willie Stargell, also collected 12 hits, hit his club's only home runs (three), drove in seven runs, and batted .400. Omar Moreno got 11 hits, and Tim Foli and Dave Parker 10 apiece. Reliever Kent Tekulve recorded three saves, setting a Series record.

1980

After three bridesmaid experiences in championship series play with the Yankees, the Kansas City Royals finally upended the New Yorkers in three straight in 1980, doing what they had been doing all year—following the smoking .390 bat of their third baseman, George Brett. Along with Brett, outfielder Willie Wilson also had an outstanding year, with 230 hits, 79 stolen bases, and a .326 batting average. Also contributing to Kansas City's first pennant were long-balling first baseman Willie Aikens, second baseman Frank White, shortstop U. L. Washington, outfielders Clint Hurdle and Amos Otis, and catcher Darrell Porter, along with DH Hal McRae. Manager Jim Frey's pitching staff was headed by right-hander Dennis Leonard, left-handers Larry Gura and Paul Splittorf, and bullpen whiz Dan Quisenberry, possessor of a baffling underhand delivery.

In the National League, the Philadelphia Phillies had broken out of a similarly dismaying pattern: after three championship series losses—all to the Los Angeles Dodgers—Dallas Green's club had at last taken the pennant by beating Houston in a stirring five-game battle, the last four games being decided in extra innings.

Galvanized by three future Hall of Famers—Pete Rose, Mike Schmidt, and Steve Carlton—the Phillies had edged out the Montreal Expos for the eastern division title by a single game. Along with Rose, Schmidt, and Carlton, the Phillies, in winning only the third pennant in their long history, got excellent years from second baseman Manny Trillo, shortstop Larry Bowa, outfielders Bake McBride and Garry Maddox, part-timers Lonnie Smith and Keith Moreland, and solid work from catcher Bob Boone. Behind Carlton, the pitching thinned out, with only right-handers Dick Ruthven and rookie Bob Walk winning in double figures. In the bullpen, Green had two strong men in righty Ron Reed and lefty Tug McGraw.

With his pitching exhausted by the Houston series, Green was forced to open the World Series in Philadelphia with Walk, the first rookie to start a World Series opener since Joe Black did it for the Dodgers in 1952. As they had been doing all year, the Phillies came from behind—from a 4–0 deficit to a 7–6 win, boosted by a three-run homer by McBride in a five-run bottom of the third. Aikens hit a pair of two-run shots for the Royals.

The Phillies came from behind again in game two, scoring four in the bottom of the eighth to pull out a 6–4 win for Carlton. The big hits in the inning were a pinch-hit double by Del Unser, another two-bagger by Schmidt, and singles by McBride and Moreland. After the game the Royals announced that Brett had been hospitalized with what became America's most famous case of hemorrhoids.

Brett was back in time for game three in Kansas City, saying that his problems "were behind" him, and proved it with a first-inning home run. It was a seesaw one-run-at-a-time game, the Royals finally winning it 4–3 in the bottom of the tenth on a single by Aikens. The Royals evened the Series the next day, doing it on the strength of a four-run first inning, winning 5–3, with Aikens again hitting a pair of home runs, making him the first ever to have a pair of two-homer games in a single Series.

The Phillies came back to take the pivotal fifth game with a two-run rally in the ninth, 4–3. The key blow in the inning was Del Unser's second clutch pinch-hit double of the Series. After Unser's double had tied it, Manny Trillo's infield single brought him in with what proved to be the winning run.

The Series returned to Philadelphia for game six, with the Phillies taking dead aim at their first championship ever. Poking away methodically at Jim Frey's pitchers, the Phillies held a 4–1 lead going into the top of the ninth. With McGraw working in relief of Carlton, the Royals loaded the bases with one out. Frank White then popped one up in front of the Phillies' dugout. First baseman Pete Rose and catcher Bob Boone raced for the ball, with Boone calling for it. With Rose standing next to him, Boone had the ball hit his glove and pop out, but the alert Rose grabbed it before it hit the ground, making two out.

The dangerous Willie Wilson was up next, but Willie had been a sitting duck for Phillie pitchers throughout the Series, with just four hits and a record 11 strikeouts. McGraw made it a record 12, and the Phillies had their long-awaited championship.

For the Royals, Amos Otis and Willie Aikens excelled in a losing cause, Otis hitting three home runs, getting 11 hits, and batting .478; Aikens hitting four homers, driving in eight runs, and batting .400. For the Phillies, Mike Schmidt drove in seven runs and batted .381, while McGraw and Carlton stood out on the mound, Steve winning two and Tug winning one and saving two.

The incomparable Roberto Clemente of the Pittsburgh Pirates. He batted .414 in the 1971 Series against Baltimore.

Celebrating Baltimore's 11–3 win in game two of the 1971 Series are, left to right, Brooks Robinson, who got three hits in the game; winning pitcher Jim Palmer; and Frank Robinson, who also got three hits in the game.

Roberto Clemente is about to make contact with this Dave McNally pitch in the fifth inning of game five, 1971. Clemente drove it into center field for a run-scoring single. Notice Clemente hitting with his right foot off the ground, a not uncommon practice of his. Elrod Hendricks is the catcher, Jim Odom the umpire.

Pittsburgh's Nelson Briles, who hurled a gem against the Orioles in the 1971 Series—a two-hit shutout in game five.

Pittsburgh's Steve Blass, hero of the 1971 World Series, beating the Orioles in games three and seven, allowing just two runs and seven hits in eighteen innings.

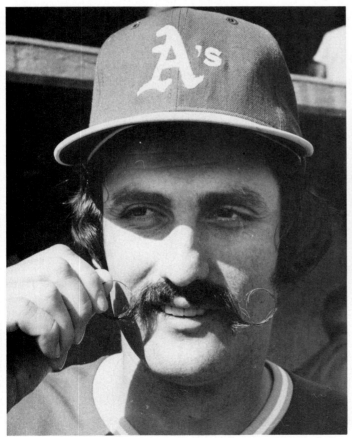

Rollie Fingers and his famous mustache. Rollie pitched for the Oakland A's six times in their seven-game Series with the Reds in 1972, winning one, losing one, and saving two.

A bit of byplay at second base during the 1972 World Series between Oakland and Cincinnati. Oakland's Joe Rudi has just been forced by the Reds' Darrel Chaney, who has fired on to first trying to double up Mike Epstein. Epstein beat the throw. The action occurred in the fourth inning of game three.

Oakland's snappy shortstop Bert Campaneris, who had nine hits and three stolen bases in the 1973 Series.

Cincinnati's Tony Perez, the leading hitter of the 1972 Series, with ten hits and a .435 batting average.

Joe Rudi's truly memorable catch of Denis Menke's bid for an extra-base hit in the bottom of the ninth inning of game two of the 1972 Series. The Reds had a man on first and no outs at the time. Oakland won it, 2–1.

Gene Tenace clouting the third of his four homers in the 1972 Series. It came in game four, against Don Gullett.

Southpaw Ken Holtzman, who beat the New York Mets twice in Oakland's seven-game World Series victory in 1973.

Catfish Hunter delivering the first pitch of game six of the 1973 Series. The batter is the Mets' Wayne Garrett. The catcher is Gene Tenace, the umpire Harry Wendelstedt.

Reggie Jackson. He started becoming "Mr. October" for the first time in the 1973 Series. The Oakland slugger had nine hits, drove in six runs, and batted .310.

Rusty Staub of the New York Mets, the leading hitter of the 1973 Series with 11 hits and a .423 batting average.

Steve Garvey of the Los Angeles Dodgers, the leading hitter of the 1974 Series between the Dodgers and Oakland. In the five-game Series Garvey had eight hits and batted .381.

Oakland's Joe Rudi, whose seventh-inning homer in game five gave his team a 3–2 win and the world championship in the 1974 Series.

An emphatic meeting at home plate in game one of the 1974 Series. Oakland's Sal Bando was trying to score from third on a fly ball to right fielder Joe Ferguson, who fired home to catcher Ray Fosse, who made the play. Umpire Tom Gorman is letting the boys know how it came out. The action occurred in the top of the eighth inning.

Oakland pinch runner Herb Washington has had it. Dodger pitcher Mike Marshall has just picked him off in the top of the ninth inning of game two of the 1974 Series. The first baseman is Steve Garvey. The pickoff finished a two-run Oakland rally as the Dodgers went on to win, 3–2.

The expression on the face of Reds catcher Johnny Bench tells you he knows he has got his man. The man is Boston's Fred Lynn. The action took place in the bottom of the sixth inning of the opening game of the 1975 World Series. Lynn was trying to score from third after a fly ball.

It's the bottom of the tenth inning of game three, 1975. The Reds' Ed Armbrister has just bunted; Carlton Fisk has just thrown off his mask and run into Armbrister. Is it interference? Home-plate umpire Larry Barnett said no. The play led to the Cincinnati win in game three.

Boston's Luis Tiant, who beat Cincinnati twice in the 1975 Series, including an opening-game shutout.

Pete Rose: ten hits and a .370 batting average in the 1975 Series.

Boston's Bernie Carbo, who blasted a dramatic, game-tying pinch-hit home run in the bottom of the eighth inning of game six of the 1975 Series.

The top of the eleventh inning of game six, 1975, and Boston right fielder Dwight Evans is about to leave his feet and make a sensational grab of Joe Morgan's bid for a tie-breaking home run. After the catch, Evans fired the ball in and doubled Ken Griffey off of first base.

Carlton Fisk has just hit the home run that gave the Red Sox the victory in the bottom of the twelfth inning of the memorable sixth game of the 1975 Series. Fisk is applying a bit of body English to make sure the ball stays fair.

Joe Morgan. His tenth-inning single won the third game of the 1975 Series for the Reds, and his ninth-inning single drove in the winning run in the seventh and final game.

The Yankees' Mickey Rivers looks slightly stunned after being picked off first base by Cincinnati pitcher Pat Zachry in the first inning of the third game of the 1976 Series. No. 32 is Yankees coach Elston Howard.

The Yankees' Thurman Munson, who batted .529 in a losing cause in the 1976 Series.

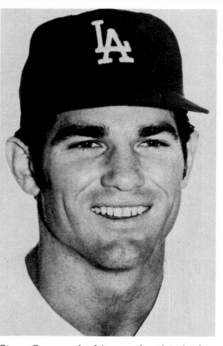

Cincinnati southpaw Don Gullett, who beat the Yankees in the opener of the 1976 Series.

Johnny Bench, batting star of the four-game 1976 World Series with eight hits, six RBIs, and a .533 batting average.

Steve Garvey, the big puncher for the Los Angeles Dodgers in the 1977 Series against the Yankees. He had nine hits and a .375 batting average.

The top four starters for the 1977 pennant-winning New York Yankees. Left to right: Ed Figueroa, Mike Torrez, Catfish Hunter, Ron Guidry.

An artfully decorated Reggie Smith of the Dodgers. He hit three home runs against the Yankees in the 1977 Series, but in the end found himself out-Reggied by the Yankees' Mr. Jackson.

Yankees third baseman Graig Nettles, whose sensational fielding was a highlight of New York's victory over Los Angeles in the 1978 World Series.

Reggie Jackson has just launched his historic third home run of game six of the 1977 Series, his fifth of the Series. The catcher is Steve Yeager, the umpire John McSherry.

Bob Welch.

Dodger shortstop Bill Russell, who had 11 hits and a .423 batting average against the Yankees in the 1978 Series.

Reggie Jackson: another outstanding Series in 1978. He hit two home runs and batted .391.

Baltimore's Doug DeCinces has just stolen second in the second inning of game four, 1979, toppling over Phil Garner in the process.

Pittsburgh's Phil Garner, who put numbers on the board in the 1979 Series: 12 hits and a record-tying .500 batting average.

Baltimore first baseman Eddie Murray has just taken Ed Ott's shot that caromed off the leg of pitcher Tim Stoddard and made the out at first. The action occurred in game four, 1979.

Pirates relief pitcher Kent Tekulve, who sparkled in the 1979 Series.

Pittsburgh's Willie Stargell being congratulated by teammate Bill Robinson after hitting the home run that put the Pirates ahead to stay in the sixth inning of the seventh game of the 1979 Series.

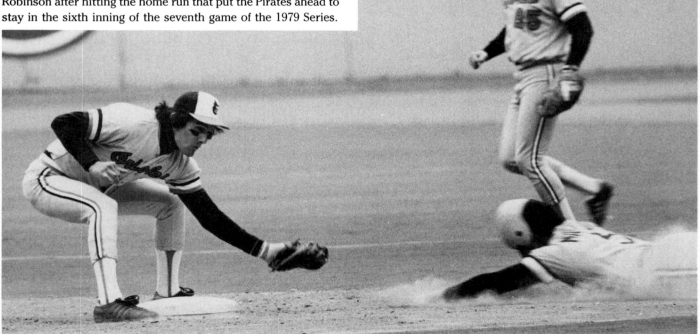

Game four action in the 1979 Series. Baltimore shortstop Kiko Garcia has the peg and is waiting for Pittsburgh's Omar Moreno to slide into it. Moreno was trying to steal second.

Kansas City's George Brett, a .375 hitter against the Phillies in the 1980 World Series.

Willie Aikens, whose bat thundered in a losing cause for the Royals in the 1980 Series. He twice hit two home runs in a game (a Series first), batted .400, and drove in eight runs.

The Phillies' Mike Schmidt, who batted .381 against the Kansas City Royals in the 1980 Series.

Tug McGraw: superb in relief for the Phillies in the 1980 Series.

Kansas City's Amos Otis is seen here clouting his third home run of the 1980 Series. It came in the sixth inning of game five. The catcher is Bob Boone, the umpire Dutch Rennert. Otis was the Series' leading hitter with 11 hits and a .478 batting average.

Bigger and Better
1981·1985

Tom Lasorda.

1981

After a depressing 50-day mid-season strike, a bizarre "second season" when play resumed, leading to playoffs to crown divisional winners, and finally championship playoffs to decide the pennant winners, the World Series opened on October 20, the latest date ever. The two surviving clubs were the New York Yankees and Los Angeles Dodgers, making it the eleventh Yankee-Dodger Series.

The infield that had played for Los Angeles in the 1974 World Series was still intact: Steve Garvey at first, Davey Lopes at second, Bill Russell at short, Ron Cey at third, along with catcher Steve Yeager. In the outfield the Dodgers had Pedro Guerrero, Dusty Baker, and Rick Monday. On the mound, skipper Tom Lasorda had the phenomenal rookie southpaw Fernando Valenzuela, left-hander Jerry Reuss, righties Bob Welch and Burt Hooton, and lefty reliever Steve Howe.

The Yankees, under Bob Lemon, had added free-agent outfielder Dave Winfield to the roster to go along with Reggie Jackson (who missed the first three games of the Series because of an injury), Graig Nettles, Willie Randolph, Lou Piniella, Rick Cerone, and Bob Watson, another free-agent signee. Lemon's top pitchers were three left-handers: Ron Guidry, Dave Righetti, and ex-Dodger Tommy John, backed up by relief right-handers Goose Gossage, Ron Davis, and George Frazier.

Opening the Series on their home ground, the Yankees got off to a rousing start on a Bob Watson three-run homer in the bottom of the first and went on to a 5–3 win behind Guidry, Davis, and Gossage— a familiar pitching litany for the Yankees that year.

The Yankees upended the Dodgers again in game two, 3–0, with John and Gossage applying the throttle. With a 4–12 record to show for their World Series history, the Dodgers were in deep trouble as the teams took off for the West Coast.

Lasorda started his best, young Valenzuela, against Lemon's swift young lefty, Righetti. Ron Cey sent the Dodgers off to a quick getaway with a three-run homer in the bottom of the first. The Yankees began pecking away at Valenzuela, however, and going into the bottom of the fifth held the lead, 4–3. The Dodgers scored twice in the bottom of the fifth and took a 5–4 lead, to which Valenzuela, despite not having his best stuff, hung on to give the Dodgers their first win of the Series. The losing pitcher was George Frazier, who would end up in the record books with three losses, matching the dubious mark set by Claude Williams of the 1919 Chicago White Sox. (Williams, of course, hadn't been trying. Frazier was.)

Reggie Jackson was back in the lineup for the Yankees for game four and immediately put on one of his "Mr. October" performances, ripping two singles and a home run and walking twice in five trips to the plate. Reggie's showing was marred, however, by a costly dropped fly in right field that kept a game-tying Dodger rally alive in the bottom of the sixth. The Dodgers ended up winning a wild scramble of a game, 8–7, tying the Series.

The Dodgers made it a home-court sweep with a 2–1 win in game five. It was a duel of left-handers, Guidry for the Yankees, Reuss for the Dodgers. Guidry had a 1–0 edge until the bottom of the seventh, when, with one out, Guerrero and Yeager hit consecutive homers, giving Reuss just enough gas to get home with.

Back in Yankee Stadium, the Dodgers made it four in a row and the championship with a 9–2 win. In spite of the runaway score, the game, in the opinion of many, pivoted on a controversial decision by Yankee skipper Bob Lemon in the bottom of the fourth. With Tommy John pitching a 1–1 tie against Burt Hooton, the Yankees were at bat with two on and two out. Lemon elected to pinch-hit for John, who stared incredulously at his manager. The pinch hitter, Bobby Murcer, flied out deep. The Yankees did not score. The Yankees bullpen immediately gave up seven runs, and the Dodgers were on their way.

1982

When Harvey Kuenn took over as manager of the Milwaukee Brewers early in the 1982 season, he told his players to "relax and have fun." They did, having so much fun swinging their bats that they became known as "Harvey's Wall Bangers." They were one of the hardest-hitting clubs of recent years, with Cecil Cooper, Jim Gantner, Robin Yount, and Paul Molitor in the infield, Gorman Thomas, Ben Oglivie, and Charlie Moore in the outfield, and Ted Simmons catching. Enjoying the support afforded by this muscular lineup were pitchers Pete Vukovich, Moose Haas, late-season pickup Don Sutton, and left-hander Mike Caldwell. (The Brewers' ace relief man, Rollie Fingers, missed the Series because of arm trouble.)

Meticulously putting together a ball club of his own design, the Cardinals' general manager–manager Whitey Herzog had emphasized speed and defense, molding it together with just enough hitting and just enough pitching. The infield was built around Ozzie Smith at shortstop and Keith Hernandez at first, a couple of defensive geniuses; and Tommy Herr at second and Ken Oberkfell at third. The outfield regulars were George Hendrick, Willie McGee, and Lonnie Smith. Darrell Porter was Herzog's solid man behind the plate. Right-handers Joaquin Andujar and Bob Forsch were the top starters for St. Louis, with Bruce Sutter and his near-unhittable split-fingered fast ball in the bullpen.

So it was to be a clash of opposites, power versus finesse: the Brewers and their 216 home runs against the defensively sound, base-stealing Cardinals.

Game one in St. Louis was a Milwaukee walkaway, Mike Caldwell shutting out the Cardinals 10–0 on a three-hitter. The Brewers rapped out 17 hits, with some record-making swatting going on at the top of the lineup when leadoff batter Paul Molitor became the first man ever to get five hits in a Series game. Making Molitor's performance even more effective was Robin Yount, batting behind Molitor, getting four hits himself.

The Cardinals came back and nudged out a 5–4 win in game two. The winning run scored in the bottom of the eighth when Milwaukee reliever Pete Ladd walked a man with the bases loaded (this underlined the fact that the loss of the injured Fingers was going to hurt the Brewers).

In Milwaukee for game three, the Cardinals turned loose Willie McGee. The St. Louis center fielder, who had hit only four home runs all season, hit two in this game and made two classy catches in the outfield that robbed Molitor and Thomas of extra base hits. With McGee driving in four runs, the Cardinals won it 6–2. The winner was Andujar, who was forced to leave the game after pitching 6⅓ shutout innings when he was struck on the leg by a Ted Simmons line drive.

In game four, the Cards led 5–1 in the bottom of the seventh when the Brewers, capitalizing on an error by pitcher Dave LaPoint, scored six runs, the big hit a two-run single by Thomas. Milwaukee's 7–5 win tied the Series.

The Brewers advanced to one win of the title with a 6–4 victory in game five. In this game, Robin Yount hit two singles, a double, and a home run to become the first man ever to collect four hits in a game twice in the same Series. In gaining his second win of the Series, Mike Caldwell, who had pitched a three-hitter in the opener, gave up 14 hits in 8⅓ innings before being bailed out by lefty Bob McClure.

Back on home ground for game six, the Cardinals

stayed alive and threw the Series into a seventh game with a 13–1 blowout behind John Stuper. For the Brewers, the agony was drawn out by a 2:39 rain delay in the middle of the game, which wasn't completed until well after midnight.

The Cardinals completed their comeback the next day with a 6–3 title clincher, with Andujar going seven innings and Sutter finishing up. The Brewers had been on top 3–1 going into the bottom of the sixth when the Cards scored three runs, the big hit being a two-run single by Hernandez. Hernandez had gone hitless his first 15 at bats, but he finished smoking, getting seven hits in his last 12 at bats and driving in eight runs. For Andujar, the seventh game had been a figurative life-or-death situation. "I win or I die," the volatile right-hander announced before the game. He survived, and so did the Cardinals.

1983

In Baltimore it was Year 1 A.W.—After Weaver. Earl had resigned at the end of the 1982 season, ending a 15-year reign as the Orioles' manager. Replacing him was Joe Altobelli, and Joe promptly went all the way: division title, pennant, world championship. With Eddie Murray and Cal Ripkin, Jr., as his bedrock regulars, Altobelli platooned at almost every other position, having particular success in left field, where John Lowenstein and Gary Roenicke combined for 34 home runs and 124 runs batted in. Altobelli's swing-shift lineup gave year-long support to a deep and talented pitching staff that featured veteran starters Scott McGregor, Mike Flanagan, and Jim Palmer, rookies Mike Boddicker and Storm Davis, and relief pitchers Tippy Martinez and Sammy Stewart.

Baltimore's opposition in the 1983 Series was the Philadelphia Phillies, managed by Paul Owens, who had stepped down from the general manager's office in mid-season to guide the club to the National League pennant. With Pete Rose, Tony Perez, and Joe Morgan on the club, the Phillies had three veterans of Cincinnati's old Big Red Machine, although some of the parts had by now rusted slightly. Along with these veterans were Mike Schmidt, Garry Maddox, Gary Matthews, Ivan DeJesus, and Bo Diaz. The Philadelphia pitching staff, as it had been for a dozen years, was anchored by Steve Carlton, along with John Denny, rookie Charles Hudson, and a strong bullpen that had Ron Reed, Willie Hernandez, and Al Holland.

The opener in Baltimore was an exchange of home run balls. Denny yielded one to Jim Dwyer in the first inning and McGregor gave up one-way tickets to Morgan in the sixth and Maddox in the eighth, and that was the ball game, 2–1. The Phillies had no way of knowing it at the time, but that was it for them.

Rookie ace Mike Boddicker drew the O's even in game two with a 4–1 three-hitter, helped along by a Lowenstein home run and a clutch double by the light-hitting catcher Rick Dempsey. Dempsey was to emerge as the Series' slugging star with four doubles, a home run, and a .385 batting average—another instance of Everyman rising to dominate a World Series.

In game three, in Philadelphia, another Dempsey double helped Baltimore squeeze by the Phillies and Steve Carlton, 3–2. A story almost as big as the game itself was the benching of Pete Rose in favor of Tony Perez. Phillies manager Paul Owens's explanation was that his club needed more offense. (Rose had singled in eight at bats over the first two games.) The move embarrassed both Rose and Perez, old and close friends. Perez got a meaningless single in four at bats in the Phillies' loss.

With Rose back in the lineup for game four, the Orioles took another one-run decision, 5–4. Rich Dauer provided the punch for the O's, driving in three runs, while relievers Stewart and Martinez came on to save the win for Davis.

Game five was never in doubt, especially once the slumping Eddie Murray went to work. After the first four games, Baltimore's most feared hitter was 2 for 16 with no RBIs. But then the big man found his groove. In the second inning he gave his club a 1–0 lead with a long home run off of Hudson. An inning later, Dempsey homered to make it 2–0. In the fourth, with Ripkin on base via a walk, Murray unloaded again, sending a 475-foot missile to right field for a 4–0 Baltimore lead. The Orioles scored one more, and Scott McGregor coasted to a 5–0 win and a Baltimore championship.

1984

Looking back, there never should have been any doubt who was going to be world champions in 1984. The Detroit Tigers won their first 9 games and 35 of their first 40, and were never out of first place for a single day. Then they ran through the Kansas City Royals in the championship series in three straight. They appeared to be one of history's unstoppable teams.

Managing the Tigers was Sparky Anderson, winning his first American League pennant after having taken four with Cincinnati in the 1970s. The Tigers boasted great "up-the-middle strength": Lance Parrish catching, Alan Trammell at short, Lou Whitaker at second, and Chet Lemon in center. Along with these regulars, the Tigers had the explosive Kirk Gibson in right field, Darrell Evans playing first and third, and various role players like Larry Herndon, Ruppert Jones, Tom Brookens, and others. On the mound, Anderson had three solid starters in Jack Morris, Dan Petry, and Milt Wilcox, and two very efficient relievers in Aurelio Lopez and Willie Hernandez.

The Series was a return match between the managers who had opposed each other in the 1972 pageant—Anderson and Dick Williams. Sparky and his Reds had been representing the National League, while Williams and his Oakland Athletics had been carrying the American League banner. Now they had reversed leagues, Williams having led the San Diego Padres to the first pennant in their history. One further bit of history was a certainty in this Series: with both managers having won a World Series in their original leagues, one of them was going to have the distinction of becoming the first manager to win a world championship in both leagues.

The Padres had invested heavily in the free-agent market, adding first baseman Steve Garvey in 1983 and relief pitcher Goose Gossage in 1984. They had also acquired from the Yankees the aging but still able Graig Nettles to play third. Along with catcher Terry Kennedy, second baseman Alan Wiggins, shortstop Garry Templeton, and outfielders Kevin McReynolds (who was injured in the championship series with the Cubs and unable to play in the World Series) and Tony Gwynn, the Padres finally had the balance they needed. Outside of reliever Gossage, however, the San Diego pitching was suspect. None of the starters—Ed Whitson, Eric Show, Mark Thurmond, or Tim Lollar—had won more than 15 games. It was a weakness that in the Series was to become glaring and fatal.

The Series opened in San Diego with Tiger ace Morris nipping the Padres 3–2 on Herndon's two-run homer in the top of the fifth. A key play occurred in San Diego's seventh inning when designated hitter Kurt Bevacqua led off with a double to right field but was cut down trying to stretch it into a triple.

Detroit started off in game two as though they would tear it irretrievably apart. They disposed of starter Whitson with a three-run first, but that was all they got. With relievers Andy Hawkins and then Craig Lefferts throttling the Tigers, San Diego began pecking away at Petry, culminating with a three-run homer by Bevacqua in the bottom of the fifth that gave the Padres a 5–3 win and a tie in the Series.

In Detroit for game three, the Tigers again struck early, knocking out Lollar with a four-run bottom of the second, and went on to a 5–2 win, Wilcox winning and Hernandez saving. It was a long, slow game, thanks to a record-tying 11 walks handed out by San Diego pitchers.

Jack Morris hurled another Tiger victory in game four, 4–2, as the Tigers again chased the Padres' starter early. This time it was Eric Show. His mistakes were blunt and to the point: he served up a pair of two-run homers to Trammell in the first and third innings, which was all Morris needed.

What had begun so stunningly for the Tigers in the spring was now about to end triumphantly for them in the fall. Following the script, they disposed of starter Mark Thurmond in the first inning of game five with three runs, two of them riding across on a Kirk Gibson homer. The Padres kept struggling, and it was 5–4 Detroit going into the bottom of the eighth. The Tigers had men on second and third and one out when Gibson came to bat. Gossage was on the mound. After a brief conference on the mound, the Padres elected to pitch to Gibson rather than walk him. It was a mistake. The keyed-up Gibson (who had never forgotten striking out against Gossage in his first major-league at bat) sent Gossage's second pitch rocketing into the upper right-field stands for a three-run home run, an 8–4 lead, and the World Series capper.

Sparky Anderson and not Dick Williams had become the first manager to win a world championship in both leagues.

1985

They called it the "I-70" World Series because of the ribbon of interstate concrete that ran between the two participating Missouri cities. The Kansas City Royals and the St. Louis Cardinals were gathering for the first all-Missouri Series since the Cardinals and Browns went at it in 1944.

While neither team was considered a powerhouse, both had demonstrated a knack for winning clutch games while running the gamut of the September pressure chamber. Kansas City's attack boasted third baseman George Brett, center fielder Willie Wilson, and power-hitting first baseman Steve Balboni. Hal McRae, one of the Royals' better hitters, was strictly a DH, and with the DH not in use in this odd-numbered year, McRae's experienced bat was reduced to pinch-hitting. Dick Howser's club also had Frank White at second base, Jim Sundberg behind the plate, and Lonnie Smith in the outfield. The Royals' pitching staff was headed by twenty-one-year-old right-hander Bret Saberhagen and three fine southpaws, Bud Black, Charlie Leibrandt, and Danny Jackson, backed up by the estimable relief ace Dan Quisenberry.

Whitey Herzog's Cardinals had stolen 314 bases, topped by rookie outfielder Vince Coleman's 110. Coleman, however, was sidelined after a freak accident during the league championship series against the Dodgers, when his leg was run over by an automatic tarpaulin. But Herzog still had a solid lineup in the league's leading hitter (.353), Willie McGee, second baseman Tommy Herr, shortstop Ozzie Smith, third baseman Terry Pendleton (all switch hitters), slugger Jack Clark at first base, and Coleman's replacement in the outfield, Tito Landrum. The Cardinals also had strong starting pitchers in lefty John Tudor and right-handers Joaquin Andujar and Danny Cox. In addition, Herzog had his "committee" in the bullpen: right-handers Bill Campbell, Todd Worrell, and Jeff Lahti and lefties Ken Dayley and Ricky Horton.

The Series opened in Kansas City with Tudor, with help from Worrell, edging the Royals 3–1, despite a strong effort from Danny Jackson. The Cardinals followed up with a 4–2 win in game two, thanks to a sudden four-run rally in the top of the ninth inning. Kansas City's Charlie Leibrandt was breezing along with a 2–0 lead when the Cards struck. A double by McGee started it, and a two-out, three-run double by Pendleton finished it.

The Series moved east to St. Louis, and the Royals took game three, 6–1, Saberhagen over Andujar. John Tudor put the Cards on the brink of the championship with a masterful five-hit, 3–0 shutout in game four. But Kansas City stayed alive with another 6–1 win in game five, Jackson going all the way.

Game six was one of the most thrilling, and controversial, Series games ever played. With Cox and Leibrandt dueling, it was scoreless going into the top of the eighth. Then, with Cardinal runners on first and second and two out, pinch hitter Brian Harper fought off an 0–2 inside pitch and sent it softly into left-center for a run-scoring single.

The Royals came up in the bottom of the ninth still trailing by that lone run. On the mound now for St. Louis was their rookie fireballer, Todd Worrell.

Pinch hitter Jorge Orta legged out an infield hit, called safe on a highly disputed call by umpire Don Denkinger. (Television's instant replay showed that Orta was out. Nevertheless.) Steve Balboni then got a life when his catchable pop foul was misplayed by Jack Clark. Balboni then singled to left. Jim Sundberg, in a bunt situation, did just that, but Worrell nipped Orta at third. With pinch hitter Hal McRae at bat, a passed ball by catcher Darrell Porter allowed the runners to move up to second and third. McRae was then intentionally walked, filling the bases. Dane Iorg was sent up to pinch-hit. Iorg, a hero of the 1982 Series for the Cardinals, hit Worrell's second pitch into right field for a single, sending in the tying and winning runs, Sundberg coming in on a headfirst slide.

Game seven saw a match-up of aces, Tudor for the Cardinals, Saberhagen for the Royals. But instead of the tight game expected, it was a Kansas City runaway. The Royals scored two in the bottom of the second on a home run by Darryl Motley and then dispatched Tudor with three more in the third. Kansas City wrapped it up with six runs in the fifth, an inning that saw relief pitcher Andujar and skipper Herzog thrown out of the game for arguing with home-plate umpire Denkinger. The final score was 11–0. Kansas City had won its first world title.

Willie Wilson, so dismal against the Phillies in the 1980 Series, led in this one with 11 hits, while George Brett, with 10 hits, led all regulars with a .370 batting average. Two-time winner Saberhagen walked off with pitching honors, logging an 0.50 earned-run average for his eighteen innings of work.

Lefty Tommy John, who pitched fine ball for the Yankees against his former Dodger teammates in the 1981 World Series.

Dodgers third baseman Ron Cey, a .350 hitter in the 1981 Series.

Dodgers third baseman Ron Cey has just made a diving grab of a pop foul bunt off the bat of Bobby Murcer. Getting to his feet, Cey was able to fire to first and double off base runner Larry Milbourne. The play occurred in the eighth inning of game three of the 1981 Series.

Steve Garvey had another fine Series against the Yankees in 1981, with ten hits and a .417 batting average.

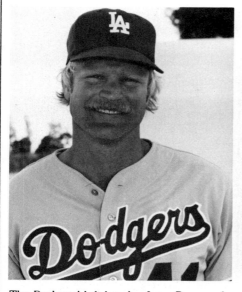

The Dodgers' left-hander Jerry Reuss, who pitched Los Angeles to a brilliant 2–1 win over the Yankees in game five, 1981.

The final out of the 1981 World Series has just been recorded and Dodgers manager Tom Lasorda (hatless, arms in the air) is rushing out of the dugout to join his players in celebration. The scene is New York's Yankee Stadium.

Ball in hand and tongue out, the Cardinals' Joaquin Andujar is at work in game three of the 1982 Series. He won it, 6–2.

It's the ninth inning of game three, 1982, and Cardinals center fielder Willie McGee is robbing Milwaukee's Gorman Thomas of what looks like a goner.

Collecting high-fives from his teammates is the Cardinals' Willie McGee after hitting the first of his two home runs in game three of the 1982 Series. The catcher is Ted Simmons.

Milwaukee's Paul Molitor, whose five hits in the first game of the 1982 Series set a record. Molitor had 11 hits and a .355 batting average for the seven-game Series.

The 1982 World Series has just become history, and catcher Darrell Porter has rushed out to congratulate reliever Bruce Sutter, who shut down the Brewers in the closing innings of game seven.

Robin Yount, whose 12 hits made him top gun in the 1982 Series. The Milwaukee shortstop batted .414.

Philadelphia's Pete Rose, whose benching by manager Paul Owens in the third game caused a furor in the 1983 World Series.

Baltimore left-hander Scott McGregor, who shut out the Phillies in the fifth and final game of the 1983 Series.

Right-hander John Denny, who won the opening game of the 1983 Series, the only game the Phillies took.

Phillies third baseman Mike Schmidt makes a valiant but vain attempt to glove Benny Ayala's pinch single in the seventh inning of game three. The hit tied the score at 2–2, and the Orioles went on to a 3–2 win.

Rick Dempsey, who did some unexpected slugging for Baltimore in the 1983 Series with four doubles and a home run.

George (Storm) Davis, Baltimore's winning pitcher in game four of the 1983 Series.

Detroit ace Jack Morris, who beat the Padres twice in the 1984 Series.

Alan Trammell, Tiger shortstop, who led all hitters in the 1984 Series with nine hits and a .450 batting average.

Detroit's Kirk Gibson smashing a two-run homer in the first inning of the fifth game of the 1984 Series. The catcher is Terry Kennedy.

An exultant Kirk Gibson after applying the crusher—his second home run of game five in the 1984 Series, a three-run shot off of San Diego's Goose Gossage in the bottom of the eighth inning that sealed Detroit's 8–4 victory, giving the Tigers the championship.

That's a world-championship victory leap Detroit's Willie Hernandez is taking. He has just recorded the final out of the 1984 World Series.

George Brett, a .370 hitter in the 1985 World Series.

The Cardinals' Willie McGee has just been tagged out on a fine relay from Willie Wilson to Frank White to George Brett. The action occurred in game one of the 1985 Series.

John Tudor.

Dane lorg, who got the biggest hit of his life in the bottom of the ninth in game six, 1985.

Bret Saberhagen, who won two games for Kansas City in the 1985 World Series, including an 11–0 title clincher in game seven.

World Series Results

(Numbers indicate games won.)

YEAR	WINNER	LOSER
1903	Boston (A.L.) 5	Pittsburgh (N.L.) 3
1904		No Series
1905	New York (N.L.) 4	Philadelphia (A.L.) 1
1906	Chicago (A.L.) 4	Chicago (N.L.) 2
1907	Chicago (N.L.) 4	Detroit (A.L.) 0; 1 tie
1908	Chicago (N.L.) 4	Detroit (A.L.) 1
1909	Pittsburgh (N.L.) 4	Detroit (A.L.) 3
1910	Philadelphia (A.L.) 4	Chicago (N.L.) 1
1911	Philadelphia (A.L.) 4	New York (N.L.) 2
1912	Boston (A.L.) 4	New York (N.L.) 3; 1 tie
1913	Philadelphia (A.L.) 4	New York (N.L.) 1
1914	Boston (N.L.) 4	Philadelphia (A.L.) 0
1915	Boston (A.L.) 4	Philadelphia (N.L.) 1
1916	Boston (A.L.) 4	Brooklyn (N.L.) 1
1917	Chicago (A.L.) 4	New York (N.L.) 2
1918	Boston (A.L.) 4	Chicago (N.L.) 2
1919	Cincinnati (N.L.) 5	Chicago (A.L.) 3
1920	Cleveland (A.L.) 5	Brooklyn (N.L.) 2
1921	New York (N.L.) 5	New York (A.L.) 3
1922	New York (N.L.) 4	New York (A.L.) 0; 1 tie
1923	New York (A.L.) 4	New York (N.L.) 2
1924	Washington (A.L.) 4	New York (N.L.) 3
1925	Pittsburgh (N.L.) 4	Washington (A.L.) 3
1926	St. Louis (N.L.) 4	New York (A.L.) 3
1927	New York (A.L.) 4	Pittsburgh (N.L.) 0
1928	New York (A.L.) 4	St. Louis (N.L.) 0
1929	Philadelphia (A.L.) 4	Chicago (N.L.) 1
1930	Philadelphia (A.L.) 4	St. Louis (N.L.) 2
1931	St. Louis (N.L.) 4	Philadelphia (A.L.) 3
1932	New York (A.L.) 4	Chicago (N.L.) 0
1933	New York (N.L.) 4	Washington (A.L.) 1
1934	St. Louis (N.L.) 4	Detroit (A.L.) 3
1935	Detroit (A.L.) 4	Chicago (N.L.) 2
1936	New York (A.L.) 4	New York (N.L.) 2
1937	New York (A.L.) 4	New York (N.L.) 1

1938	New York (A.L.) 4	Chicago (N.L.) 0
1939	New York (A.L.) 4	Cincinnati (N.L.) 0
1940	Cincinnati (N.L.) 4	Detroit (A.L.) 3
1941	New York (A.L.) 4	Brooklyn (N.L.) 1
1942	St. Louis (N.L.) 4	New York (A.L.) 1
1943	New York (A.L.) 4	St. Louis (N.L.) 1
1944	St. Louis (N.L.) 4	St. Louis (A.L.) 2
1945	Detroit (A.L.) 4	Chicago (N.L.) 3
1946	St. Louis (N.L.) 4	Boston (A.L.) 3
1947	New York (A.L.) 4	Brooklyn (N.L.) 3
1948	Cleveland (A.L.) 4	Boston (N.L.) 2
1949	New York (A.L.) 4	Brooklyn (N.L.) 1
1950	New York (A.L.) 4	Philadelphia (N.L.) 0
1951	New York (A.L.) 4	New York (N.L.) 2
1952	New York (A.L.) 4	Brooklyn (N.L.) 3
1953	New York (A.L.) 4	Brooklyn (N.L.) 2
1954	New York (N.L.) 4	Cleveland (A.L.) 0
1955	Brooklyn (N.L.) 4	New York (A.L.) 3
1956	New York (A.L.) 4	Brooklyn (N.L.) 3
1957	Milwaukee (N.L.) 4	New York (A.L.) 3
1958	New York (A.L.) 4	Milwaukee (N.L.) 3
1959	Los Angeles (N.L.) 4	Chicago (A.L.) 2
1960	Pittsburgh (N.L.) 4	New York (A.L.) 3
1961	New York (A.L.) 4	Cincinnati (N.L.) 1
1962	New York (A.L.) 4	San Francisco (N.L.) 3
1963	Los Angeles (N.L.) 4	New York (A.L.) 0
1964	St. Louis (N.L.) 4	New York (A.L.) 3
1965	Los Angeles (N.L.) 4	Minnesota (A.L.) 3
1966	Baltimore (A.L.) 4	Los Angeles (N.L.) 0
1967	St. Louis (N.L.) 4	Boston (A.L.) 3
1968	Detroit (A.L.) 4	St. Louis (N.L.) 3
1969	New York (N.L.) 4	Baltimore (A.L.) 1
1970	Baltimore (A.L.) 4	Cincinnati (N.L.) 1
1971	Pittsburgh (N.L.) 4	Baltimore (A.L.) 3
1972	Oakland (A.L.) 4	Cincinnati (N.L.) 3
1973	Oakland (A.L.) 4	New York (N.L.) 3
1974	Oakland (A.L.) 4	Los Angeles (N.L.) 1
1975	Cincinnati (N.L.) 4	Boston (A.L.) 3
1976	Cincinnati (N.L.) 4	New York (A.L.) 0
1977	New York (A.L.) 4	Los Angeles (N.L.) 2
1978	New York (A.L.) 4	Los Angeles (N.L.) 2

1979	Pittsburgh (N.L.) 4	Baltimore (A.L.) 3
1980	Philadelphia (N.L.) 4	Kansas City (A.L.) 2
1981	Los Angeles (N.L.) 4	New York (A.L.) 2
1982	St. Louis (N.L.) 4	Milwaukee (A.L.) 3
1983	Baltimore (A.L.) 4	Philadelphia (N.L.) 1
1984	Detroit (A.L.) 4	San Diego (N.L.) 1
1985	Kansas City (A.L.) 4	St. Louis (N.L.) 3

World Series trophy.

Index

The numbers in italics refer to photographs.